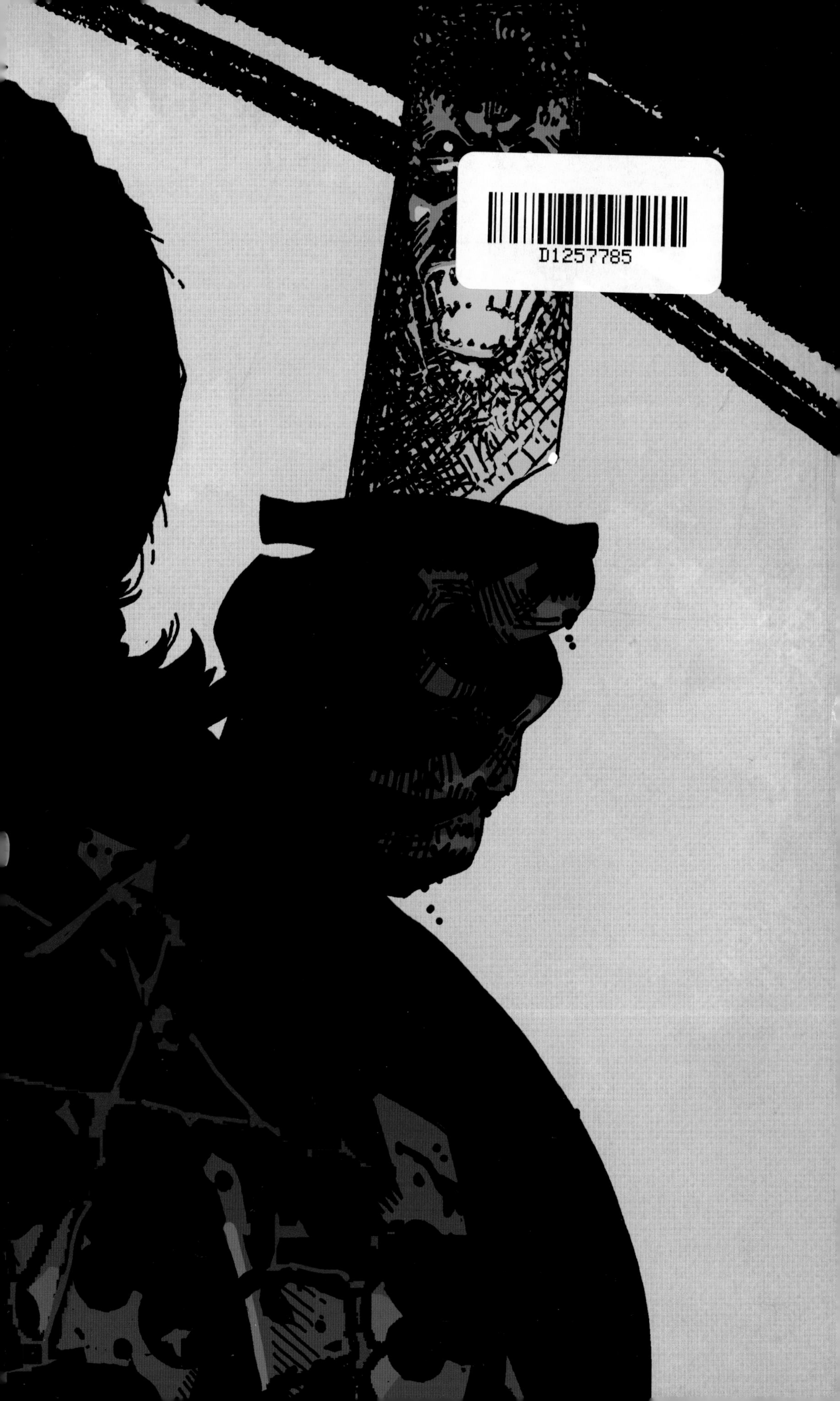

publisher
MIKE RICHARDSON

editor
MEGAN WALKER

assistant editor
JUDY KHUU

designer
SKYLER WEISSENFLUH

digital art technician
ADAM PRUETT

KILL WHITEY DONOVAN

This volume collects issues #1 through #5 of the Dark Horse Comics series *Kill Whitey Donovan*.

Published by Dark Horse Books
A division of Dark Horse Comics LLC
10956 SE Main Street, Milwaukie, OR 97222

DarkHorse.com
12GaugeComics.com

 Facebook.com/DarkHorseComics
 Twitter.com/DarkHorseComics

To find a comics shop in your area, visit comicshoplocator.com

First Edition: March 2021
Ebook ISBN 978-1-50671-651-0
Trade Paperback ISBN 978-1-50671-650-3

10 9 8 7 6 5 4 3 2 1
Printed in China

Library of Congress Cataloging-in-Publication Data

Names: Duncan, Sydney (Fiction writer), author. | Barahona, Natalie, artist. | Peteri, Troy, letterer.
Title: Kill Whitey Donovan / script, Sydney Duncan ; art & colors, Natalie Barahona ; letters, Troy Peteri.
Description: First edition. | Milwaukie, OR : Dark Horse Books, 2020. | "This volume collects issues #1 through #5 of the Dark Horse Comics series Kill Whitey Donovan" | Summary: "After Anna Hoyt's sister commits suicide, Anna sets off for Atlanta to kill the man responsible for destroying her family-her fiancé, Jim 'Whitey' Donovan. But Anna, a spirited though pampered daughter of a prominent doctor, can't do it alone. To get through the hell that lay between her Alabama home and Atlanta, she makes a deal with one of the Donovan slaves, Hattie Virgil, who has an agenda all her own. In exchange for a chance at freedom, Hattie, a survivor, will lead this unlikely pair on a quest that will change them both forever. Don't miss this exciting and unapologetic adventure story, starring two powerful women who will stop at nothing to get the justice they seek, set during a time when America was at war for its own soul."-- Provided by publisher.
Identifiers: LCCN 2020002805 | ISBN 9781506716503 (trade paperback)
Subjects: LCSH: Comic books, strips, etc.
Classification: LCC PN6728.K5439 D86 2020 | DDC 741.5/973--dc23
LC record available at https://lccn.loc.gov/2020002805

DARK HORSE BOOKS
PRESENTS
A 12-GAUGE COMICS PRODUCTION

~~KILL~~ WHITEY DONOVAN ™

script
SYDNEY DUNCAN

art & colors
NATALIE BARAHONA

cover art
JASON PEARSON

letters
TROY PETERI

12-gauge comics editorial
**BRIAN STELFREEZE
& KEVEN GARDNER**

Dark Horse Books

FOREWORD

BRIAN STELFREEZE

"I've already agreed, but I'll wait for you to stop asking."

It's exhilarating when a project puts itself together faster than you can assemble it. In fact, it creates an uncomfortable ease. That describes the entire process of producing *Kill Whitey Donovan*. Sure, it's customary to use words like *create* and *produce*, but this project almost felt as though it was discovered.

Keven Gardner had brought Sydney Duncan's name up to me several times before, and I knew her work had that 12-Gauge feel to it, but there wasn't a specific project we had for her to write. This is a common thing with 12-Gauge; there are always a few creators in the ether that seem perfect but we are just waiting for something to solidify.

Then, one afternoon, Keven called to tell me about a novel Sydney was writing; he had asked if she'd consider doing it as a comic book or graphic novel, and he wanted to bounce it off of me. He mentioned the working title, *Kill Whitey*, and I immediately said, "I'm in." He went on to describe the setup and I repeated, "Dude, I'm in." He then followed with a brief overview of the plot, and again, "Hell yes, let's do it." He just kept on trying to convince me to sign on to edit the project and I kept trying to convince him that I had already agreed.

Of course, this immediately solidified Natalie Barahona from the 12-Gauge ether as well. I've long hosted a figure drawing group in Atlanta and it's attended by a great number of talented individuals, all passionate about learning. Natalie walked in one day with a quiet and unassuming personality that belied her cacophony of talent. She was scary good already, but wanted to learn more. She was a manager at an animation company, but she also had a wide range of interests. One day we had a serious conversation about career pursuits and she said she was really interested in doing a comic book. There wasn't anything currently available at 12-Gauge, but I kept her in mind . . .

Perhaps it was a year later when I offered her the *Kill Whitey* project. Oddly, I think she agreed within the first few minutes, but I kept trying to convince her how cool it would be. When I finally got the message that she had accepted the project, it was her turn to try to convince me that she could handle the entire art production from inks to colors. This is not usually the case for a first-time artist, but this was Natalie and she was something else. I agreed immediately, but you know what happened after that . . .

And I have to thank our editor, Megan Walker, who championed the book and got it on the slate at Dark Horse (I haven't asked her, but I bet they agreed to publish it immediately and she just kept telling them all the reasons they needed to say yes).

Sydney and Natalie were so much fun to work with, and that shows on every page throughout the book. I love it when you can look back at a project and find it was just as fulfilling as what you were looking forward to on day one.

—Brian

CHAPTER ONE

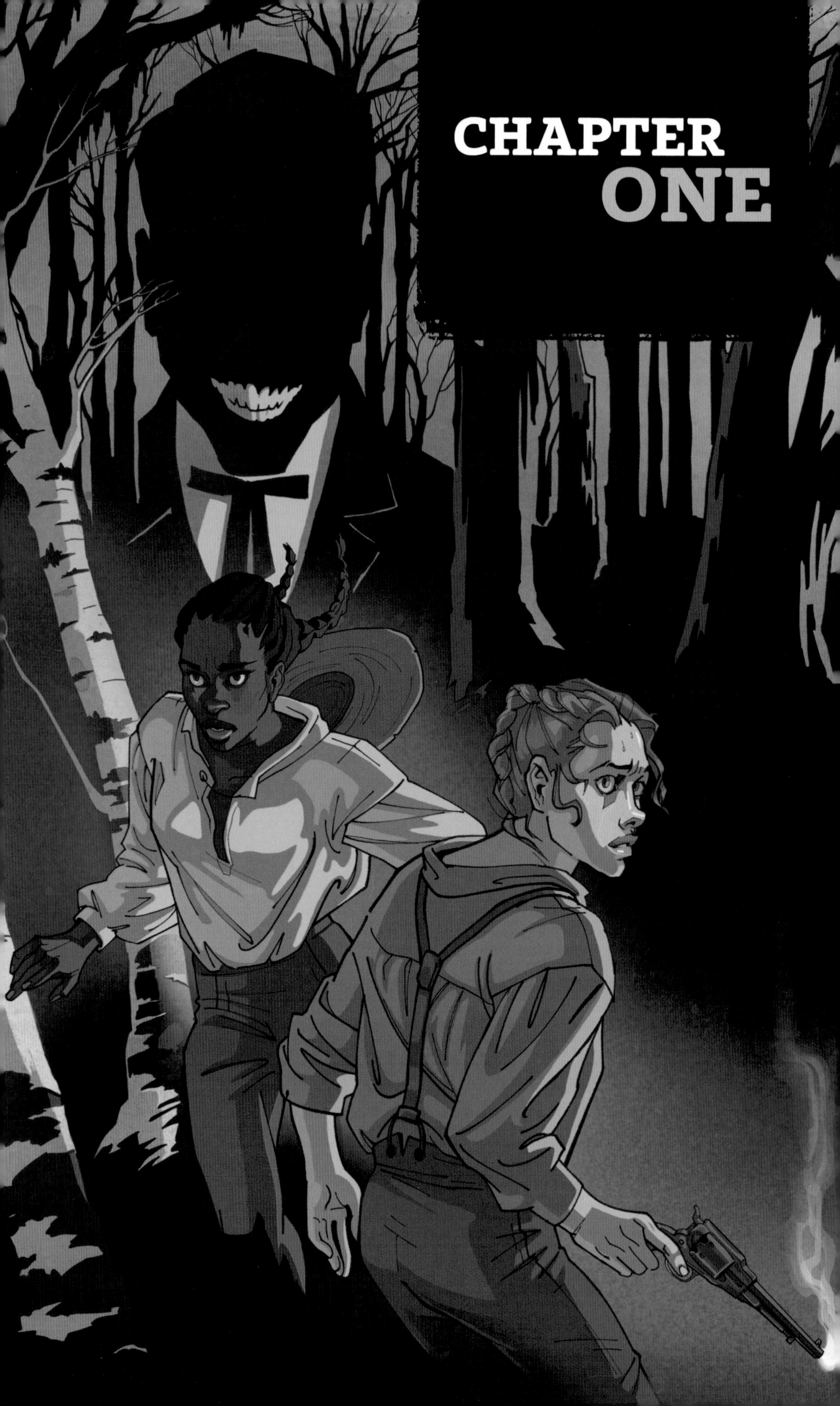

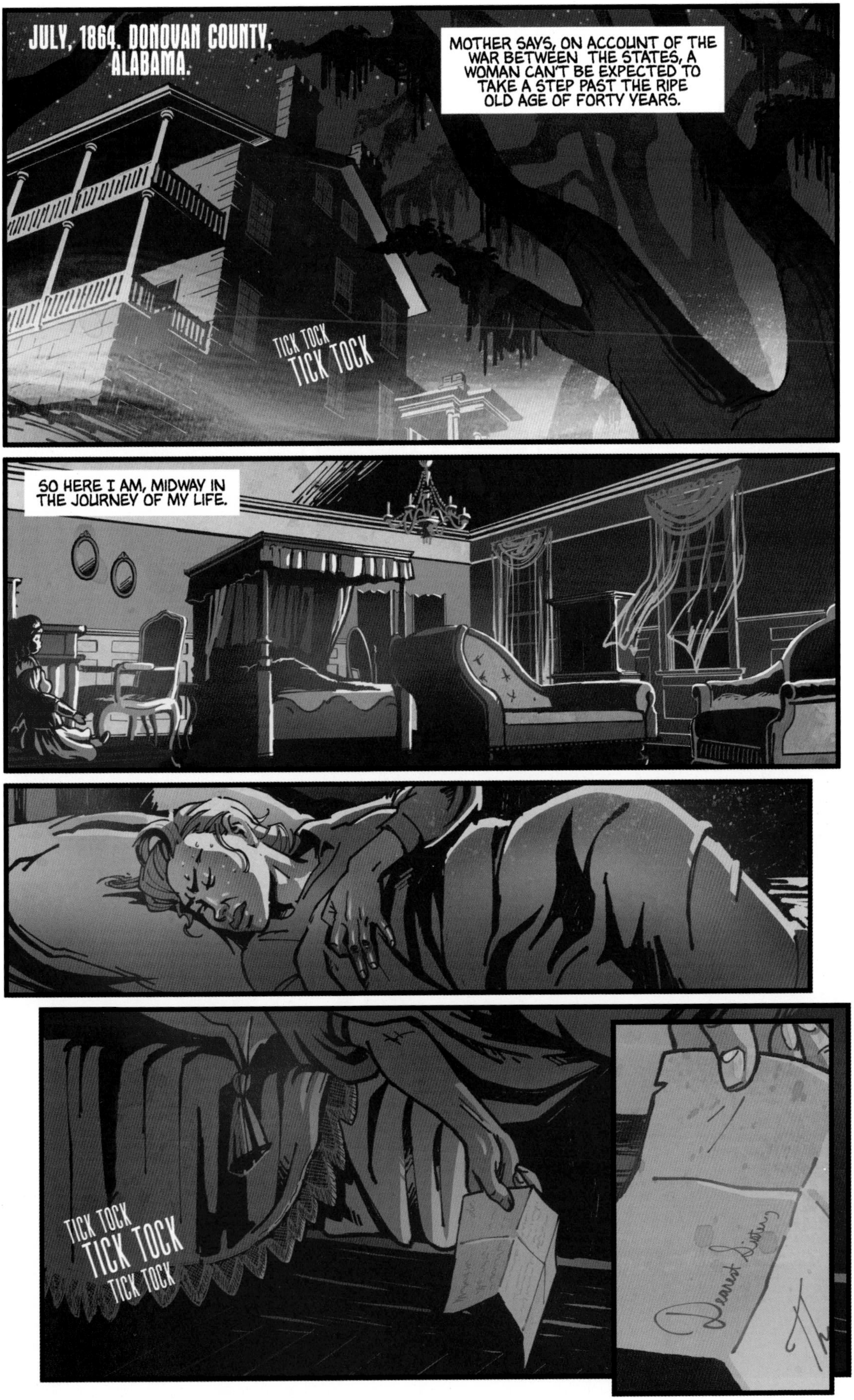
JULY, 1864. DONOVAN COUNTY, ALABAMA.
MOTHER SAYS, ON ACCOUNT OF THE WAR BETWEEN THE STATES, A WOMAN CAN'T BE EXPECTED TO TAKE A STEP PAST THE RIPE OLD AGE OF FORTY YEARS.
TICK TOCK
TICK TOCK
SO HERE I AM, MIDWAY IN THE JOURNEY OF MY LIFE.
TICK TOCK
TICK TOCK
TICK TOCK
Dearest Sister

NEARLY THE SAME AGE AS SHE WAS WHEN SHE FIRST FOUND HERSELF STUCK IN THIS GOD-FORSAKEN TOWN, WEARIN' THE MASK OF THE QUIET WIFE AND TAKING WHATEVER BEATING FATE GAVE HER.

TICK TOCK
TICK TOCK

BOOM...
BOOM...
BOOM...

WELL, I AIN'T HER. AND FATE CAN KISS MY ASS.

GET UP, ANNA. DAMN YOU, GET UP AND GO.

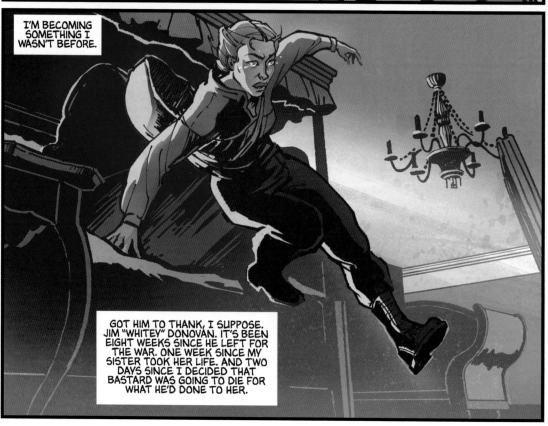

I'M BECOMING SOMETHING I WASN'T BEFORE.

GOT HIM TO THANK, I SUPPOSE. JIM "WHITEY" DONOVAN. IT'S BEEN EIGHT WEEKS SINCE HE LEFT FOR THE WAR. ONE WEEK SINCE MY SISTER TOOK HER LIFE. AND TWO DAYS SINCE I DECIDED THAT BASTARD WAS GOING TO DIE FOR WHAT HE'D DONE TO HER.

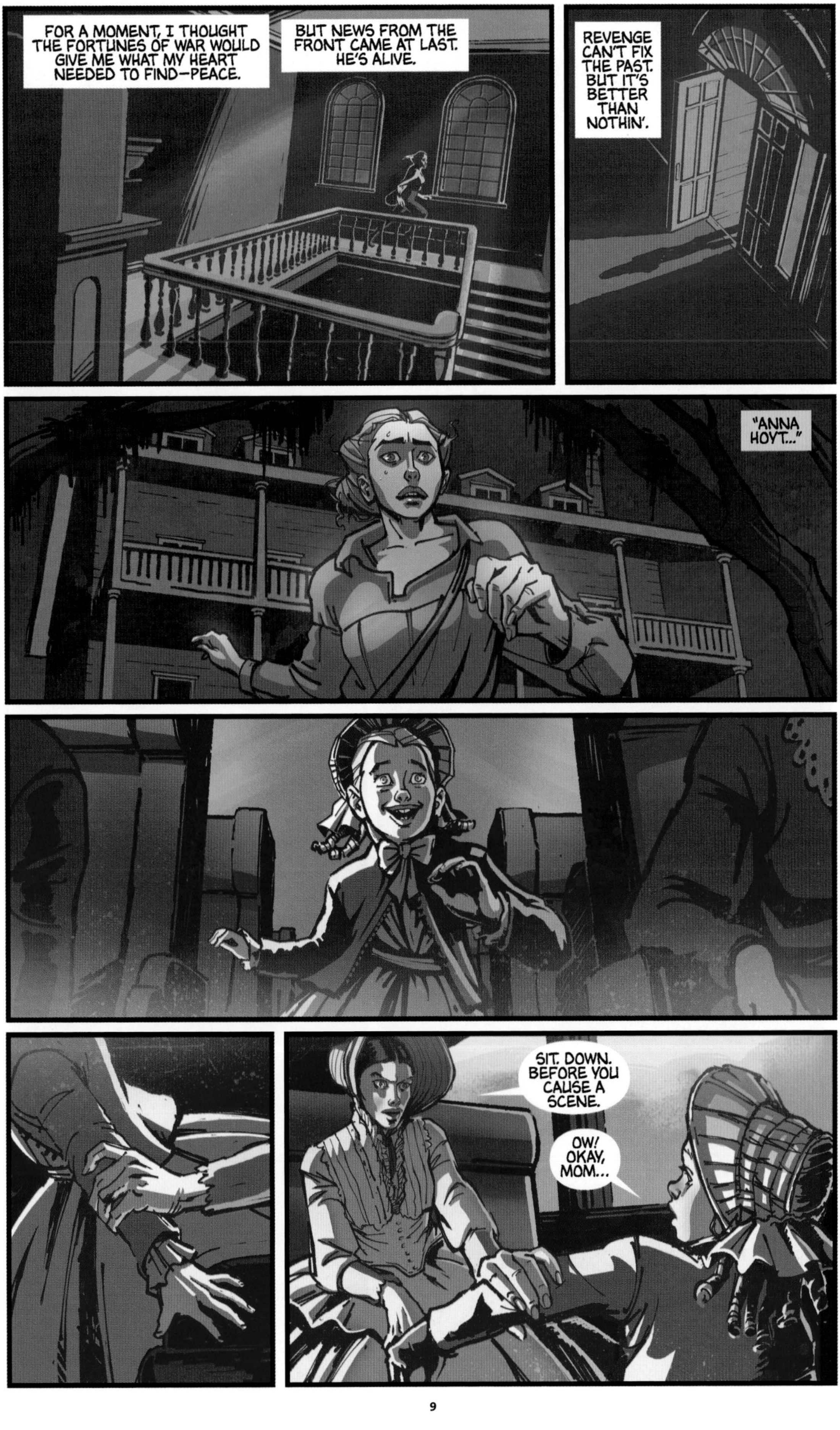
FOR A MOMENT, I THOUGHT THE FORTUNES OF WAR WOULD GIVE ME WHAT MY HEART NEEDED TO FIND—PEACE.
BUT NEWS FROM THE FRONT CAME AT LAST. HE'S ALIVE.
REVENGE CAN'T FIX THE PAST. BUT IT'S BETTER THAN NOTHIN'.
"ANNA HOYT..."
SIT. DOWN. BEFORE YOU CAUSE A SCENE.
OW! OKAY, MOM...

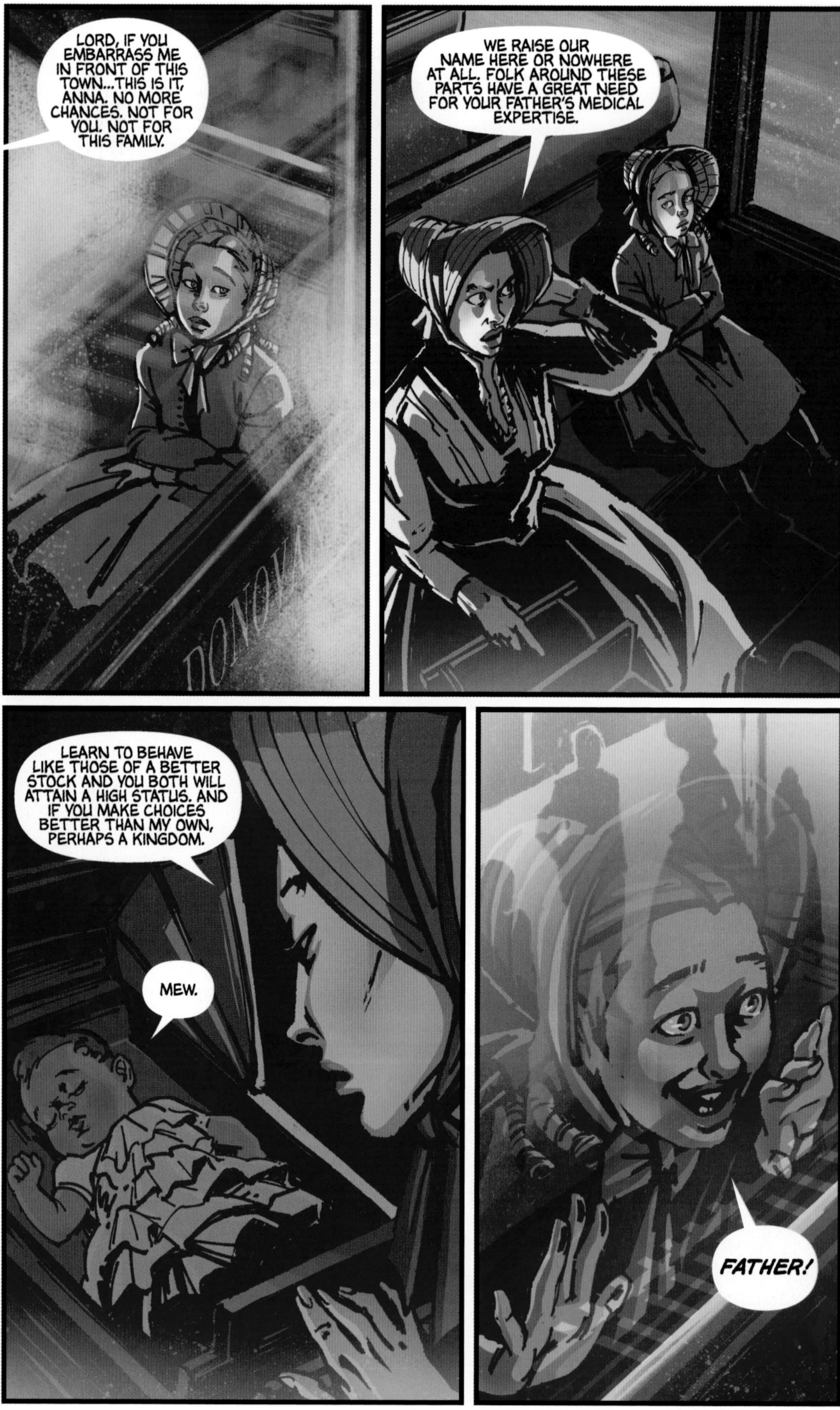
LORD, IF YOU EMBARRASS ME IN FRONT OF THIS TOWN...THIS IS IT, ANNA. NO MORE CHANCES. NOT FOR YOU. NOT FOR THIS FAMILY.
DONOVA
WE RAISE OUR NAME HERE OR NOWHERE AT ALL. FOLK AROUND THESE PARTS HAVE A GREAT NEED FOR YOUR FATHER'S MEDICAL EXPERTISE.
LEARN TO BEHAVE LIKE THOSE OF A BETTER STOCK AND YOU BOTH WILL ATTAIN A HIGH STATUS. AND IF YOU MAKE CHOICES BETTER THAN MY OWN, PERHAPS A KINGDOM.
MEW.
FATHER!

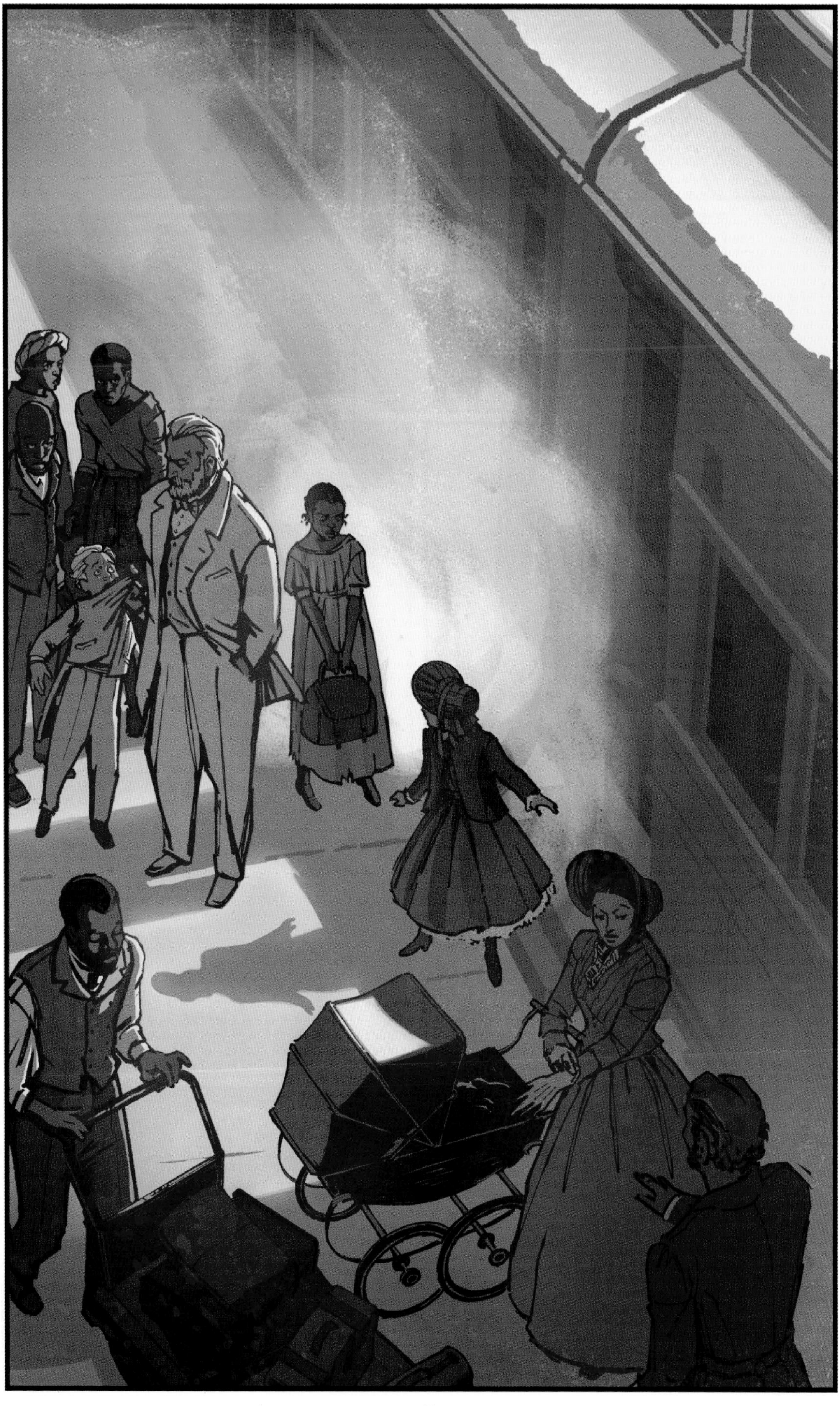

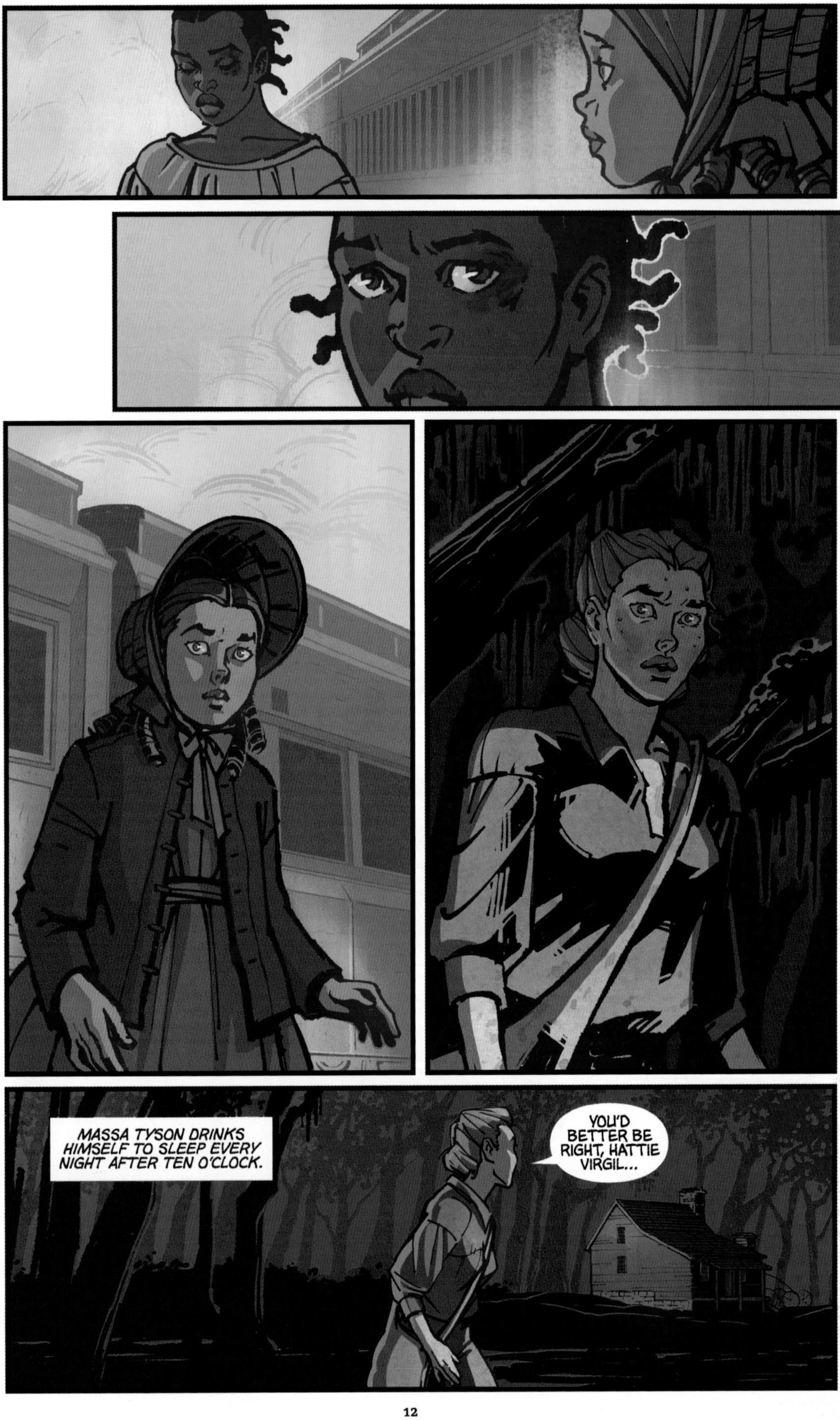
MASSA TYSON DRINKS HIMSELF TO SLEEP EVERY NIGHT AFTER TEN O'CLOCK.
YOU'D BETTER BE RIGHT, HATTIE VIRGIL...

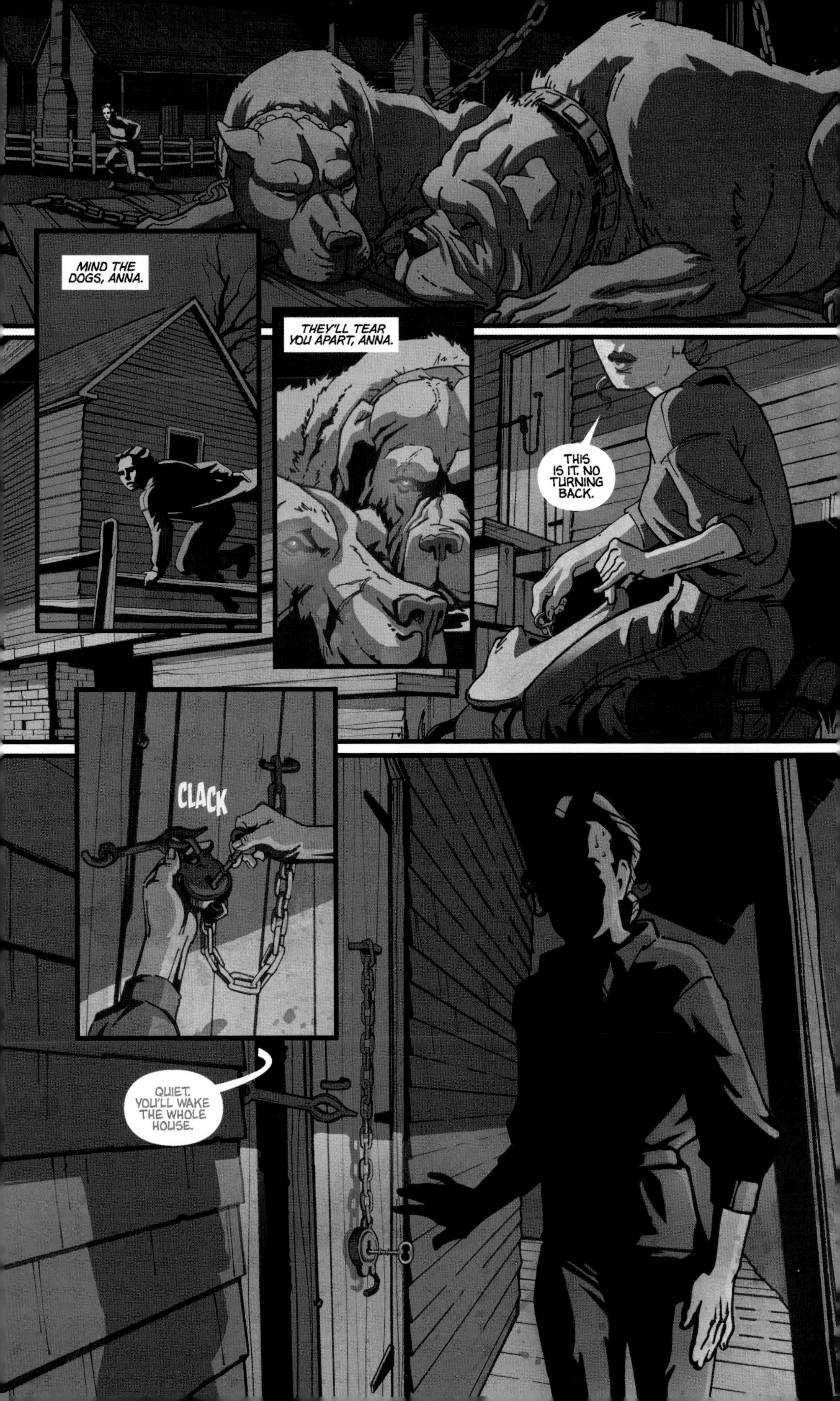
MIND THE DOGS, ANNA.
THEY'LL TEAR YOU APART, ANNA.
THIS IS IT. NO TURNING BACK.
CLACK
QUIET. YOU'LL WAKE THE WHOLE HOUSE.

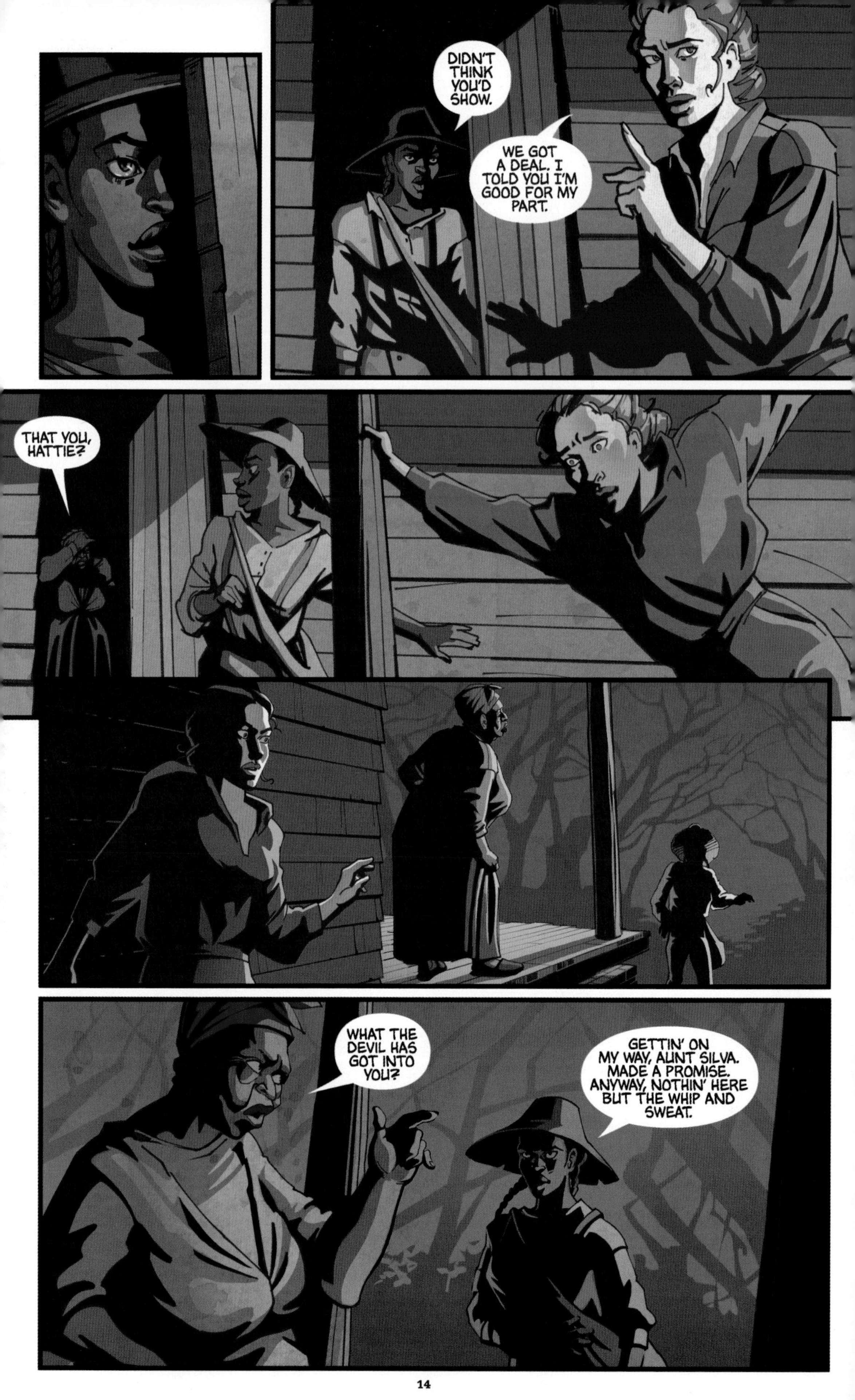
DIDN'T THINK YOU'D SHOW.
WE GOT A DEAL. I TOLD YOU I'M GOOD FOR MY PART.
THAT YOU, HATTIE?
WHAT THE DEVIL HAS GOT INTO YOU?
GETTIN' ON MY WAY, AUNT SILVA. MADE A PROMISE. ANYWAY, NOTHIN' HERE BUT THE WHIP AND SWEAT.

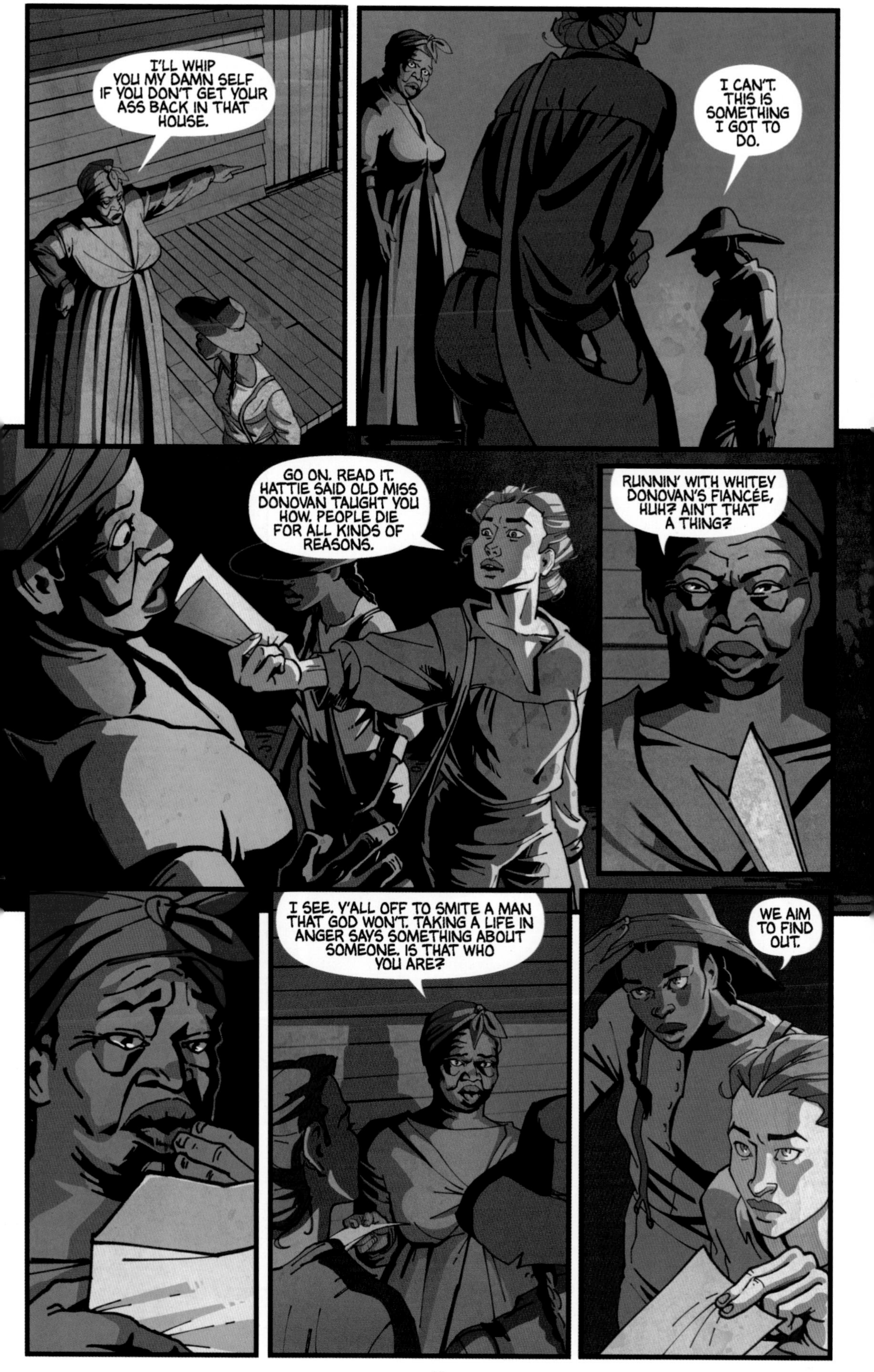
I'LL WHIP YOU MY DAMN SELF IF YOU DON'T GET YOUR ASS BACK IN THAT HOUSE.
I CAN'T. THIS IS SOMETHING I GOT TO DO.
GO ON. READ IT. HATTIE SAID OLD MISS DONOVAN TAUGHT YOU HOW. PEOPLE DIE FOR ALL KINDS OF REASONS.
RUNNIN' WITH WHITEY DONOVAN'S FIANCÉE, HUH? AIN'T THAT A THING?
I SEE. Y'ALL OFF TO SMITE A MAN THAT GOD WON'T. TAKING A LIFE IN ANGER SAYS SOMETHING ABOUT SOMEONE. IS THAT WHO YOU ARE?
WE AIM TO FIND OUT.

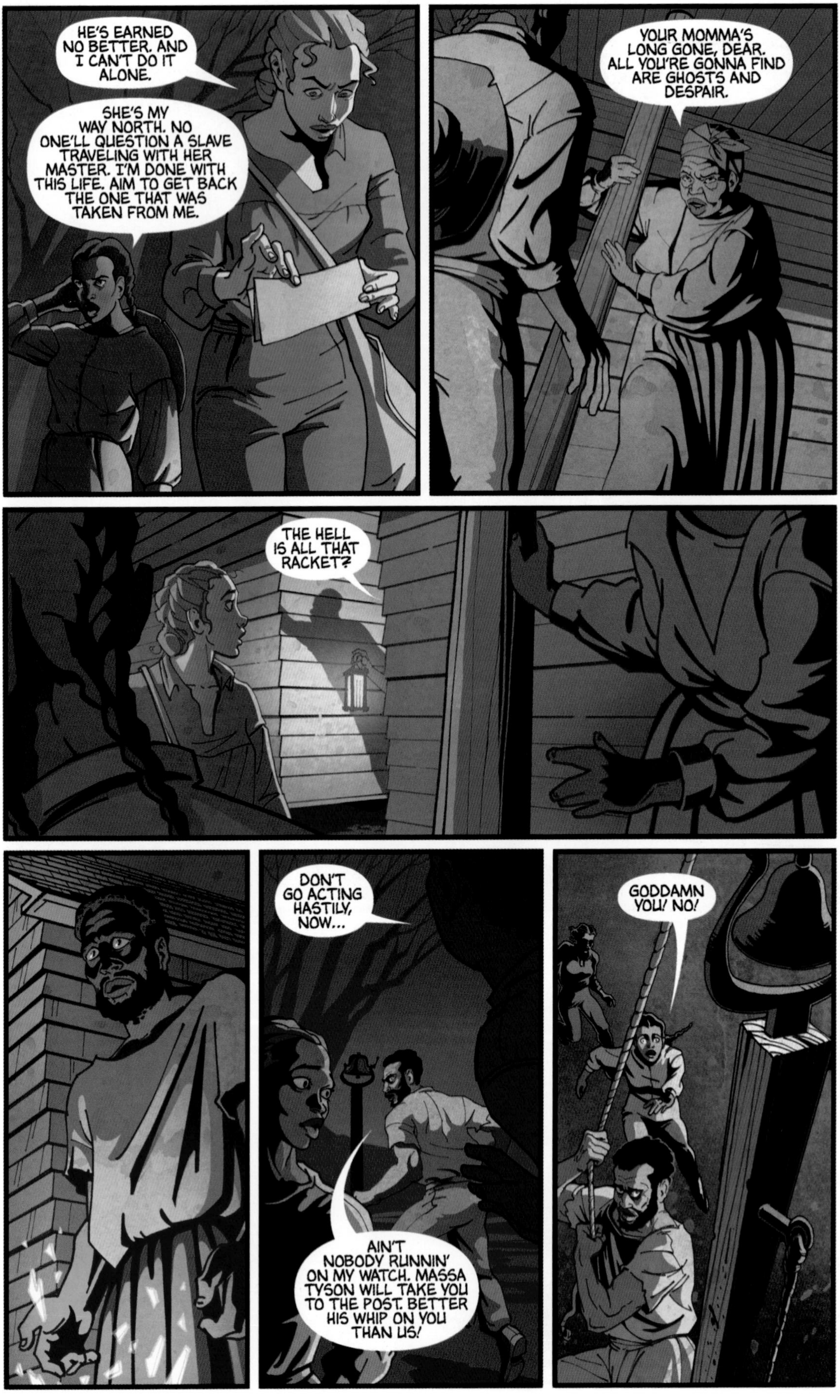
HE'S EARNED NO BETTER. AND I CAN'T DO IT ALONE.
SHE'S MY WAY NORTH. NO ONE'LL QUESTION A SLAVE TRAVELING WITH HER MASTER. I'M DONE WITH THIS LIFE. AIM TO GET BACK THE ONE THAT WAS TAKEN FROM ME.
YOUR MOMMA'S LONG GONE, DEAR. ALL YOU'RE GONNA FIND ARE GHOSTS AND DESPAIR.
THE HELL IS ALL THAT RACKET?
DON'T GO ACTING HASTILY, NOW...
AIN'T NOBODY RUNNIN' ON MY WATCH. MASSA TYSON WILL TAKE YOU TO THE POST. BETTER HIS WHIP ON YOU THAN US!
GODDAMN YOU! NO!

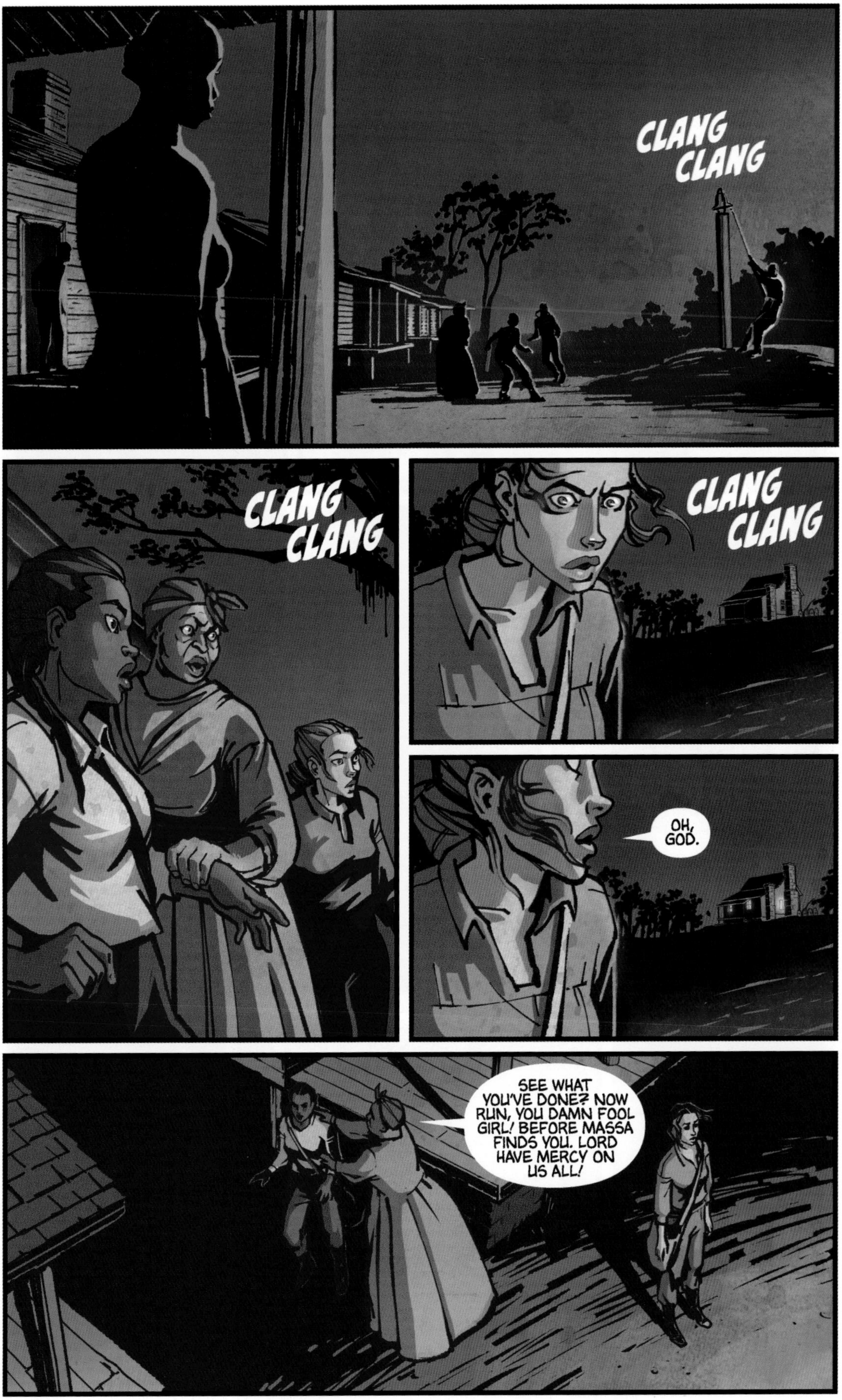
CLANG
CLANG
CLANG
CLANG
CLANG
CLANG
OH, GOD.
SEE WHAT YOU'VE DONE? NOW RUN, YOU DAMN FOOL GIRL! BEFORE MASSA FINDS YOU. LORD HAVE MERCY ON US ALL!

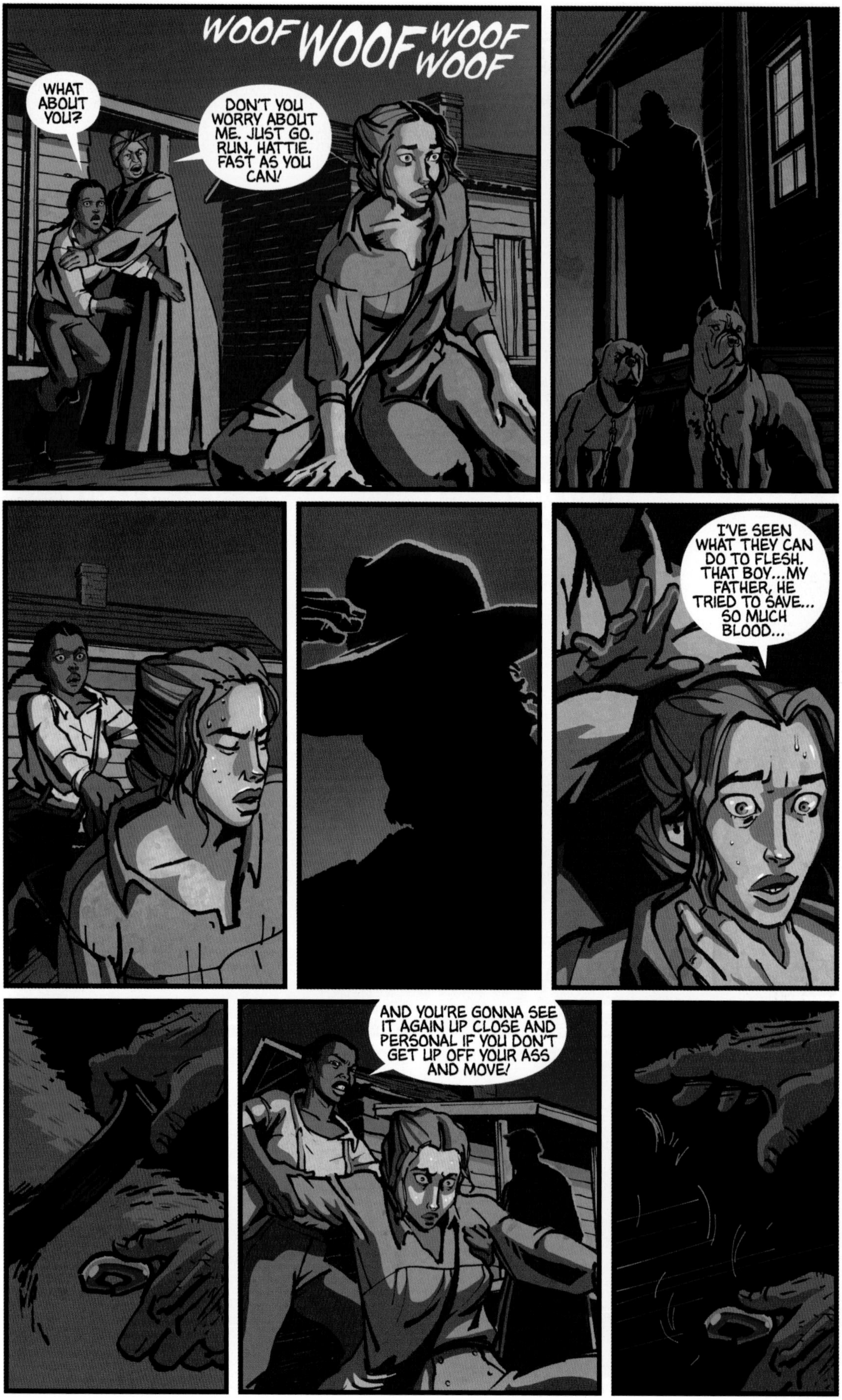
WOOF WOOF WOOF WOOF
WHAT ABOUT YOU?
DON'T YOU WORRY ABOUT ME. JUST GO. RUN, HATTIE. FAST AS YOU CAN!
I'VE SEEN WHAT THEY CAN DO TO FLESH. THAT BOY...MY FATHER, HE TRIED TO SAVE... SO MUCH BLOOD...
AND YOU'RE GONNA SEE IT AGAIN UP CLOSE AND PERSONAL IF YOU DON'T GET UP OFF YOUR ASS AND MOVE!

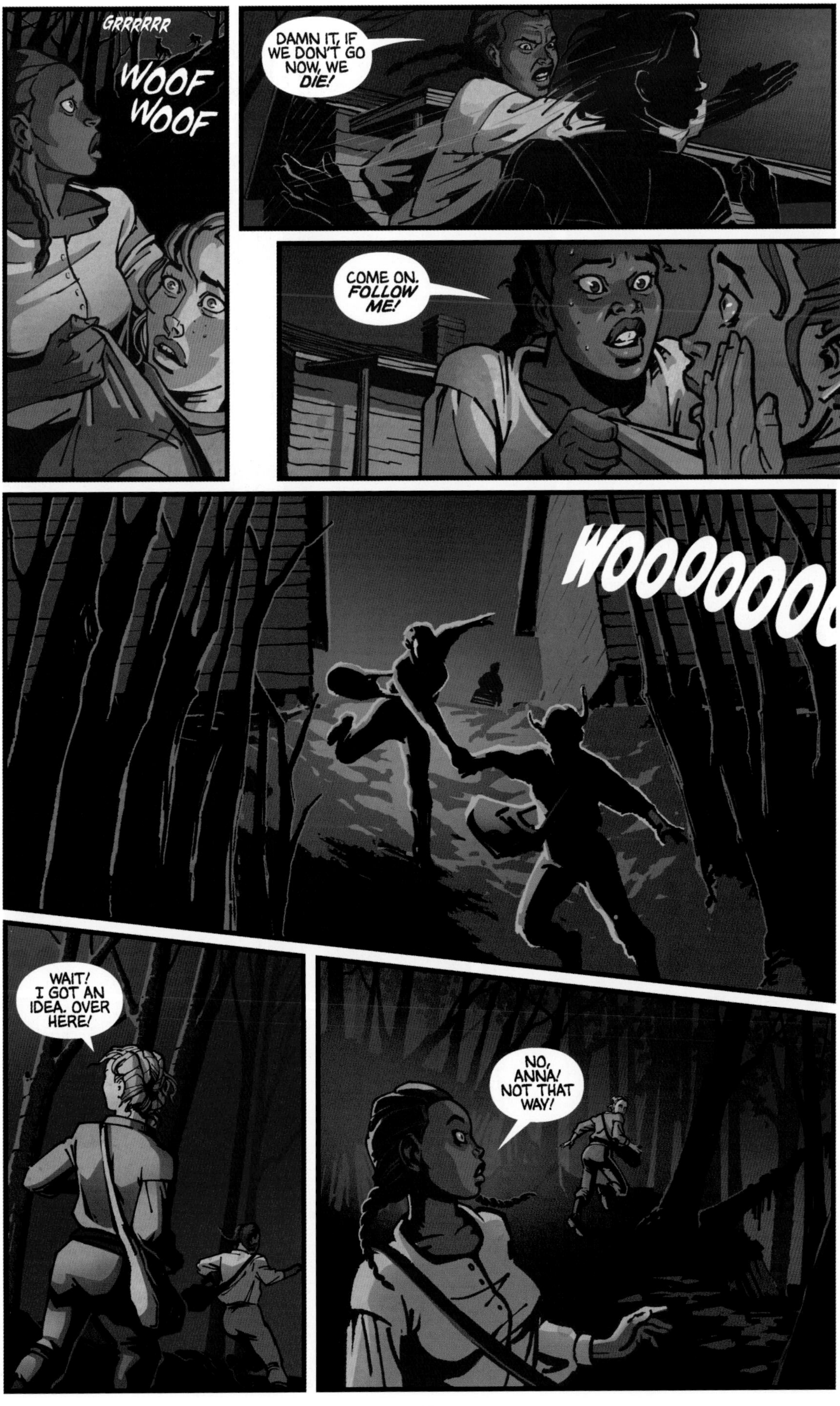
GRRRRRR
WOOF WOOF
DAMN IT, IF WE DON'T GO NOW, WE DIE!
COME ON. FOLLOW ME!
WOOOOOOO
WAIT! I GOT AN IDEA. OVER HERE!
NO, ANNA! NOT THAT WAY!

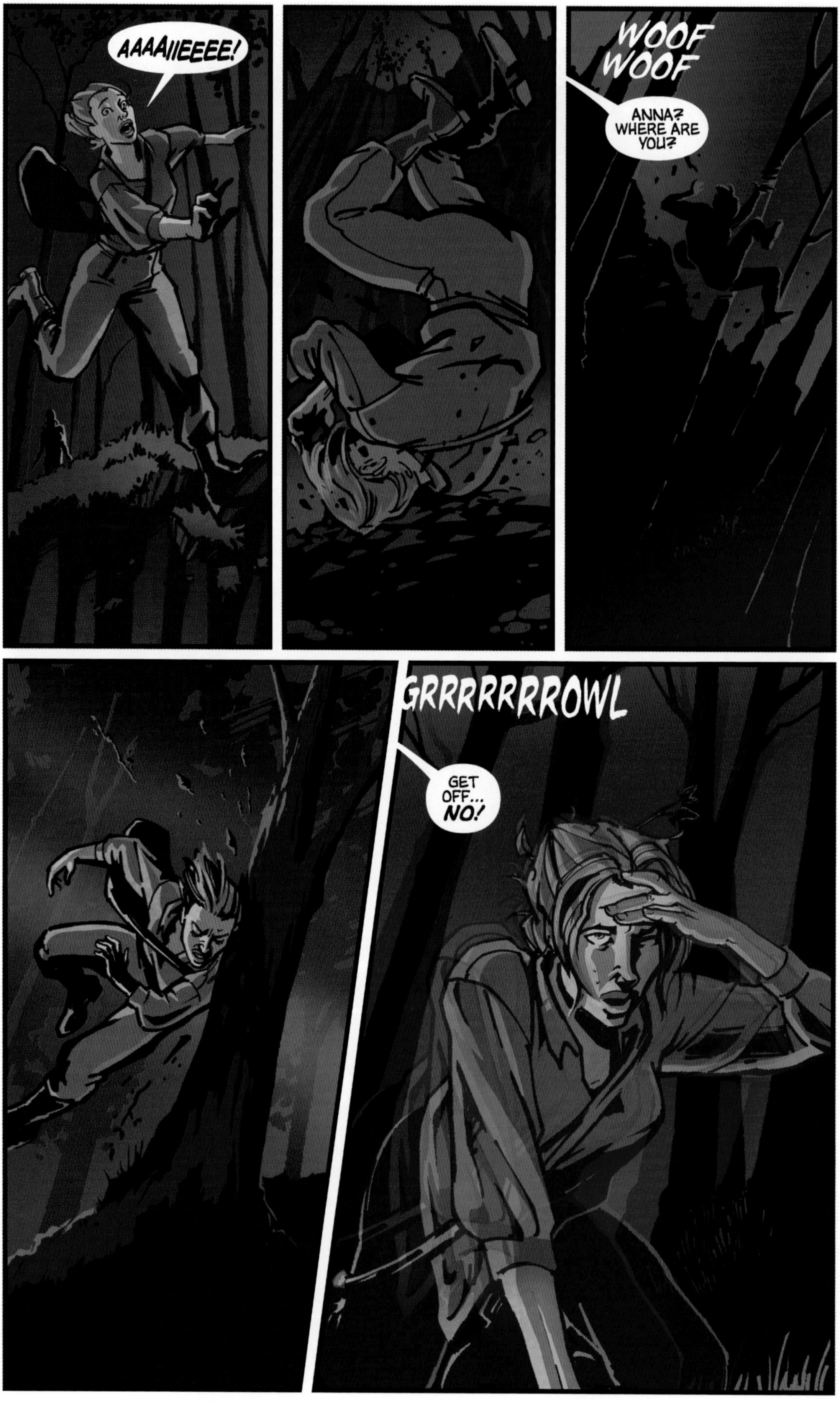
AAAAIIEEEE!
WOOF WOOF
ANNA? WHERE ARE YOU?
GRRRRRRROWL
GET OFF... NO!

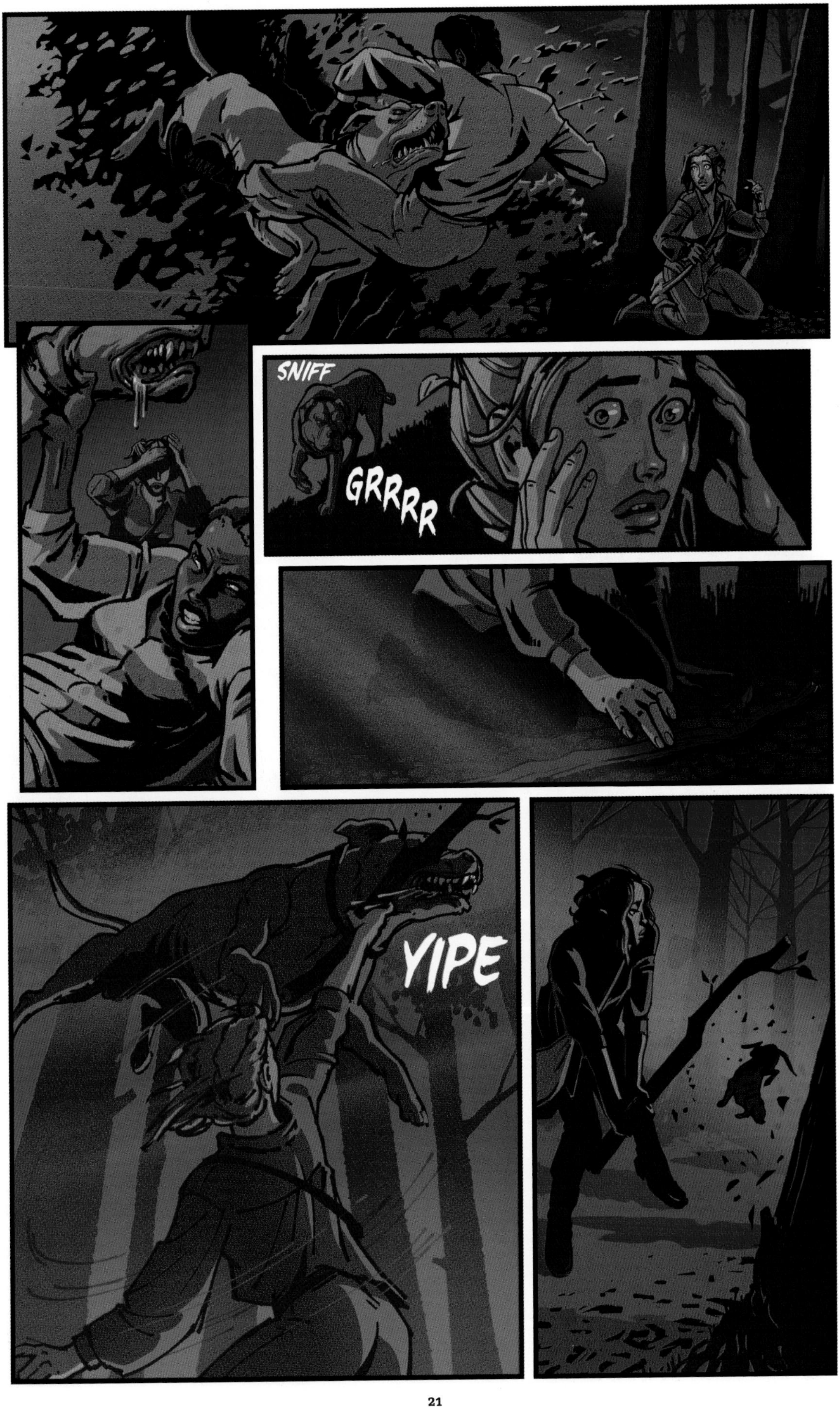
SNIFF
GRRRRR
YIPE

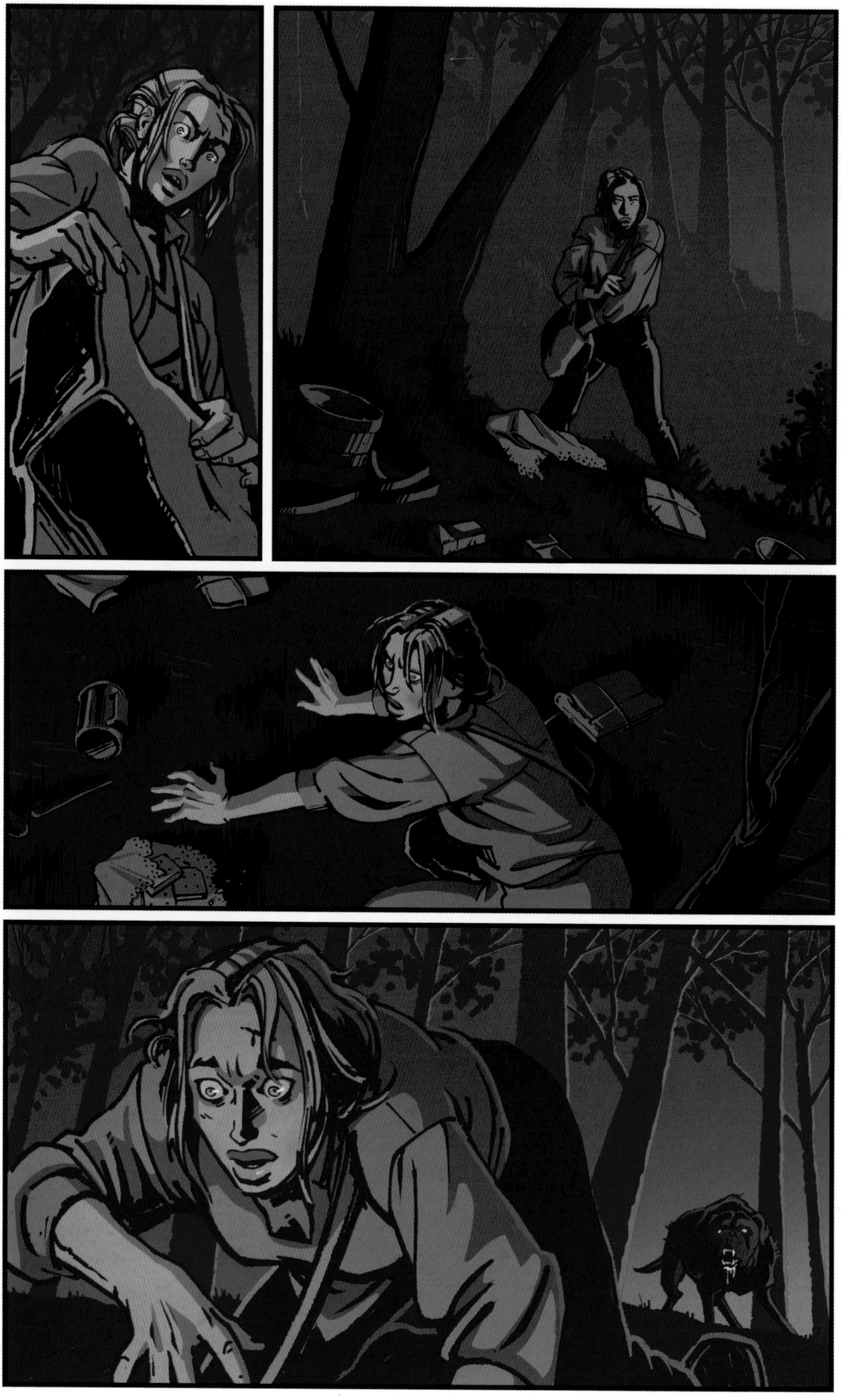

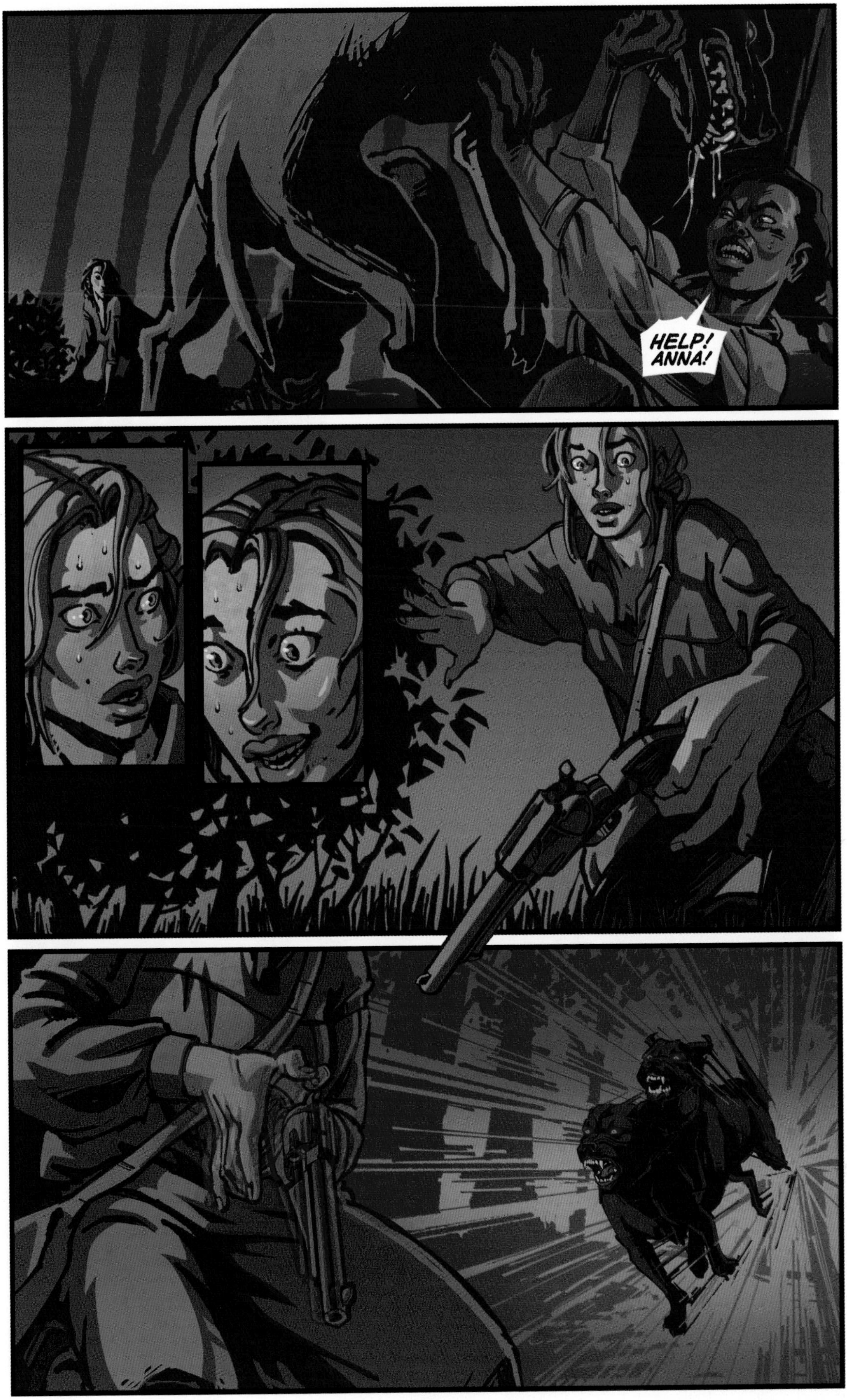
HELP! ANNA!

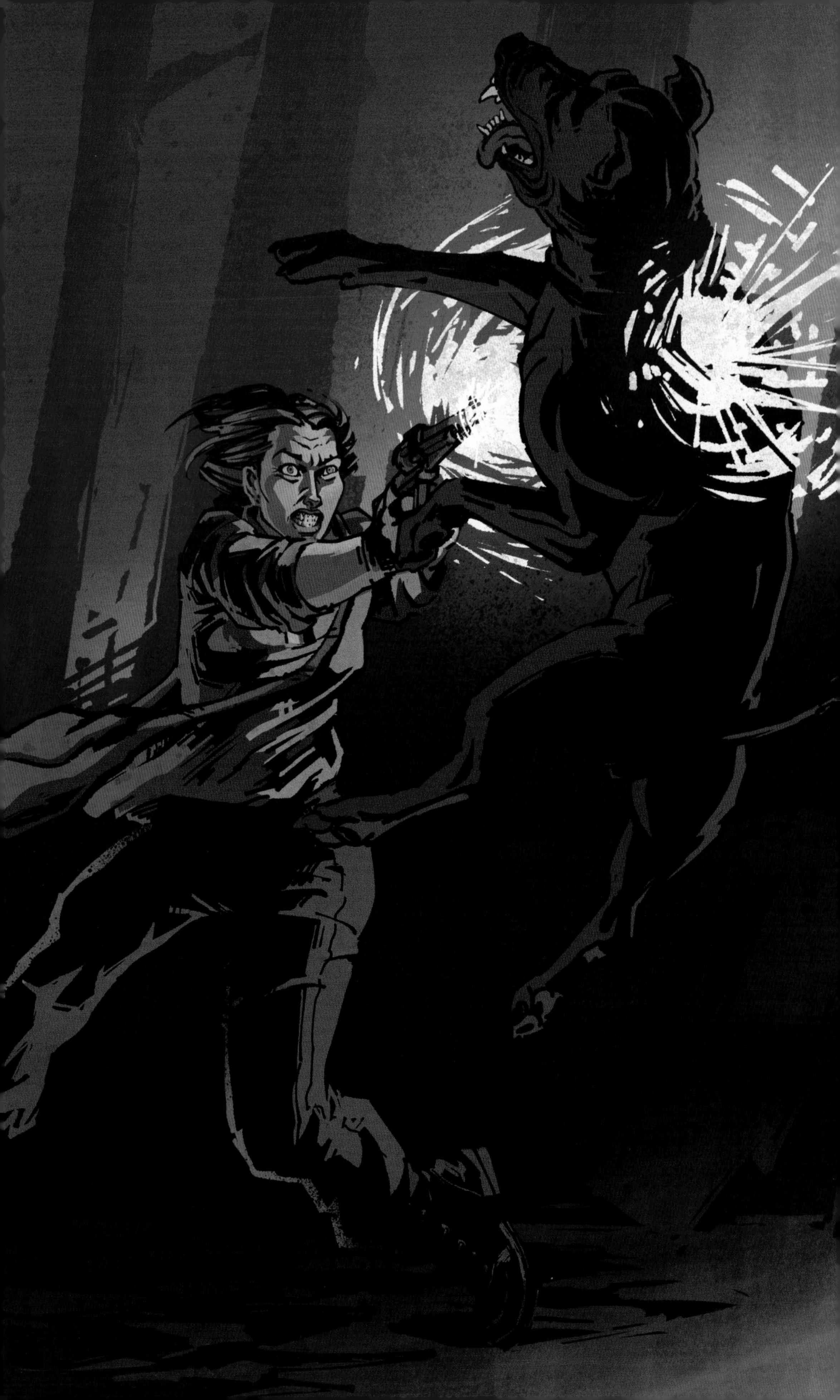

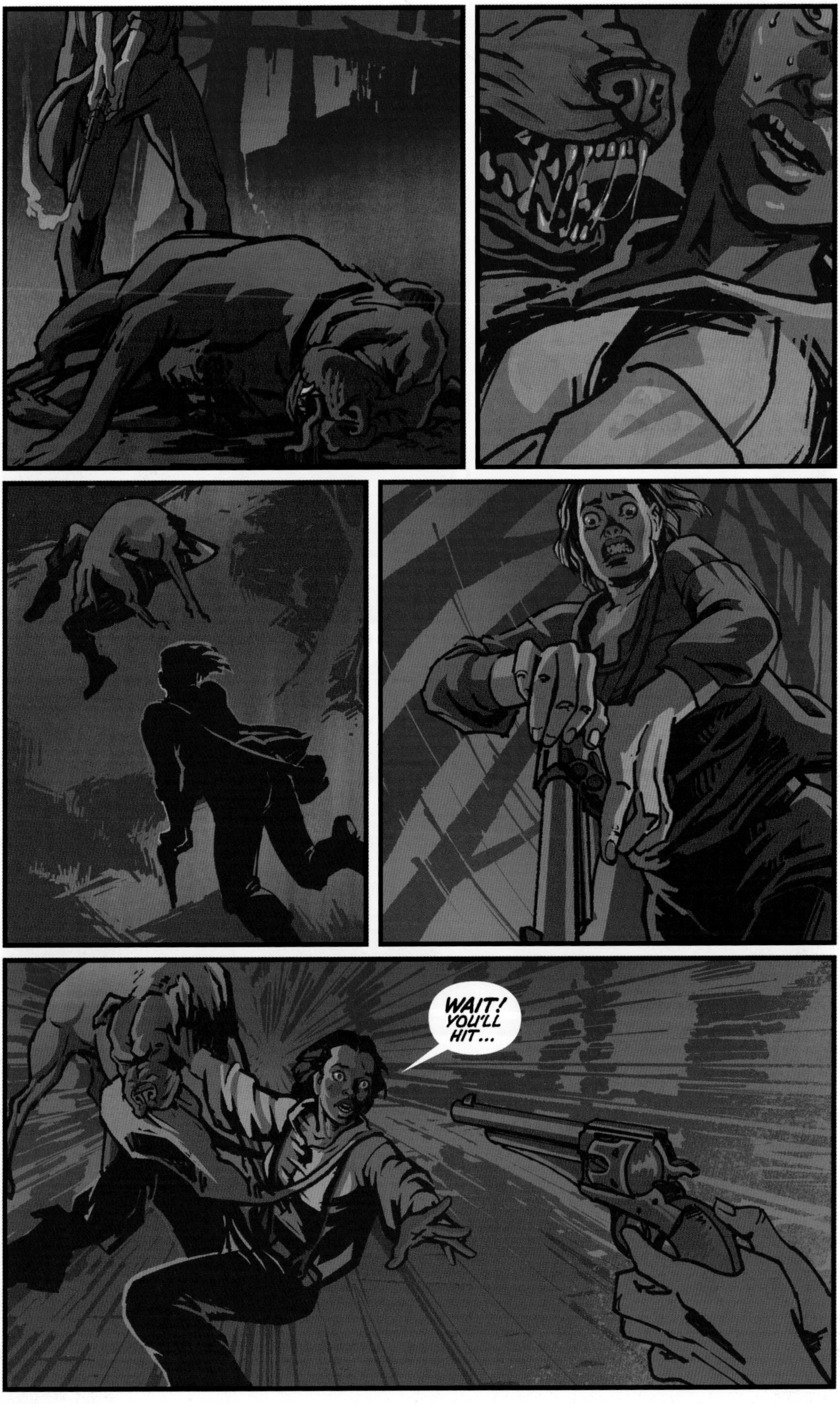
WAIT! YOU'LL HIT...

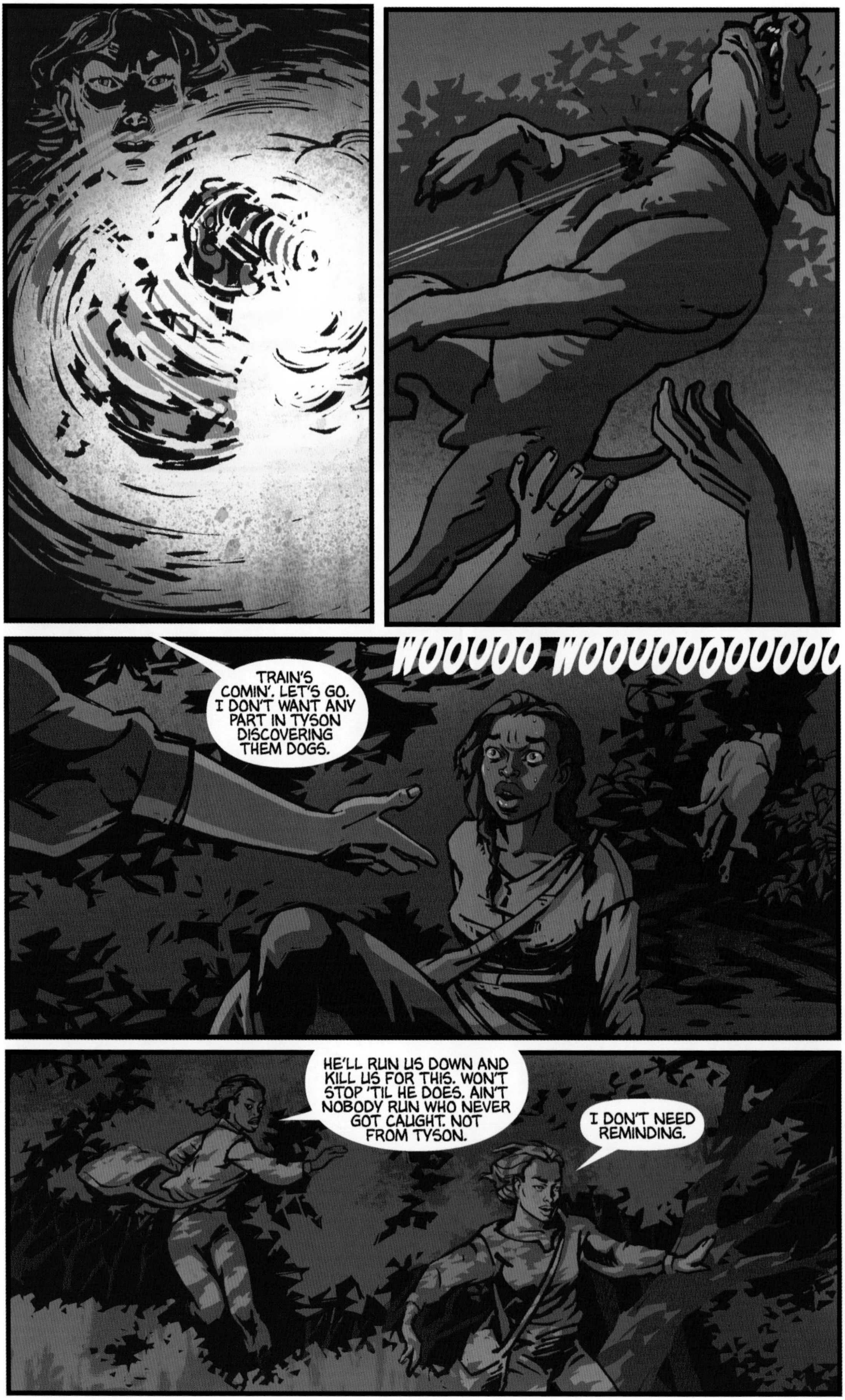
WOOOOO WOOOOOOOOOOO
TRAIN'S COMIN'. LET'S GO. I DON'T WANT ANY PART IN TYSON DISCOVERING THEM DOGS.
HE'LL RUN US DOWN AND KILL US FOR THIS. WON'T STOP 'TIL HE DOES. AIN'T NOBODY RUN WHO NEVER GOT CAUGHT. NOT FROM TYSON.
I DON'T NEED REMINDING.

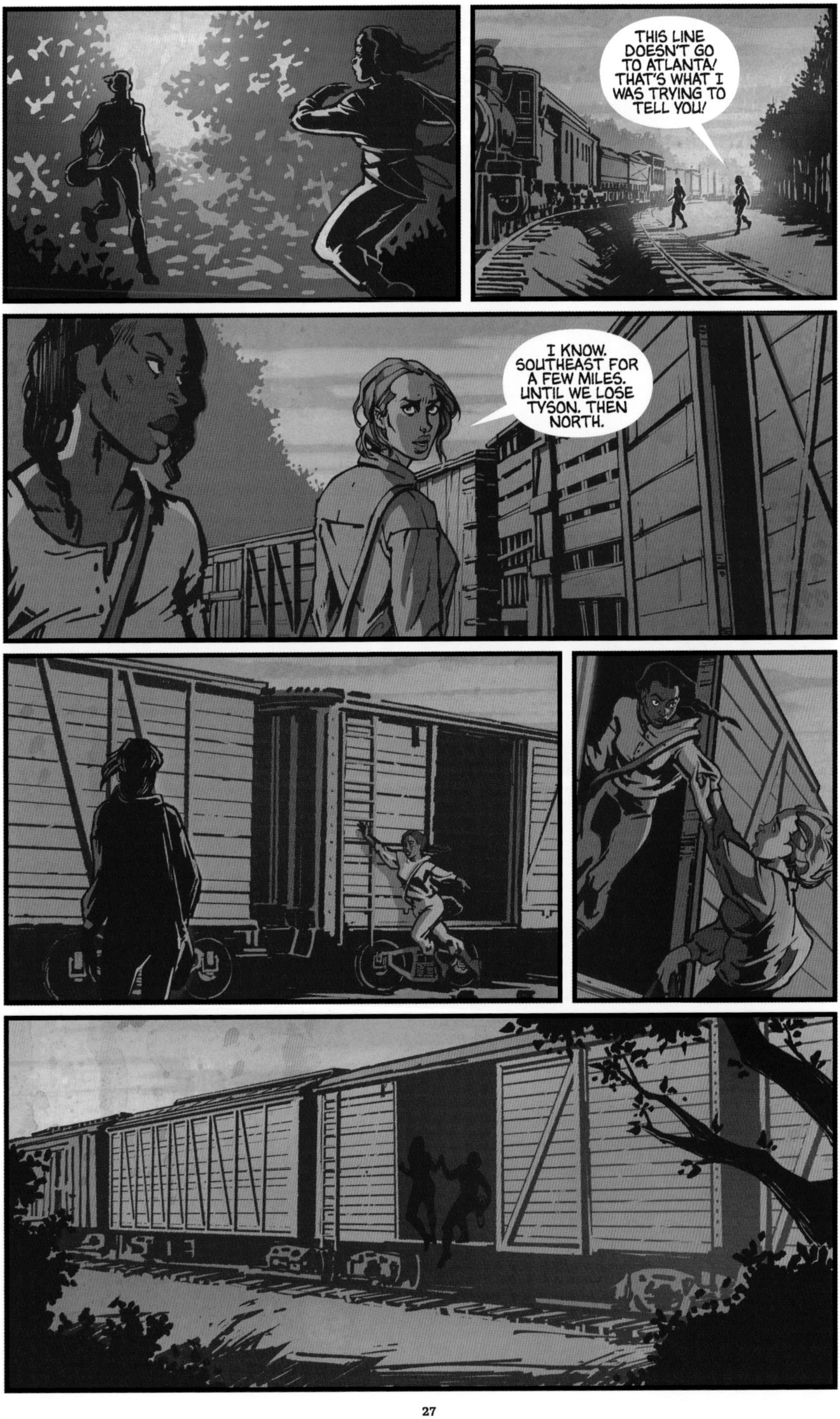
THIS LINE DOESN'T GO TO ATLANTA! THAT'S WHAT I WAS TRYING TO TELL YOU!
I KNOW. SOUTHEAST FOR A FEW MILES. UNTIL WE LOSE TYSON. THEN NORTH.

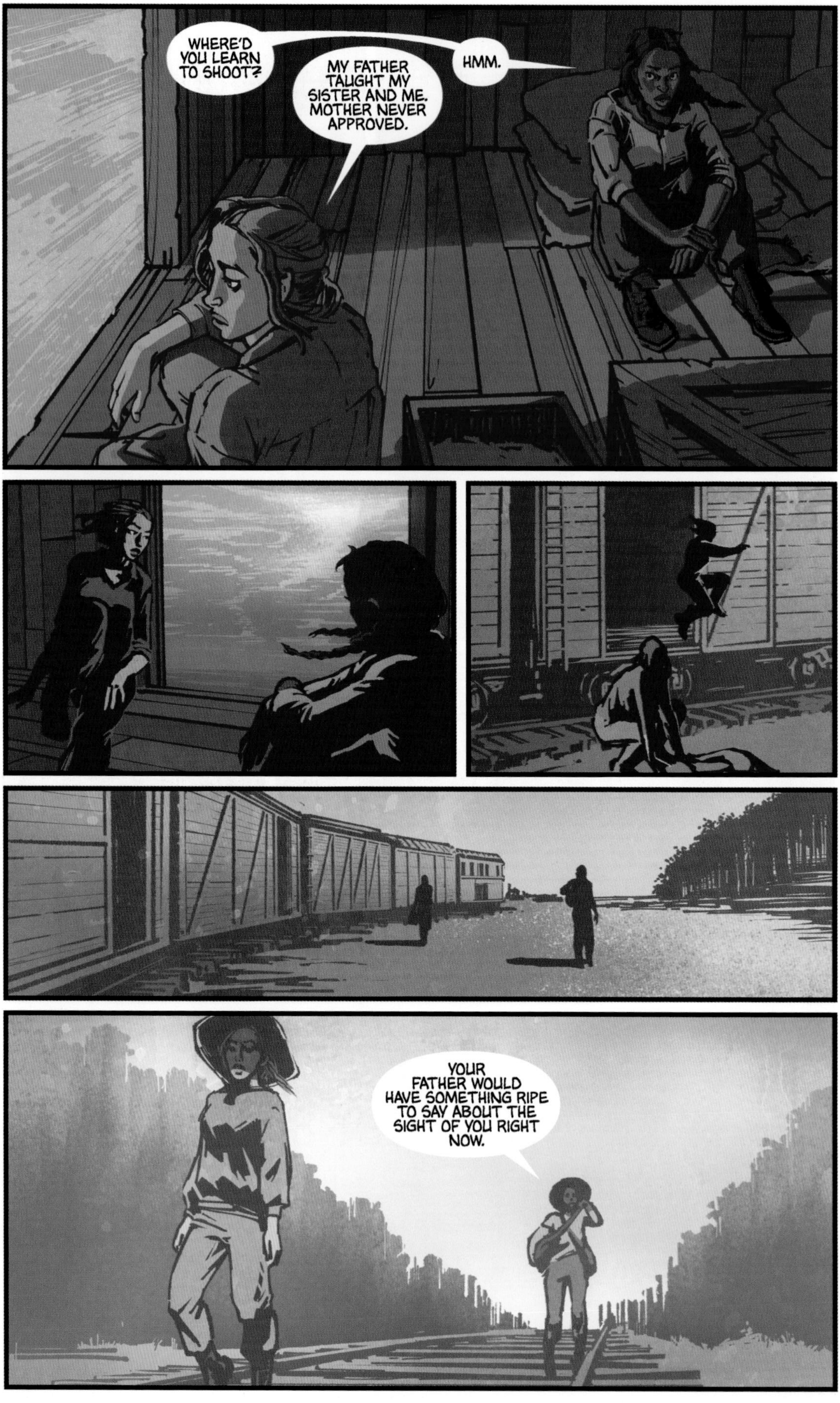
WHERE'D YOU LEARN TO SHOOT?
MY FATHER TAUGHT MY SISTER AND ME. MOTHER NEVER APPROVED.
HMM.
YOUR FATHER WOULD HAVE SOMETHING RIPE TO SAY ABOUT THE SIGHT OF YOU RIGHT NOW.

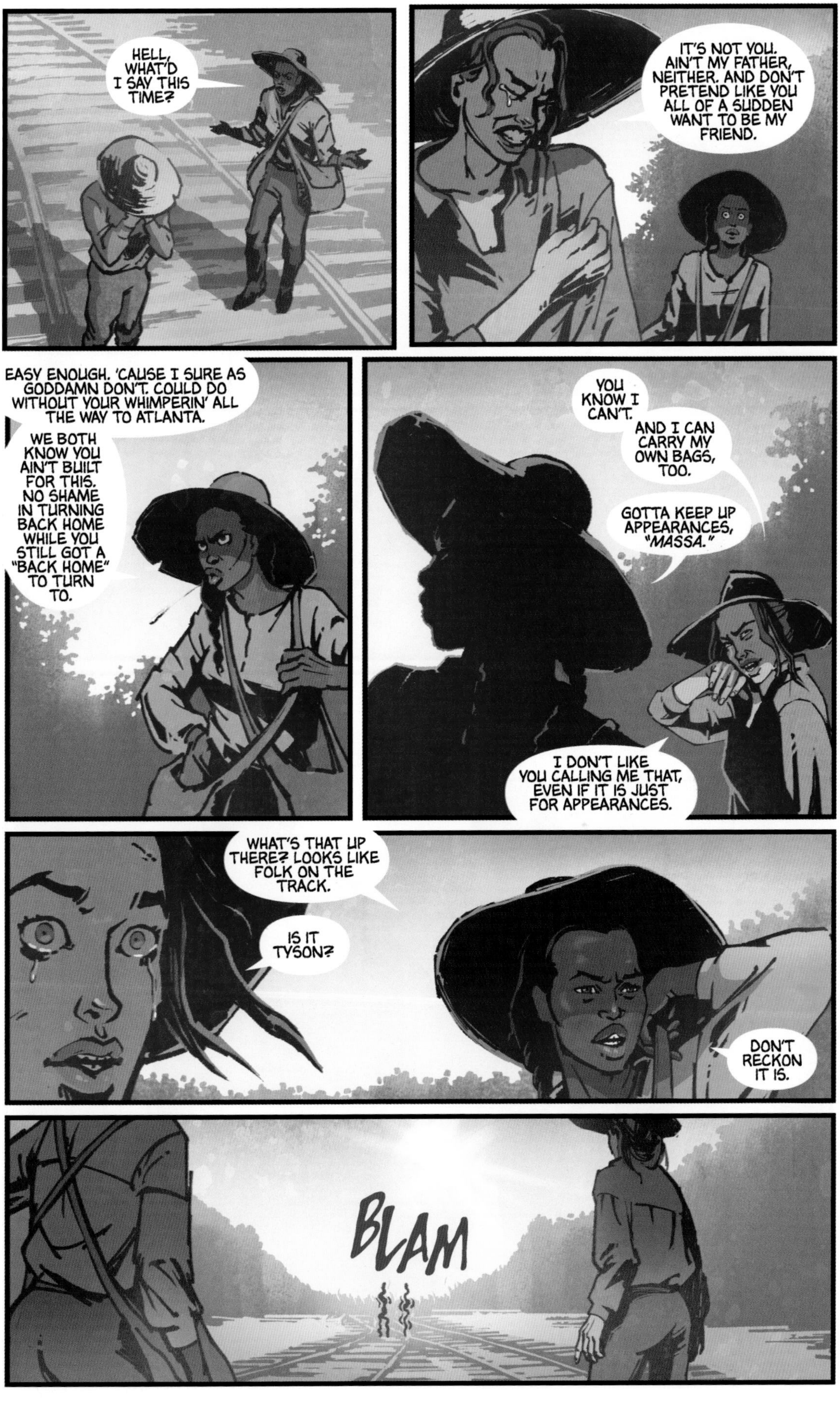

HELL, WHAT'D I SAY THIS TIME?
IT'S NOT YOU. AIN'T MY FATHER, NEITHER. AND DON'T PRETEND LIKE YOU ALL OF A SUDDEN WANT TO BE MY FRIEND.
EASY ENOUGH. 'CAUSE I SURE AS GODDAMN DON'T. COULD DO WITHOUT YOUR WHIMPERIN' ALL THE WAY TO ATLANTA.
WE BOTH KNOW YOU AIN'T BUILT FOR THIS. NO SHAME IN TURNING BACK HOME WHILE YOU STILL GOT A "BACK HOME" TO TURN TO.
YOU KNOW I CAN'T.
AND I CAN CARRY MY OWN BAGS, TOO.
GOTTA KEEP UP APPEARANCES, "MASSA."
I DON'T LIKE YOU CALLING ME THAT, EVEN IF IT IS JUST FOR APPEARANCES.
WHAT'S THAT UP THERE? LOOKS LIKE FOLK ON THE TRACK.
IS IT TYSON?
DON'T RECKON IT IS.
BLAM

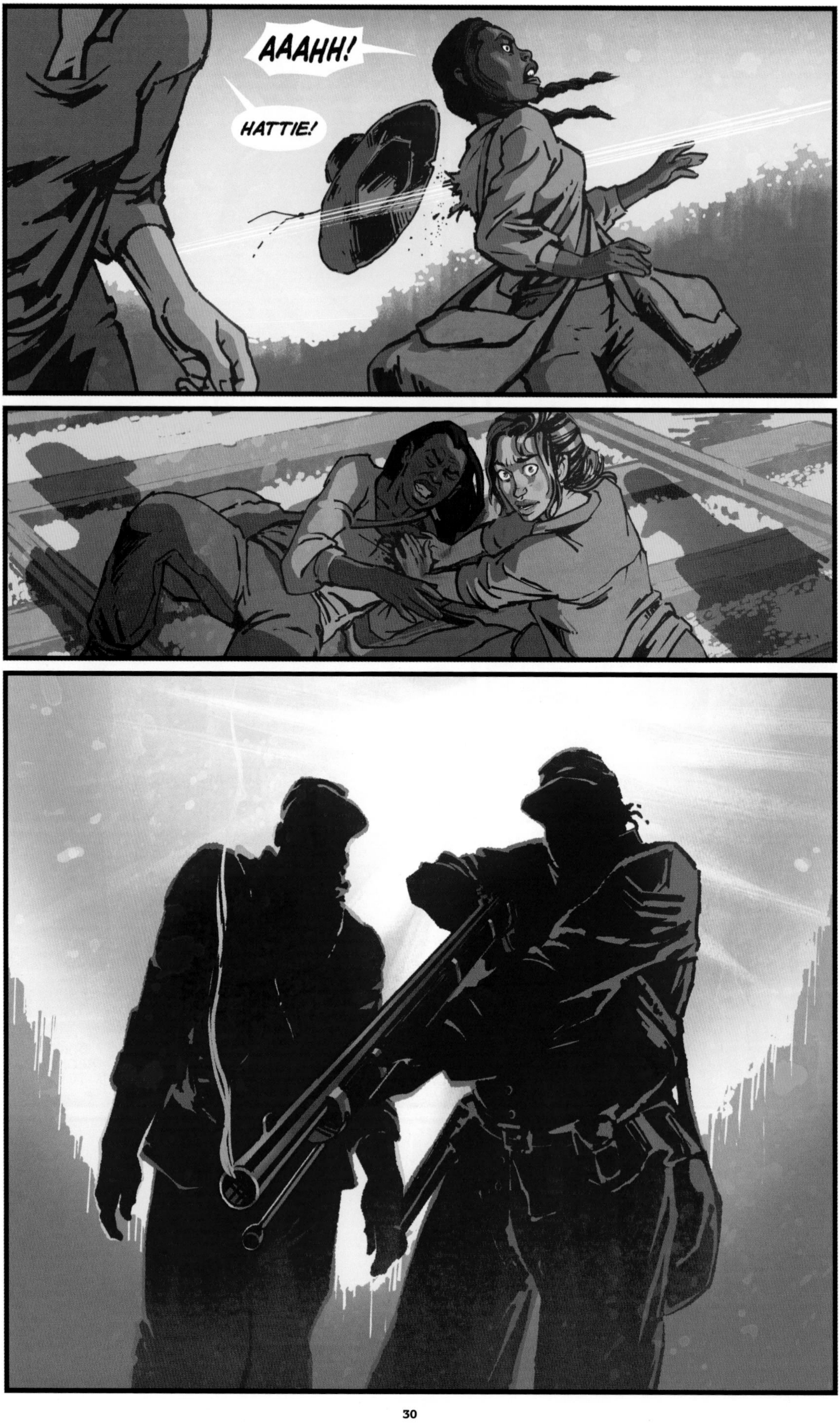
AAAHH!
HATTIE!

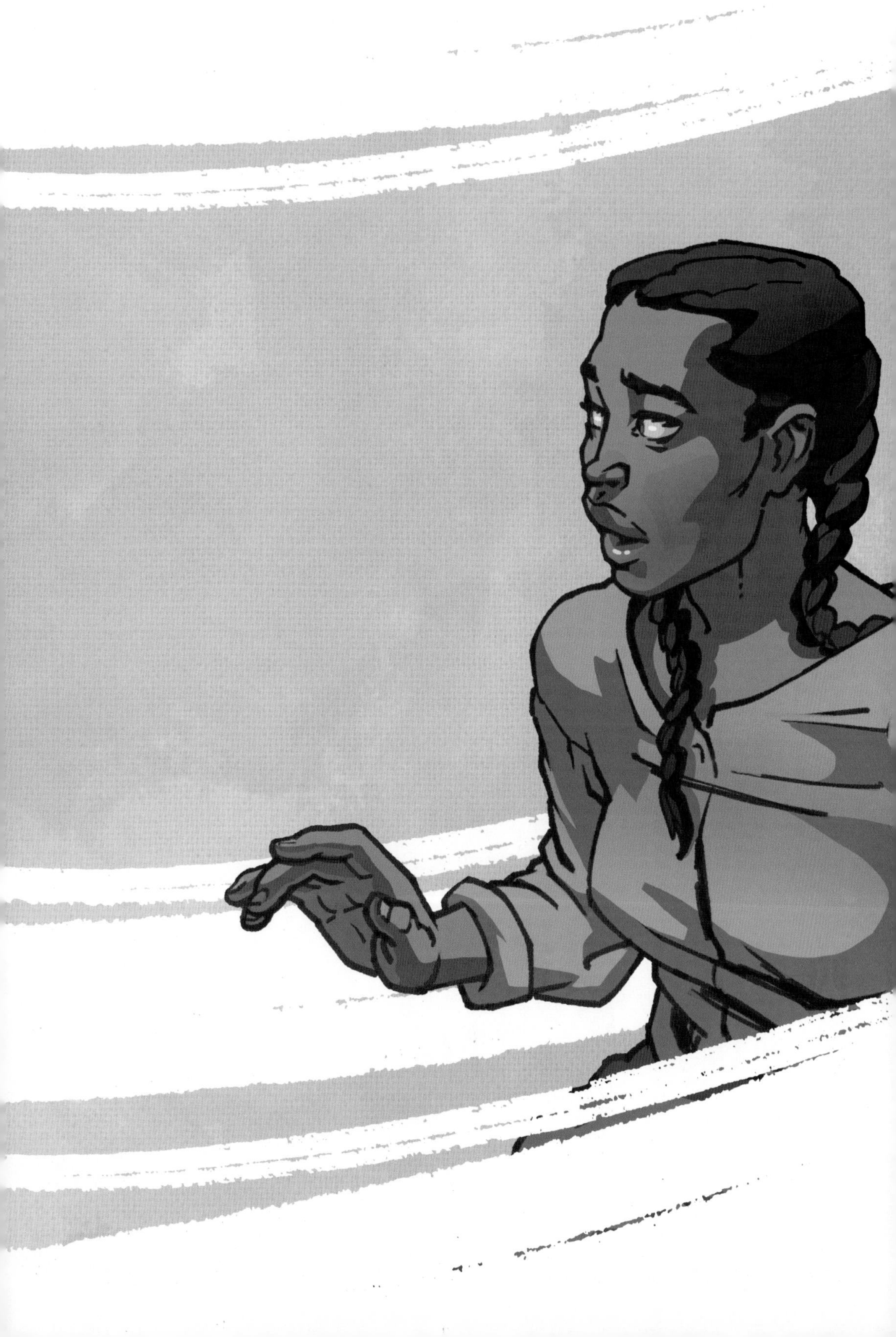

CHAPTER TWO

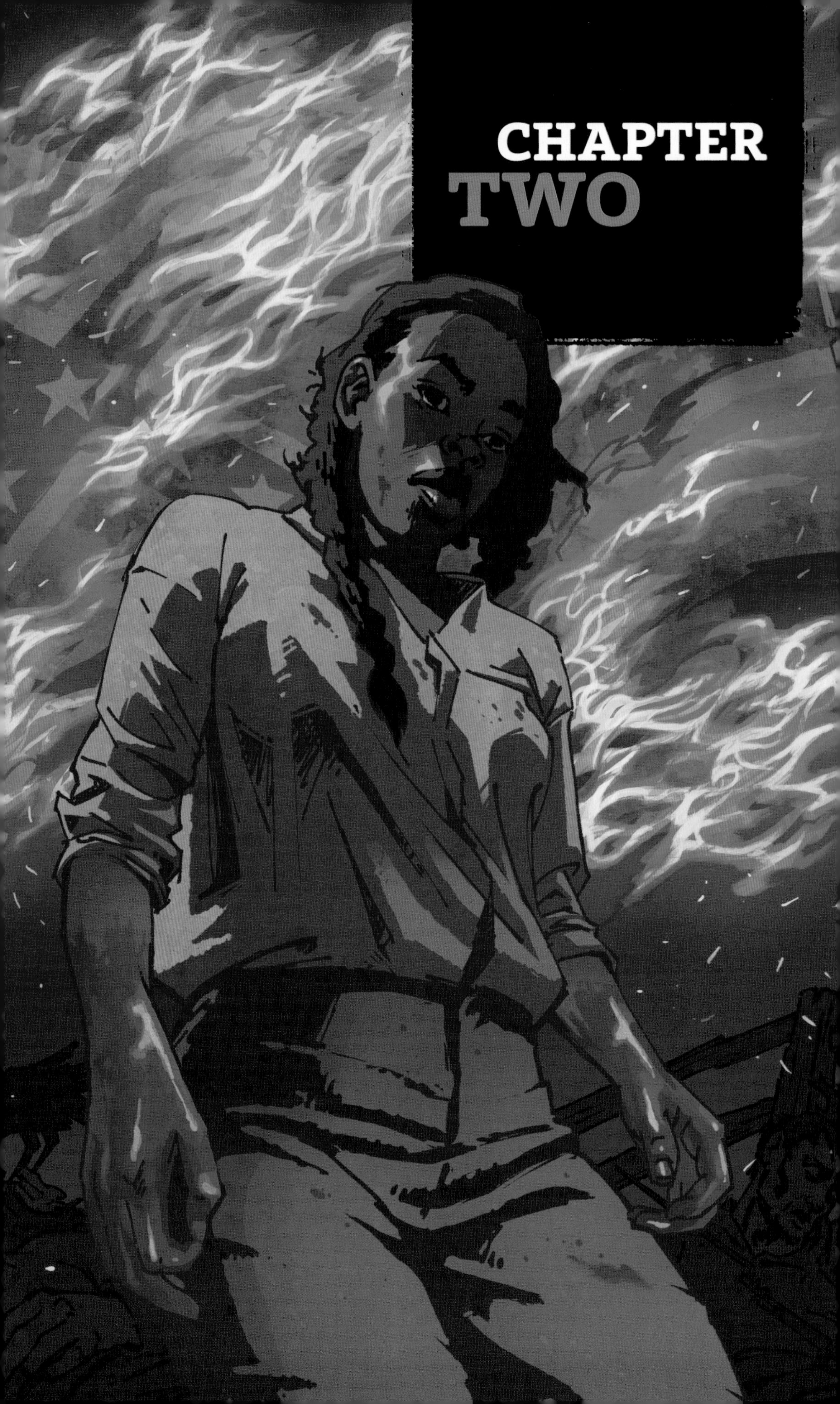

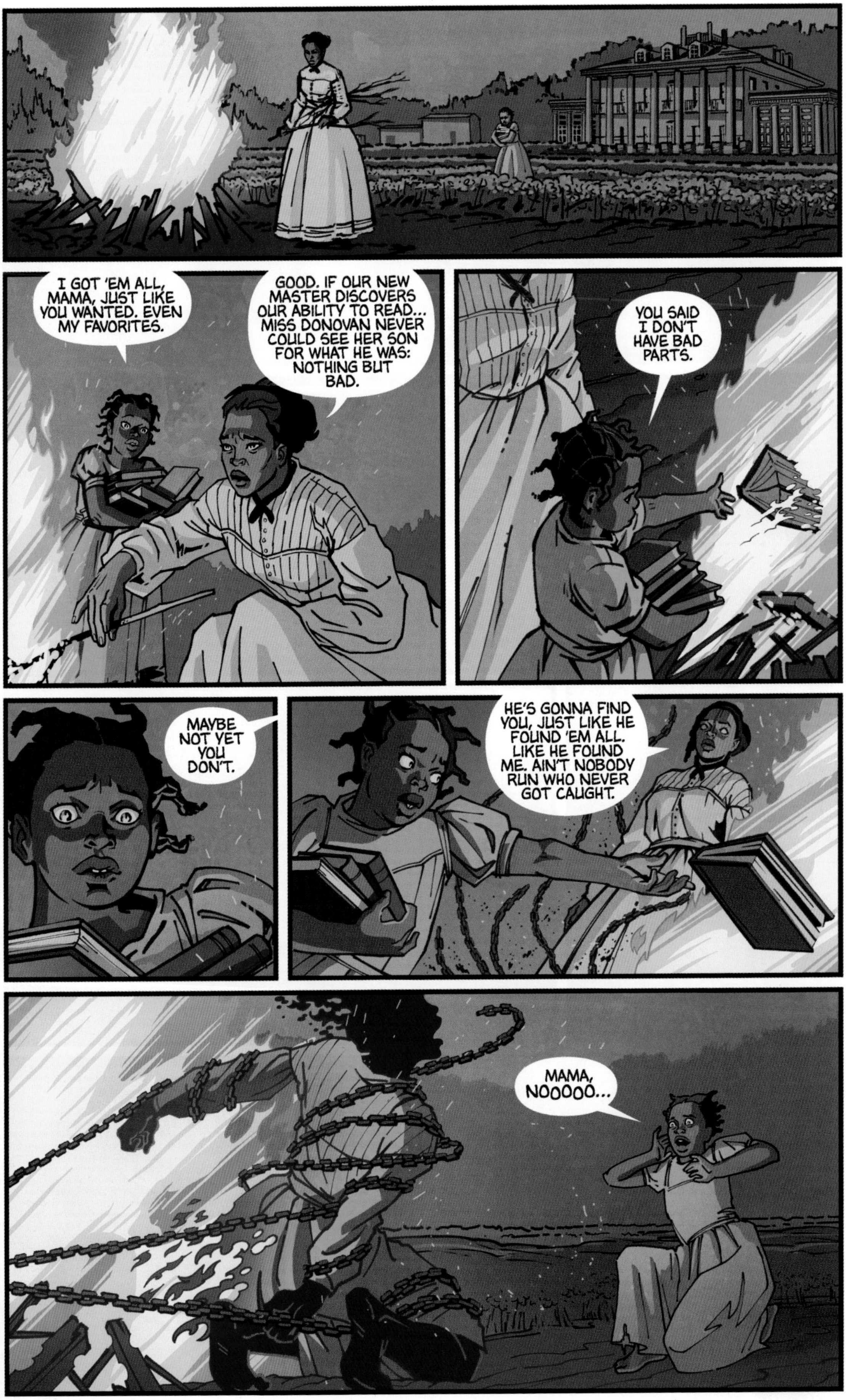

I GOT 'EM ALL, MAMA, JUST LIKE YOU WANTED. EVEN MY FAVORITES.
GOOD. IF OUR NEW MASTER DISCOVERS OUR ABILITY TO READ... MISS DONOVAN NEVER COULD SEE HER SON FOR WHAT HE WAS: NOTHING BUT BAD.
YOU SAID I DON'T HAVE BAD PARTS.
MAYBE NOT YET YOU DON'T.
HE'S GONNA FIND YOU, JUST LIKE HE FOUND 'EM ALL. LIKE HE FOUND ME. AIN'T NOBODY RUN WHO NEVER GOT CAUGHT.
MAMA, NOOOOO...

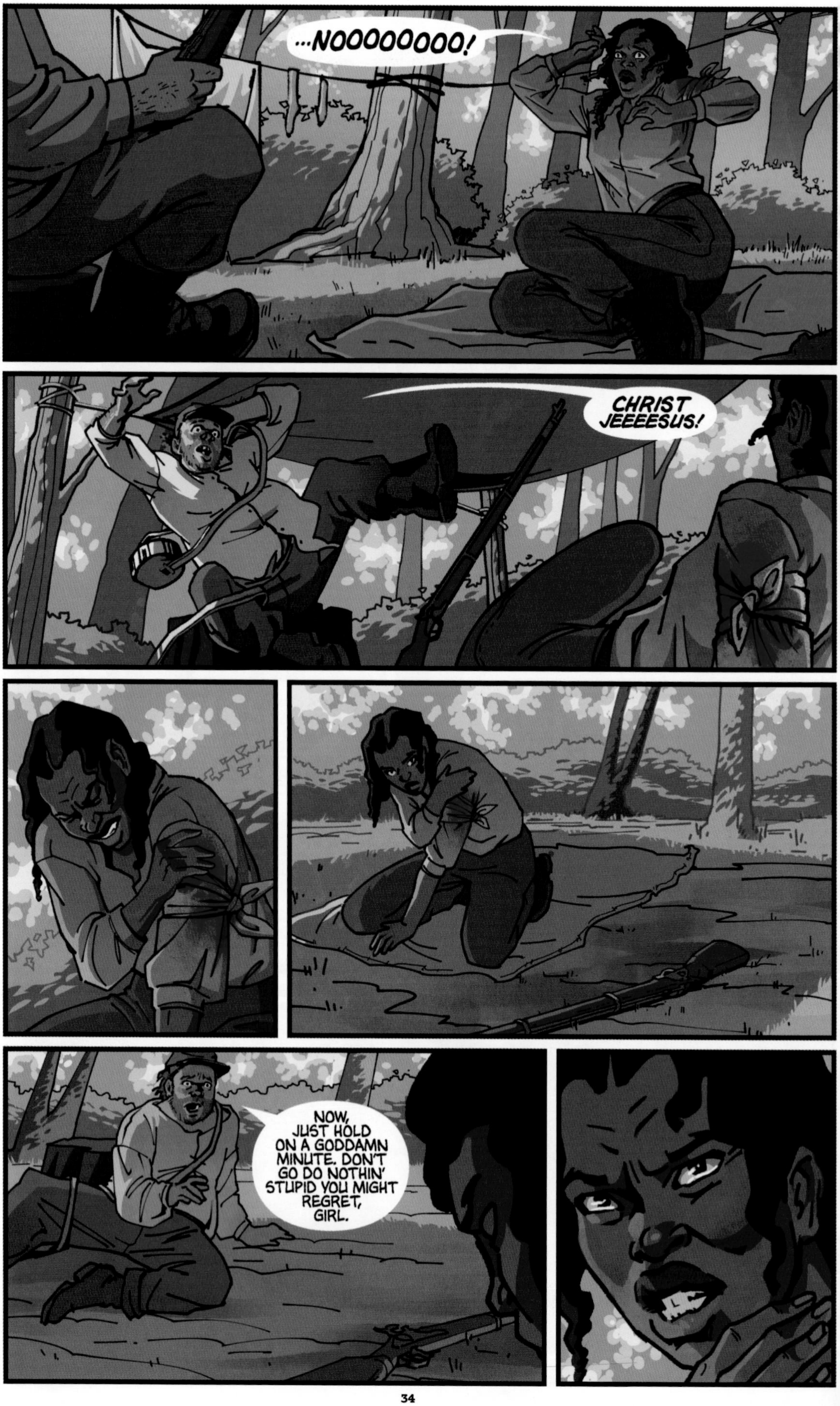
...NOOOOOOOO!
CHRIST JEEEESUS!
NOW, JUST HOLD ON A GODDAMN MINUTE. DON'T GO DO NOTHIN' STUPID YOU MIGHT REGRET, GIRL.

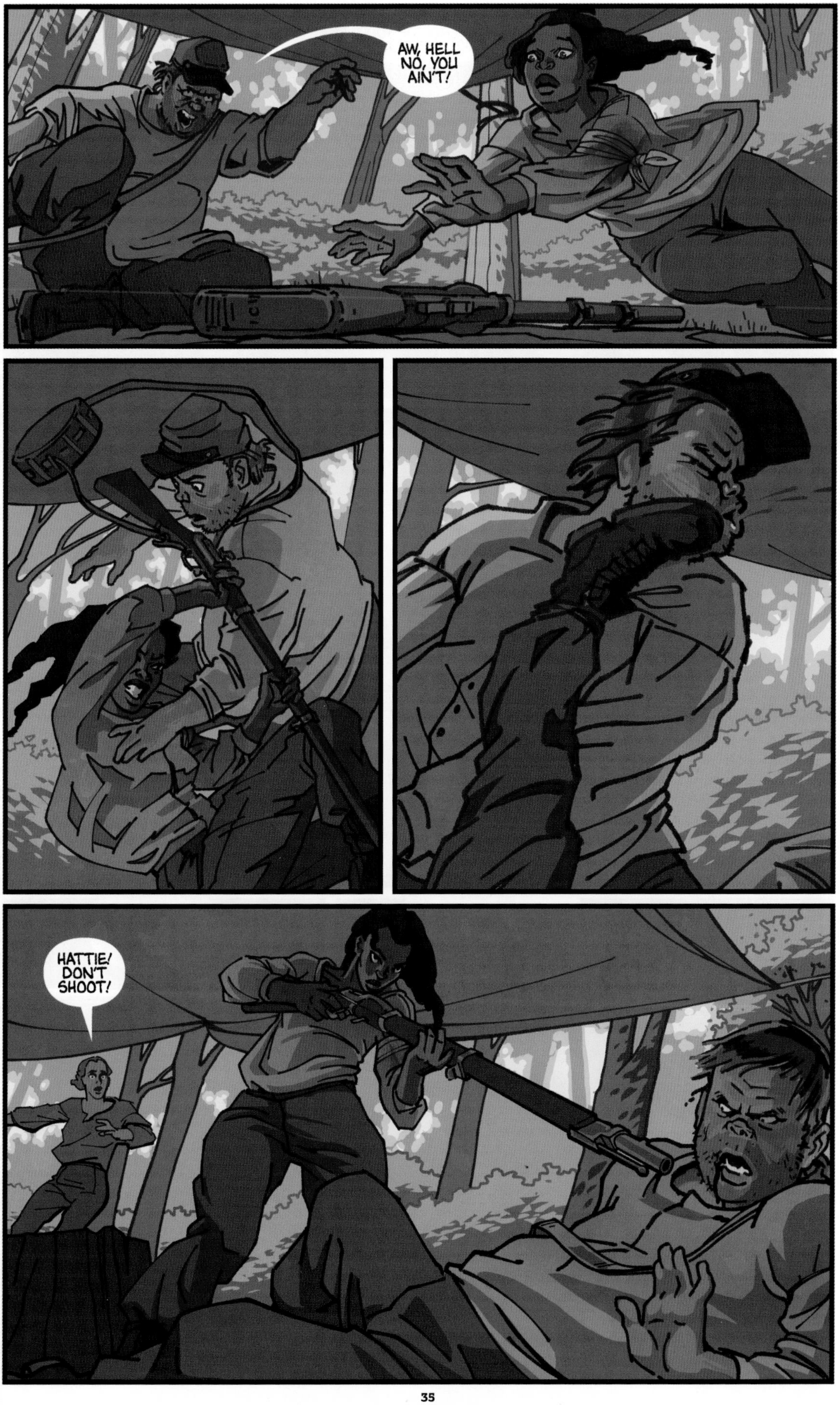
AW, HELL NO, YOU AIN'T!
HATTIE! DON'T SHOOT!

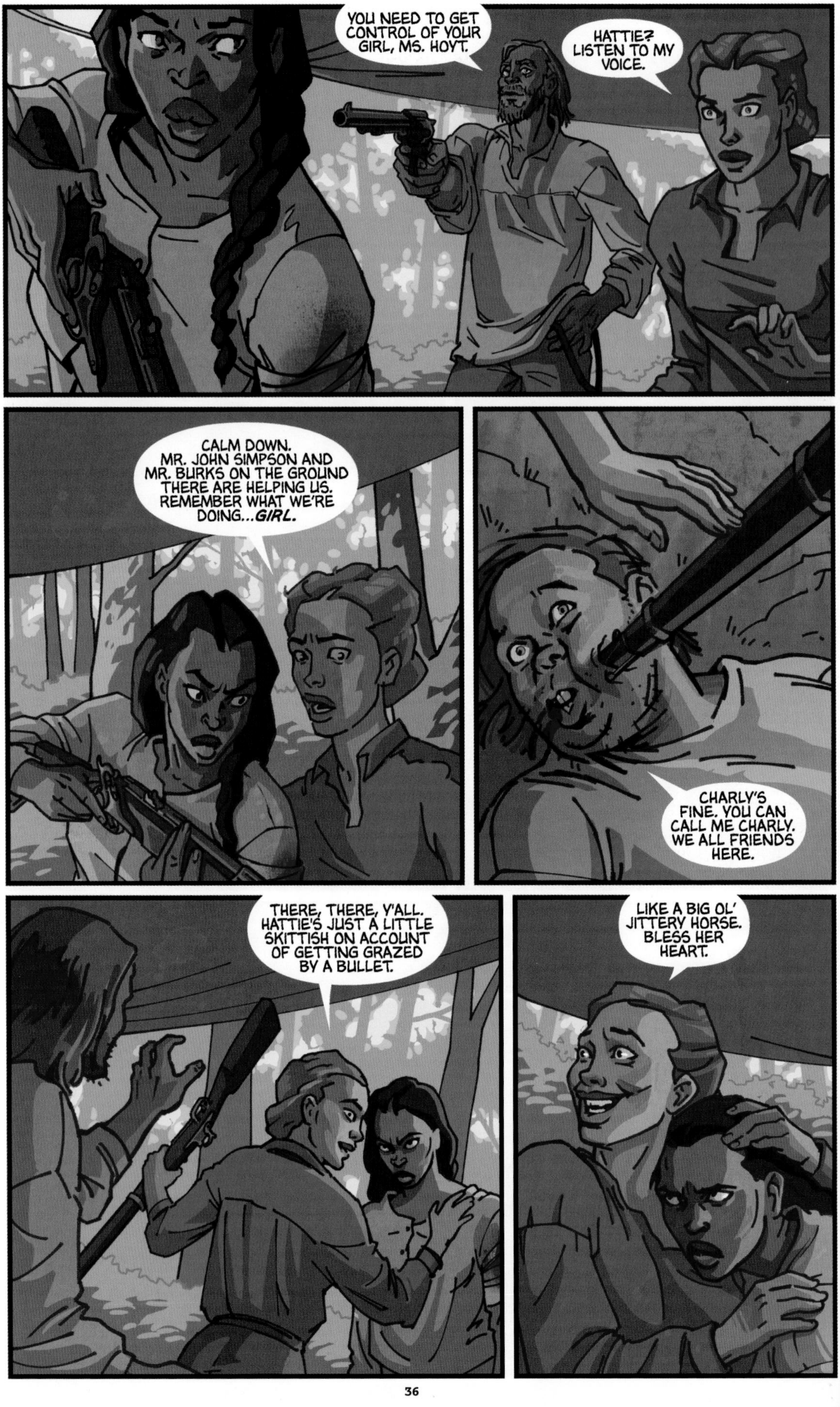
YOU NEED TO GET CONTROL OF YOUR GIRL, MS. HOYT.
HATTIE? LISTEN TO MY VOICE.
CALM DOWN. MR. JOHN SIMPSON AND MR. BURKS ON THE GROUND THERE ARE HELPING US. REMEMBER WHAT WE'RE DOING... GIRL.
CHARLY'S FINE. YOU CAN CALL ME CHARLY. WE ALL FRIENDS HERE.
THERE, THERE, Y'ALL. HATTIE'S JUST A LITTLE SKITTISH ON ACCOUNT OF GETTING GRAZED BY A BULLET.
LIKE A BIG OL' JITTERY HORSE. BLESS HER HEART.

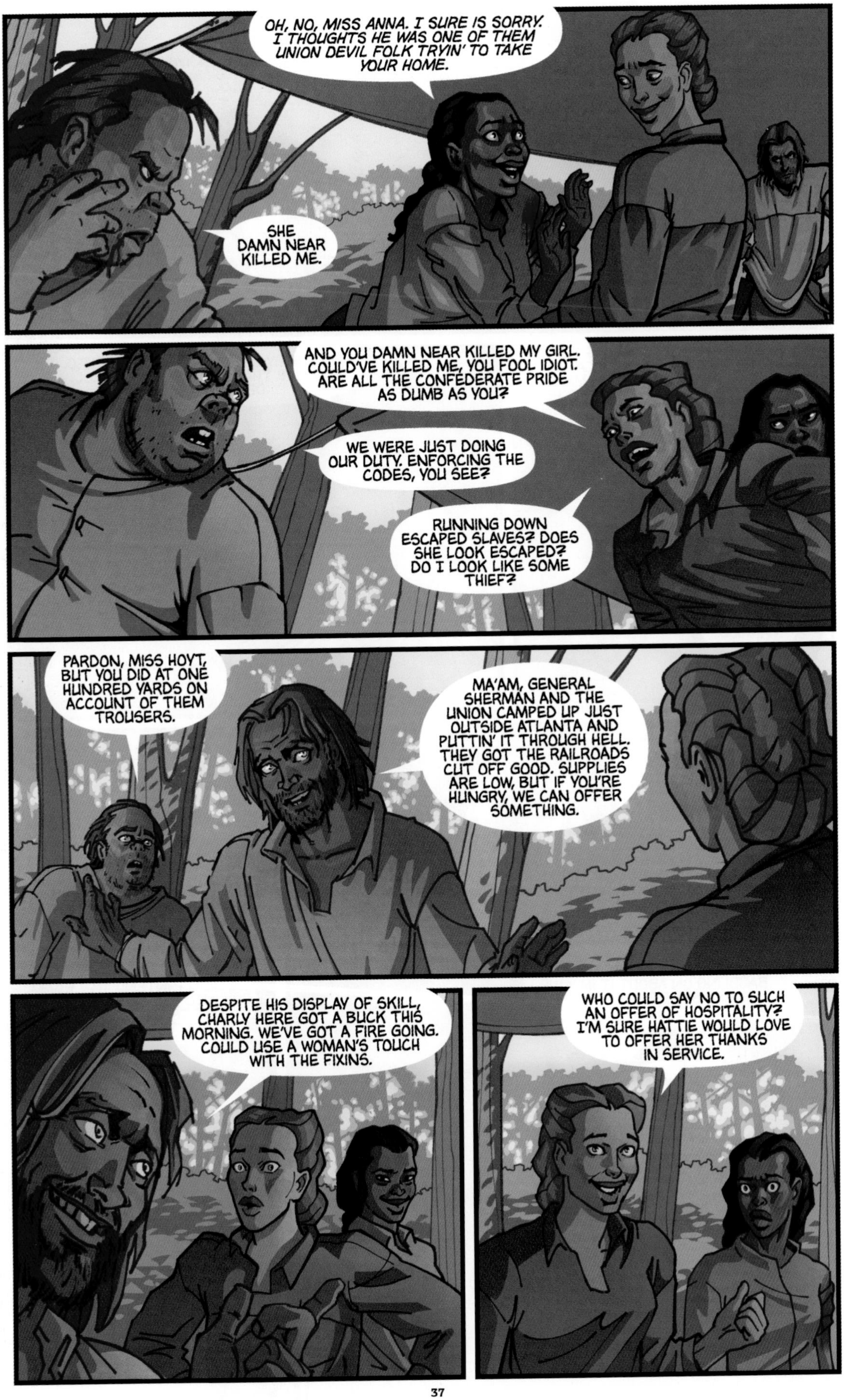
OH, NO, MISS ANNA. I SURE IS SORRY. I THOUGHTS HE WAS ONE OF THEM UNION DEVIL FOLK TRYIN' TO TAKE YOUR HOME.
SHE DAMN NEAR KILLED ME.
AND YOU DAMN NEAR KILLED MY GIRL. COULD'VE KILLED ME, YOU FOOL IDIOT. ARE ALL THE CONFEDERATE PRIDE AS DUMB AS YOU?
WE WERE JUST DOING OUR DUTY. ENFORCING THE CODES, YOU SEE?
RUNNING DOWN ESCAPED SLAVES? DOES SHE LOOK ESCAPED? DO I LOOK LIKE SOME THIEF?
PARDON, MISS HOYT, BUT YOU DID AT ONE HUNDRED YARDS ON ACCOUNT OF THEM TROUSERS.
MA'AM, GENERAL SHERMAN AND THE UNION CAMPED UP JUST OUTSIDE ATLANTA AND PUTTIN' IT THROUGH HELL. THEY GOT THE RAILROADS CUT OFF GOOD. SUPPLIES ARE LOW, BUT IF YOU'RE HUNGRY, WE CAN OFFER SOMETHING.
DESPITE HIS DISPLAY OF SKILL, CHARLY HERE GOT A BUCK THIS MORNING. WE'VE GOT A FIRE GOING. COULD USE A WOMAN'S TOUCH WITH THE FIXINS.
WHO COULD SAY NO TO SUCH AN OFFER OF HOSPITALITY? I'M SURE HATTIE WOULD LOVE TO OFFER HER THANKS IN SERVICE.

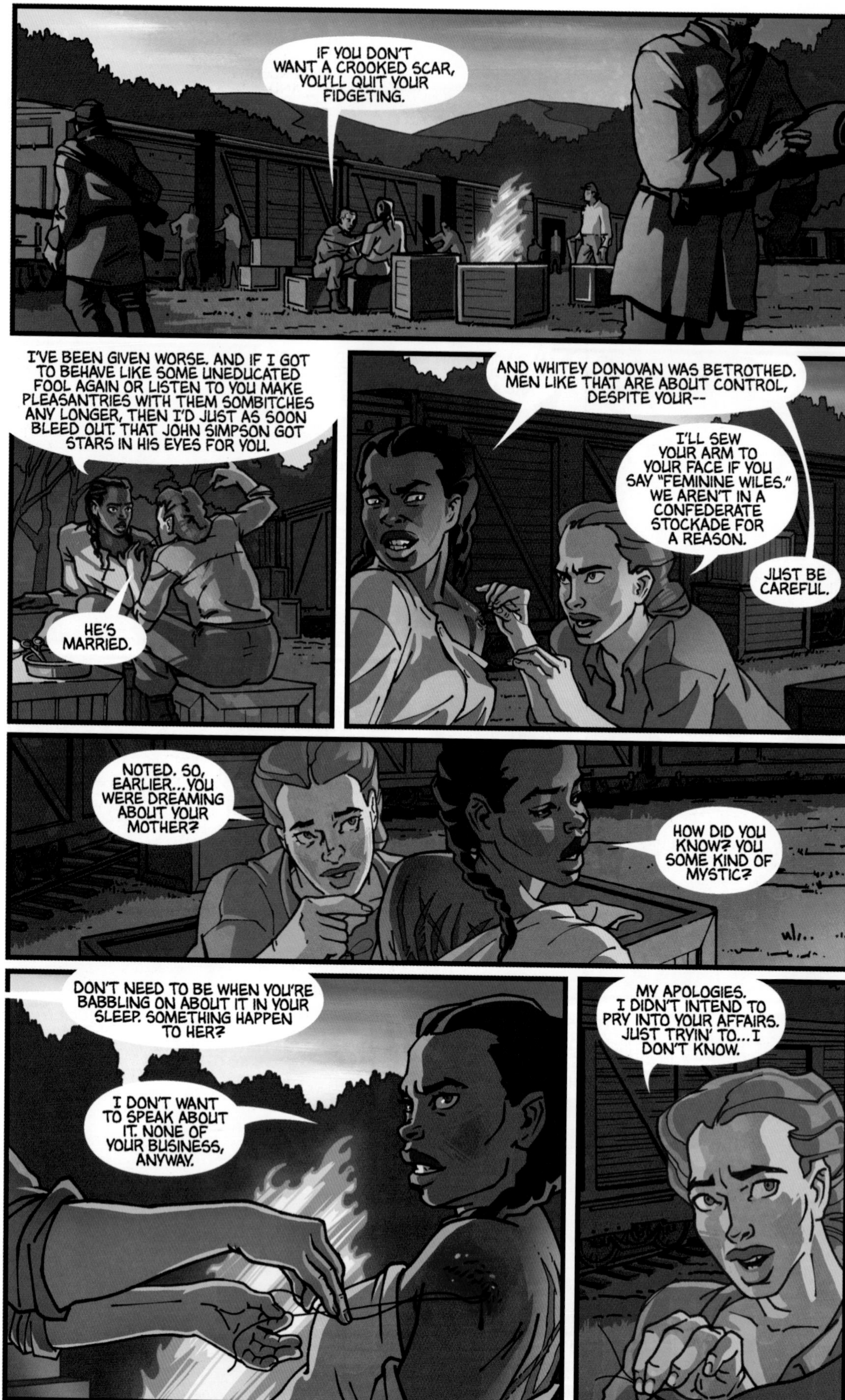

IF YOU DON'T WANT A CROOKED SCAR, YOU'LL QUIT YOUR FIDGETING.
I'VE BEEN GIVEN WORSE. AND IF I GOT TO BEHAVE LIKE SOME UNEDUCATED FOOL AGAIN OR LISTEN TO YOU MAKE PLEASANTRIES WITH THEM SOMBITCHES ANY LONGER, THEN I'D JUST AS SOON BLEED OUT. THAT JOHN SIMPSON GOT STARS IN HIS EYES FOR YOU.
HE'S MARRIED.
AND WHITEY DONOVAN WAS BETROTHED. MEN LIKE THAT ARE ABOUT CONTROL, DESPITE YOUR--
I'LL SEW YOUR ARM TO YOUR FACE IF YOU SAY "FEMININE WILES." WE AREN'T IN A CONFEDERATE STOCKADE FOR A REASON.
JUST BE CAREFUL.
NOTED. SO, EARLIER... YOU WERE DREAMING ABOUT YOUR MOTHER?
HOW DID YOU KNOW? YOU SOME KIND OF MYSTIC?
DON'T NEED TO BE WHEN YOU'RE BABBLING ON ABOUT IT IN YOUR SLEEP. SOMETHING HAPPEN TO HER?
I DON'T WANT TO SPEAK ABOUT IT. NONE OF YOUR BUSINESS, ANYWAY.
MY APOLOGIES. I DIDN'T INTEND TO PRY INTO YOUR AFFAIRS. JUST TRYIN' TO... I DON'T KNOW.

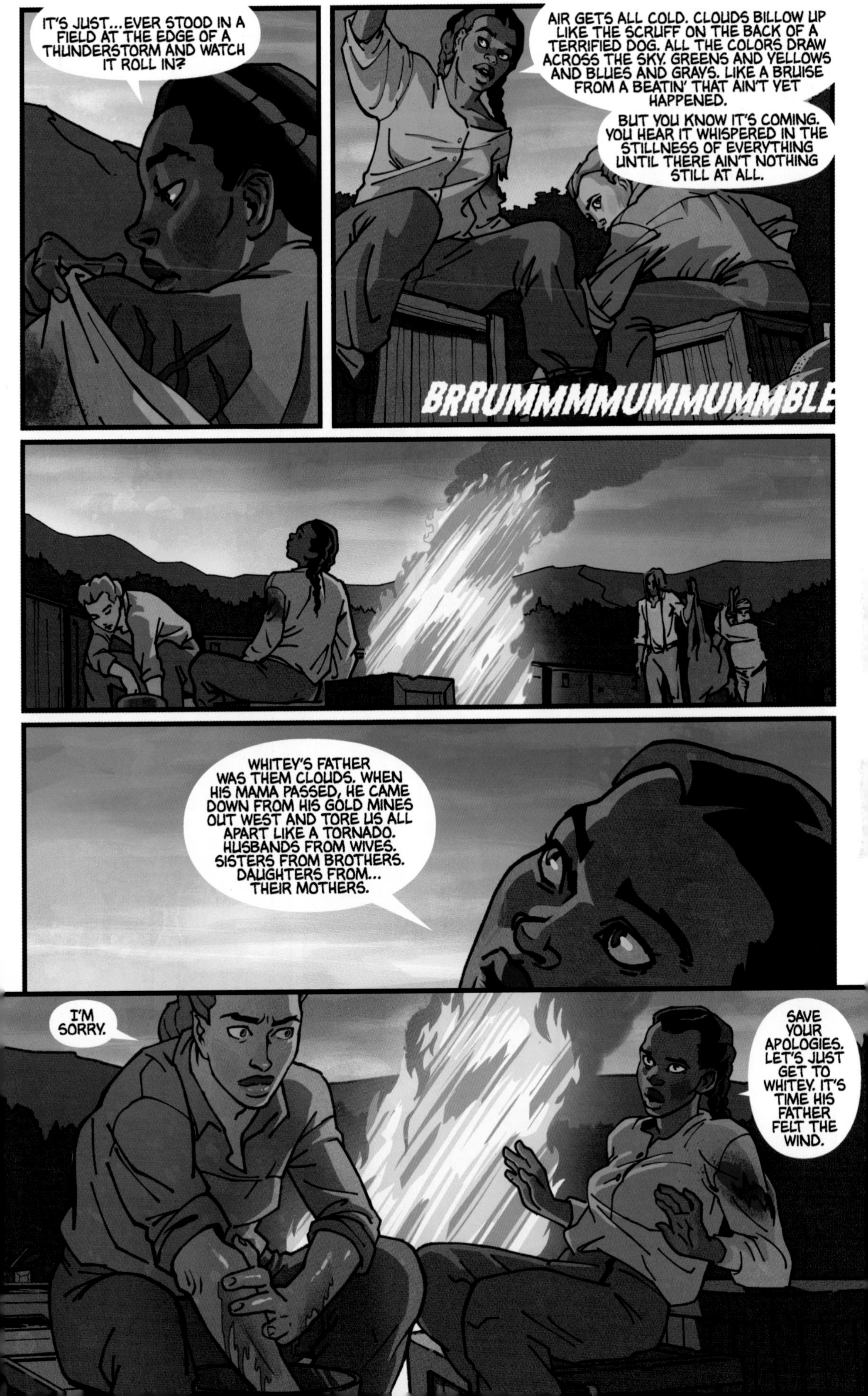
IT'S JUST... EVER STOOD IN A FIELD AT THE EDGE OF A THUNDERSTORM AND WATCH IT ROLL IN?
AIR GETS ALL COLD. CLOUDS BILLOW UP LIKE THE SCRUFF ON THE BACK OF A TERRIFIED DOG. ALL THE COLORS DRAW ACROSS THE SKY. GREENS AND YELLOWS AND BLUES AND GRAYS. LIKE A BRUISE FROM A BEATIN' THAT AIN'T YET HAPPENED.
BUT YOU KNOW IT'S COMING. YOU HEAR IT WHISPERED IN THE STILLNESS OF EVERYTHING UNTIL THERE AIN'T NOTHING STILL AT ALL.
BRRUMMMMUMMUMMBLE
WHITEY'S FATHER WAS THEM CLOUDS. WHEN HIS MAMA PASSED, HE CAME DOWN FROM HIS GOLD MINES OUT WEST AND TORE US ALL APART LIKE A TORNADO. HUSBANDS FROM WIVES. SISTERS FROM BROTHERS. DAUGHTERS FROM... THEIR MOTHERS.
I'M SORRY.
SAVE YOUR APOLOGIES. LET'S JUST GET TO WHITEY. IT'S TIME HIS FATHER FELT THE WIND.

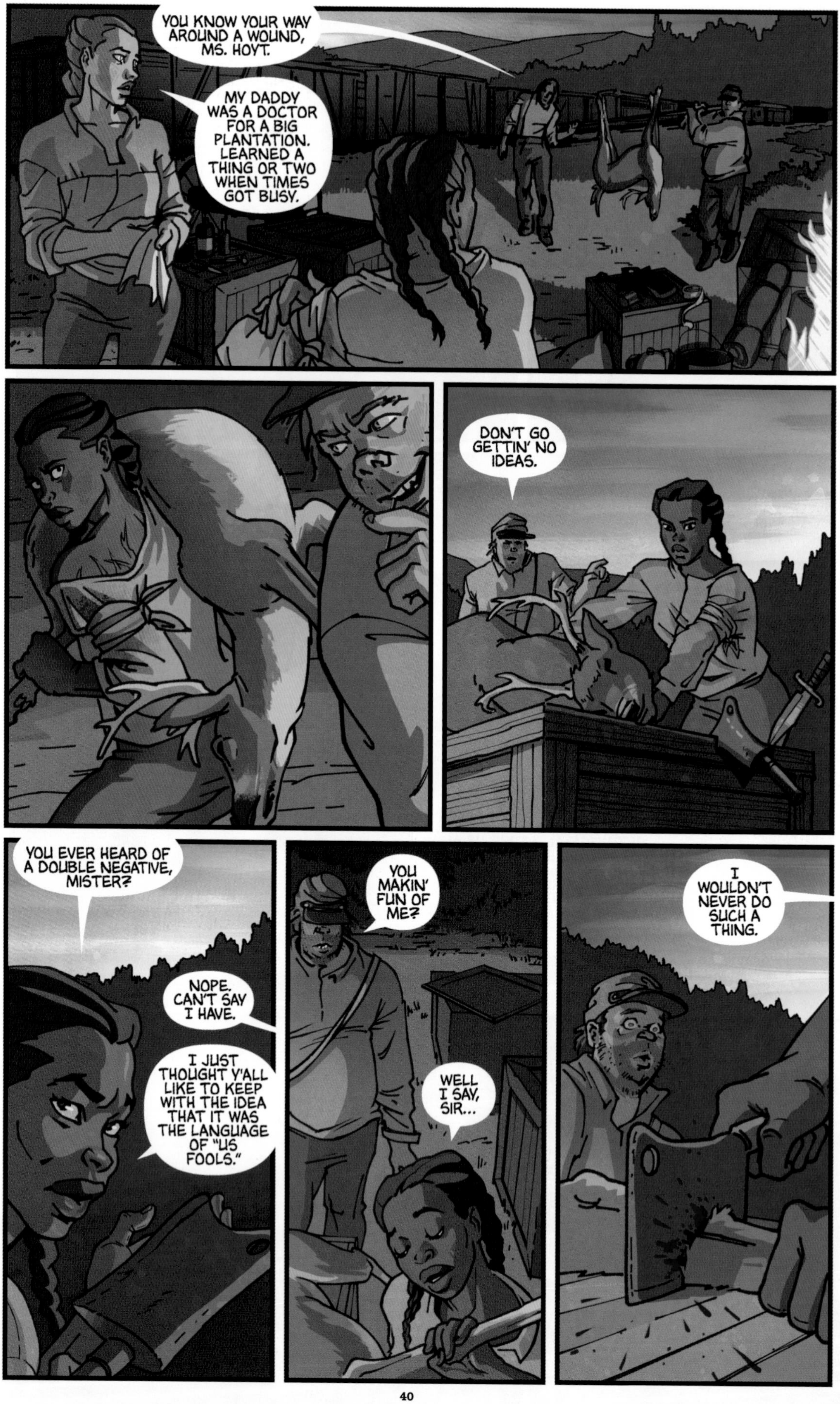
YOU KNOW YOUR WAY AROUND A WOUND, MS. HOYT.
MY DADDY WAS A DOCTOR FOR A BIG PLANTATION. LEARNED A THING OR TWO WHEN TIMES GOT BUSY.
DON'T GO GETTIN' NO IDEAS.
YOU EVER HEARD OF A DOUBLE NEGATIVE, MISTER?
NOPE. CAN'T SAY I HAVE.
I JUST THOUGHT Y'ALL LIKE TO KEEP WITH THE IDEA THAT IT WAS THE LANGUAGE OF "US FOOLS."
YOU MAKIN' FUN OF ME?
WELL I SAY, SIR...
I WOULDN'T NEVER DO SUCH A THING.

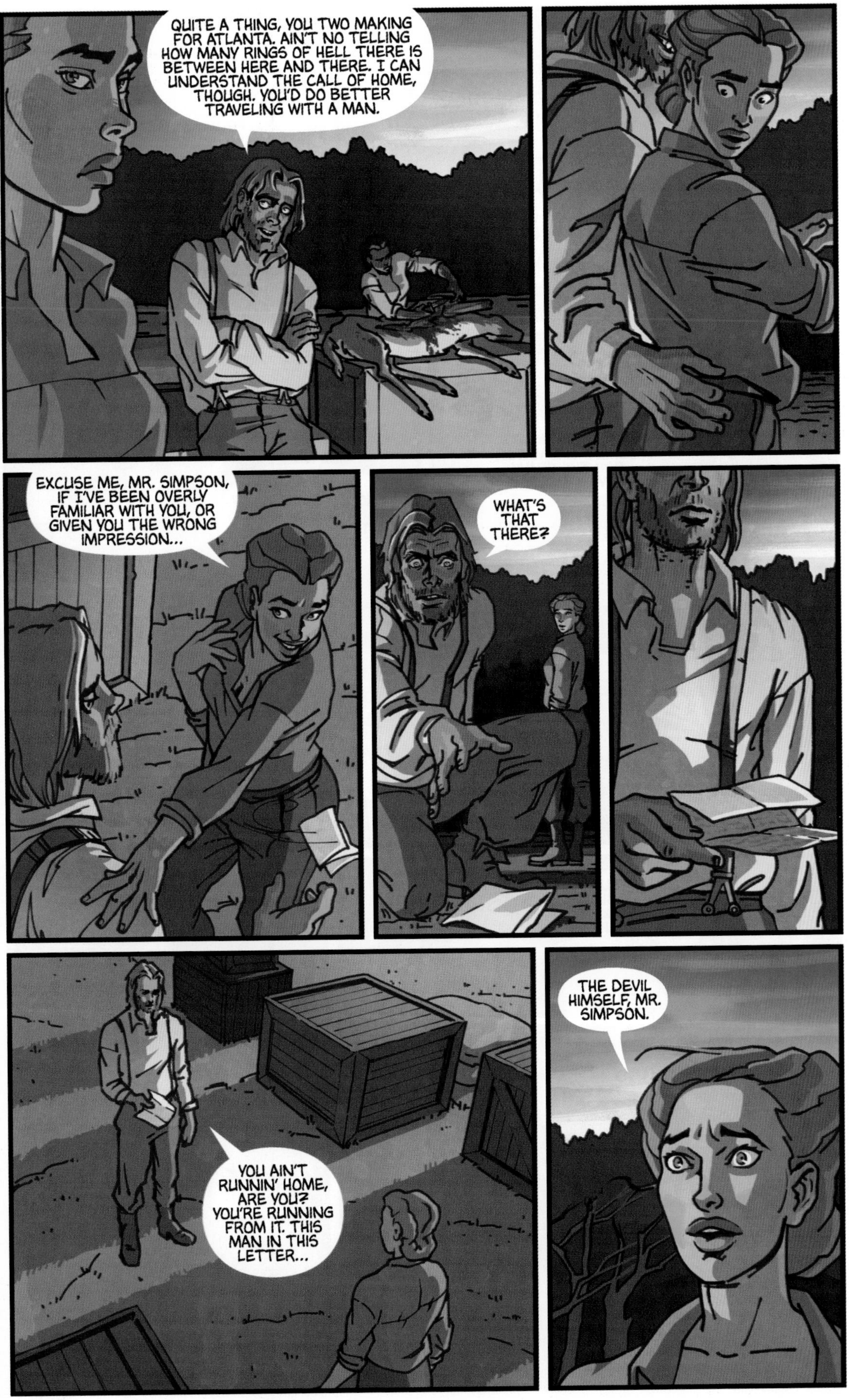
QUITE A THING, YOU TWO MAKING FOR ATLANTA. AIN'T NO TELLING HOW MANY RINGS OF HELL THERE IS BETWEEN HERE AND THERE. I CAN UNDERSTAND THE CALL OF HOME, THOUGH. YOU'D DO BETTER TRAVELING WITH A MAN.
EXCUSE ME, MR. SIMPSON, IF I'VE BEEN OVERLY FAMILIAR WITH YOU, OR GIVEN YOU THE WRONG IMPRESSION...
WHAT'S THAT THERE?
YOU AIN'T RUNNIN' HOME, ARE YOU? YOU'RE RUNNING FROM IT. THIS MAN IN THIS LETTER...
THE DEVIL HIMSELF, MR. SIMPSON.

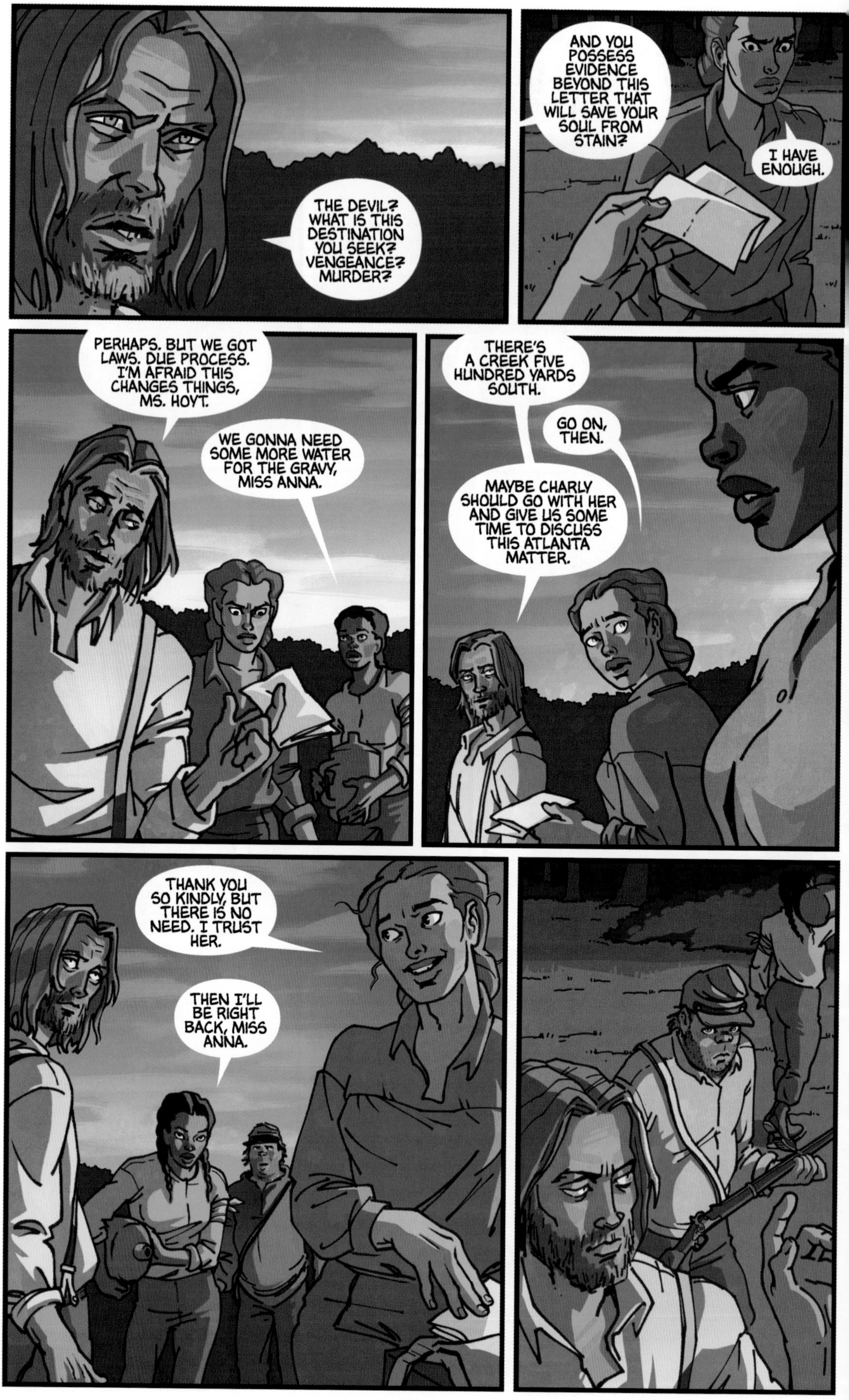
THE DEVIL? WHAT IS THIS DESTINATION YOU SEEK? VENGEANCE? MURDER?
AND YOU POSSESS EVIDENCE BEYOND THIS LETTER THAT WILL SAVE YOUR SOUL FROM STAIN?
I HAVE ENOUGH.
PERHAPS. BUT WE GOT LAWS. DUE PROCESS. I'M AFRAID THIS CHANGES THINGS, MS. HOYT.
WE GONNA NEED SOME MORE WATER FOR THE GRAVY, MISS ANNA.
THERE'S A CREEK FIVE HUNDRED YARDS SOUTH.
GO ON, THEN.
MAYBE CHARLY SHOULD GO WITH HER AND GIVE US SOME TIME TO DISCUSS THIS ATLANTA MATTER.
THANK YOU SO KINDLY, BUT THERE IS NO NEED. I TRUST HER.
THEN I'LL BE RIGHT BACK, MISS ANNA.

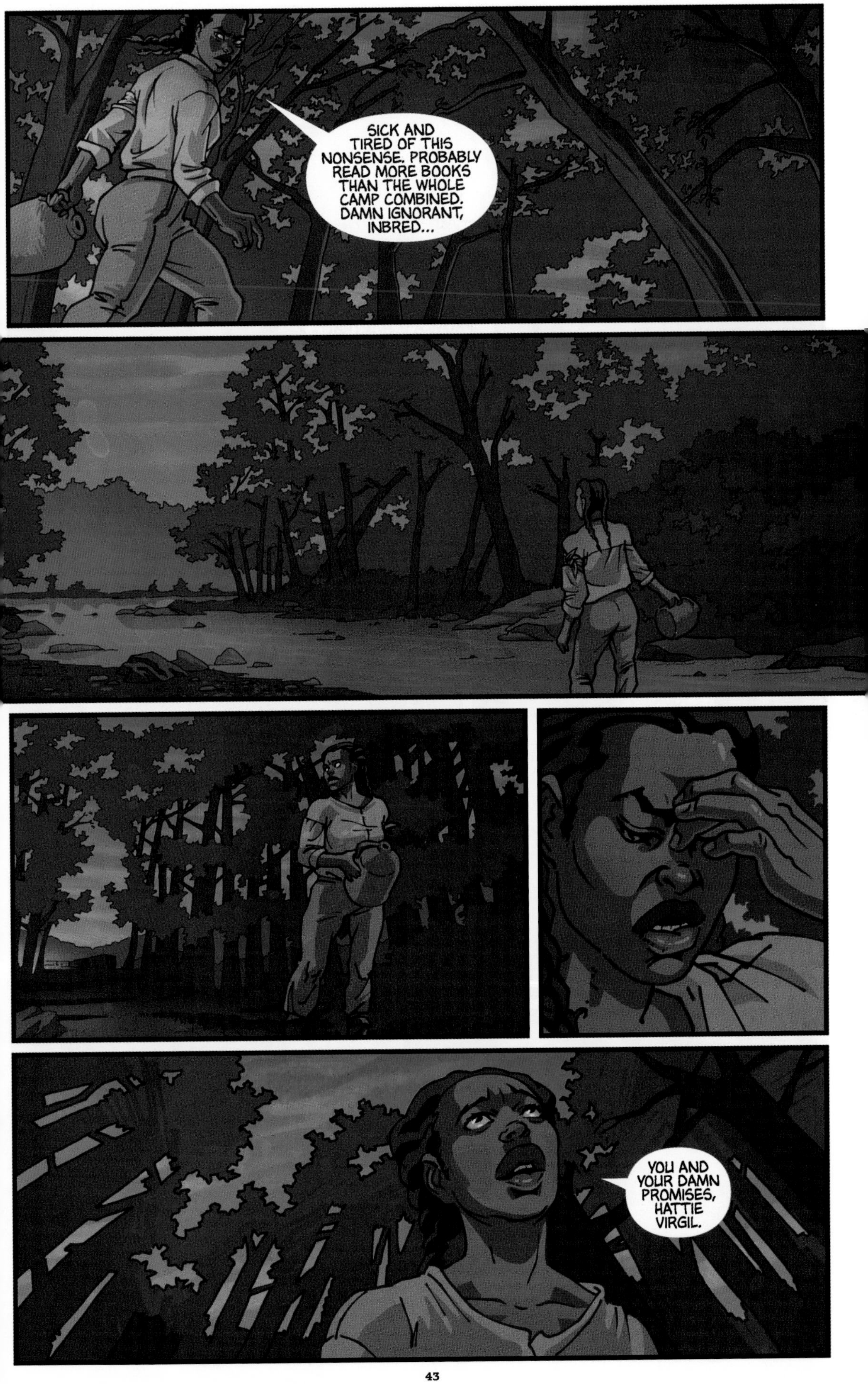
SICK AND TIRED OF THIS NONSENSE. PROBABLY READ MORE BOOKS THAN THE WHOLE CAMP COMBINED. DAMN IGNORANT, INBRED...
YOU AND YOUR DAMN PROMISES, HATTIE VIRGIL.

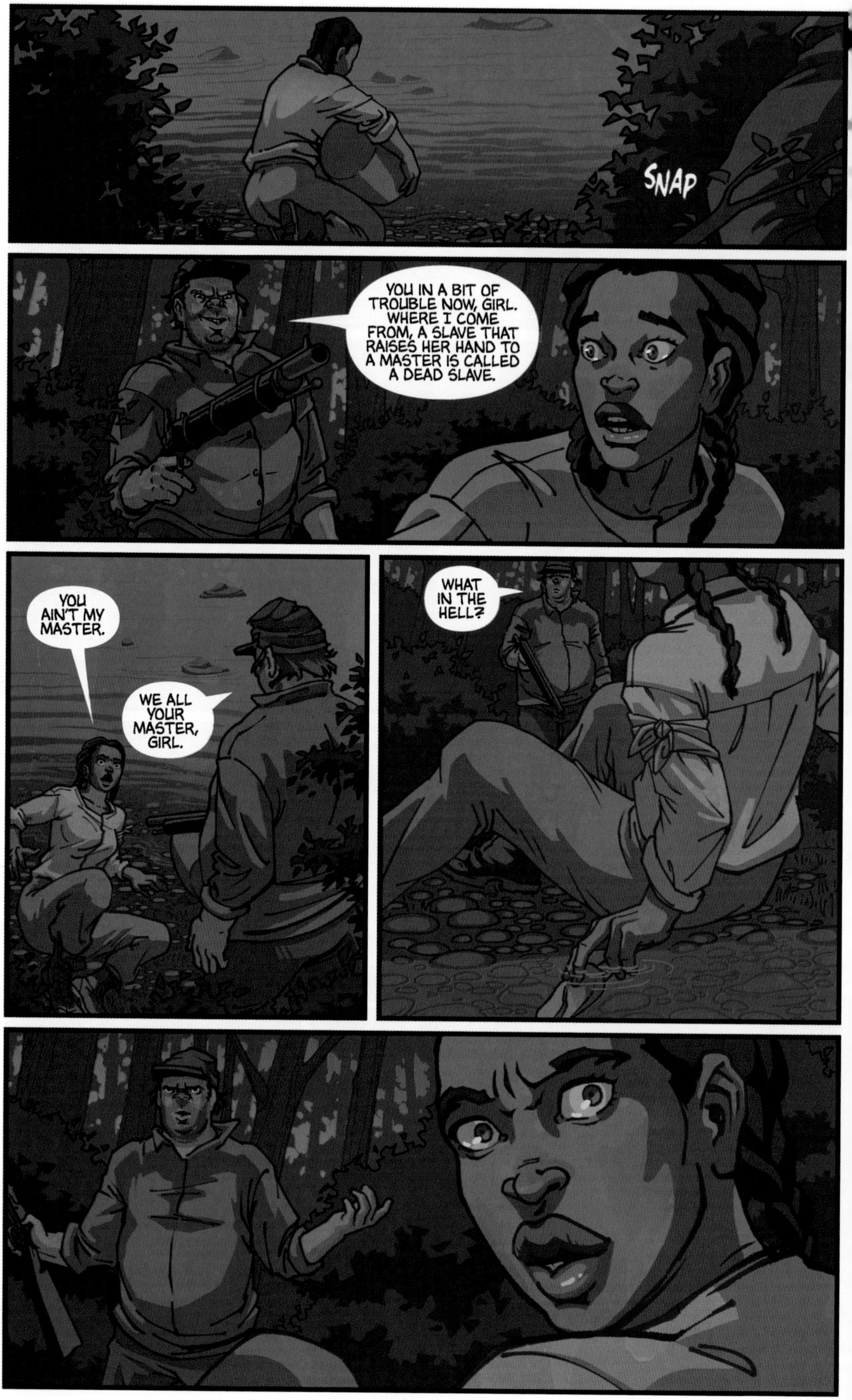
SNAP
YOU IN A BIT OF TROUBLE NOW, GIRL. WHERE I COME FROM, A SLAVE THAT RAISES HER HAND TO A MASTER IS CALLED A DEAD SLAVE.
YOU AIN'T MY MASTER.
WE ALL YOUR MASTER, GIRL.
WHAT IN THE HELL?

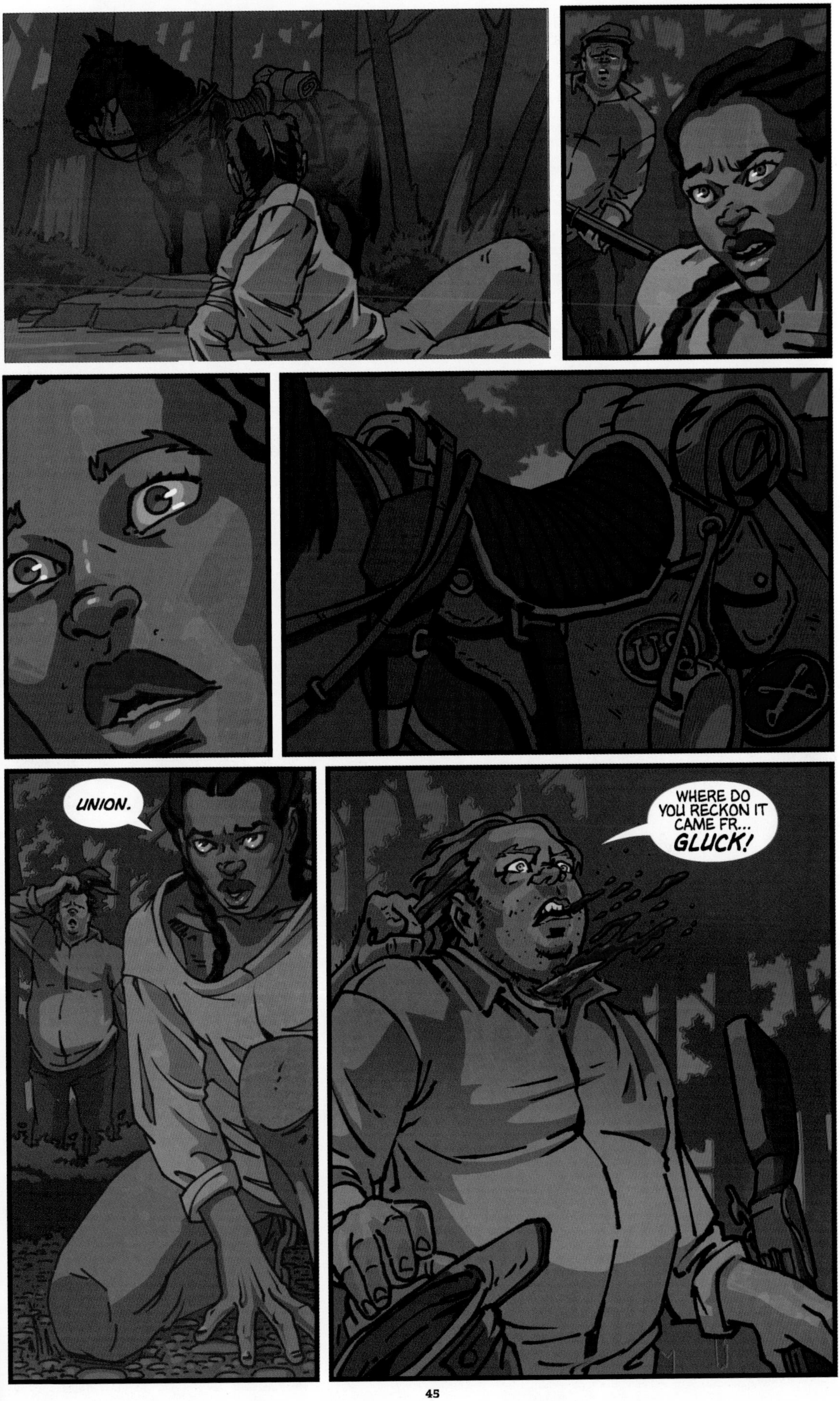
UNION.
WHERE DO YOU RECKON IT CAME FR... GLUCK!

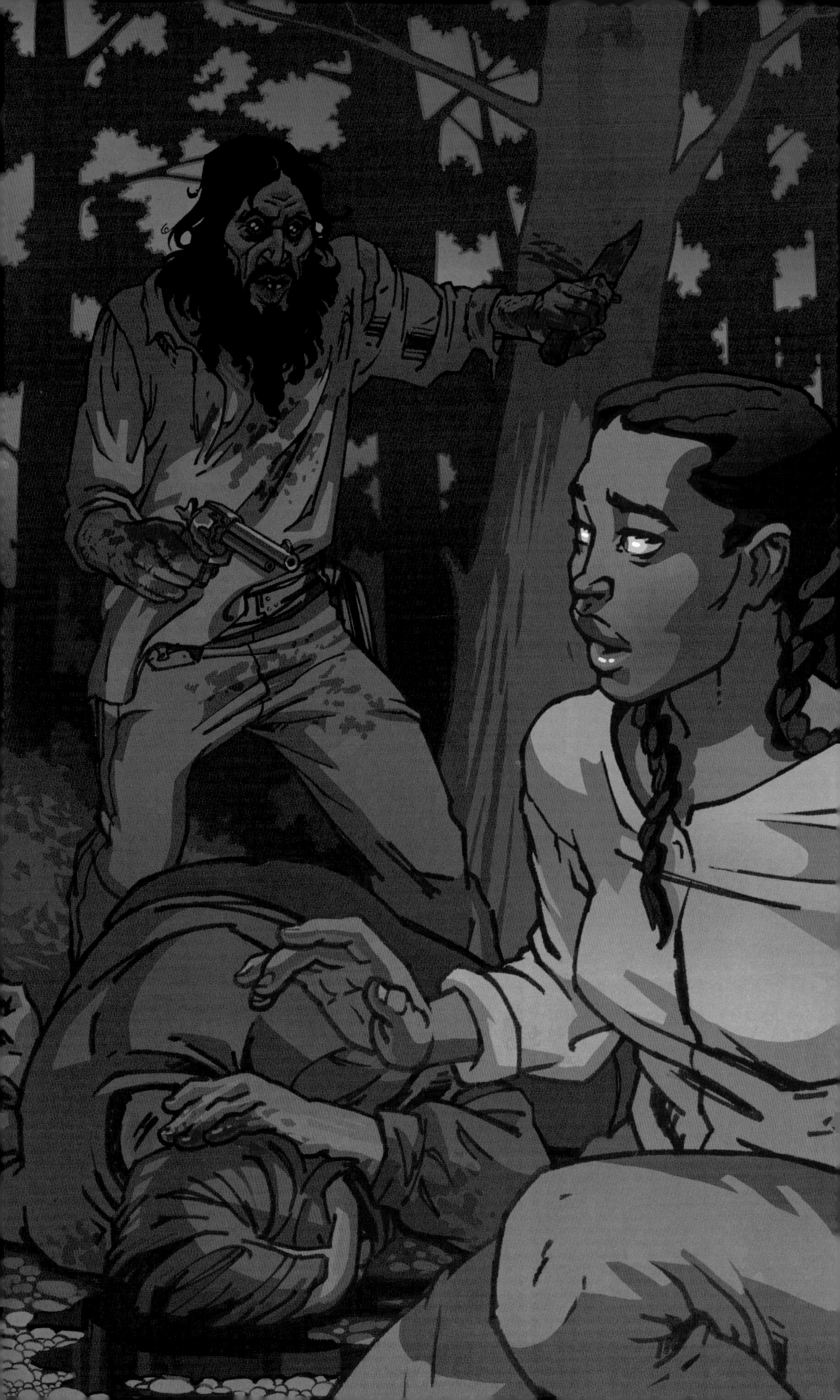

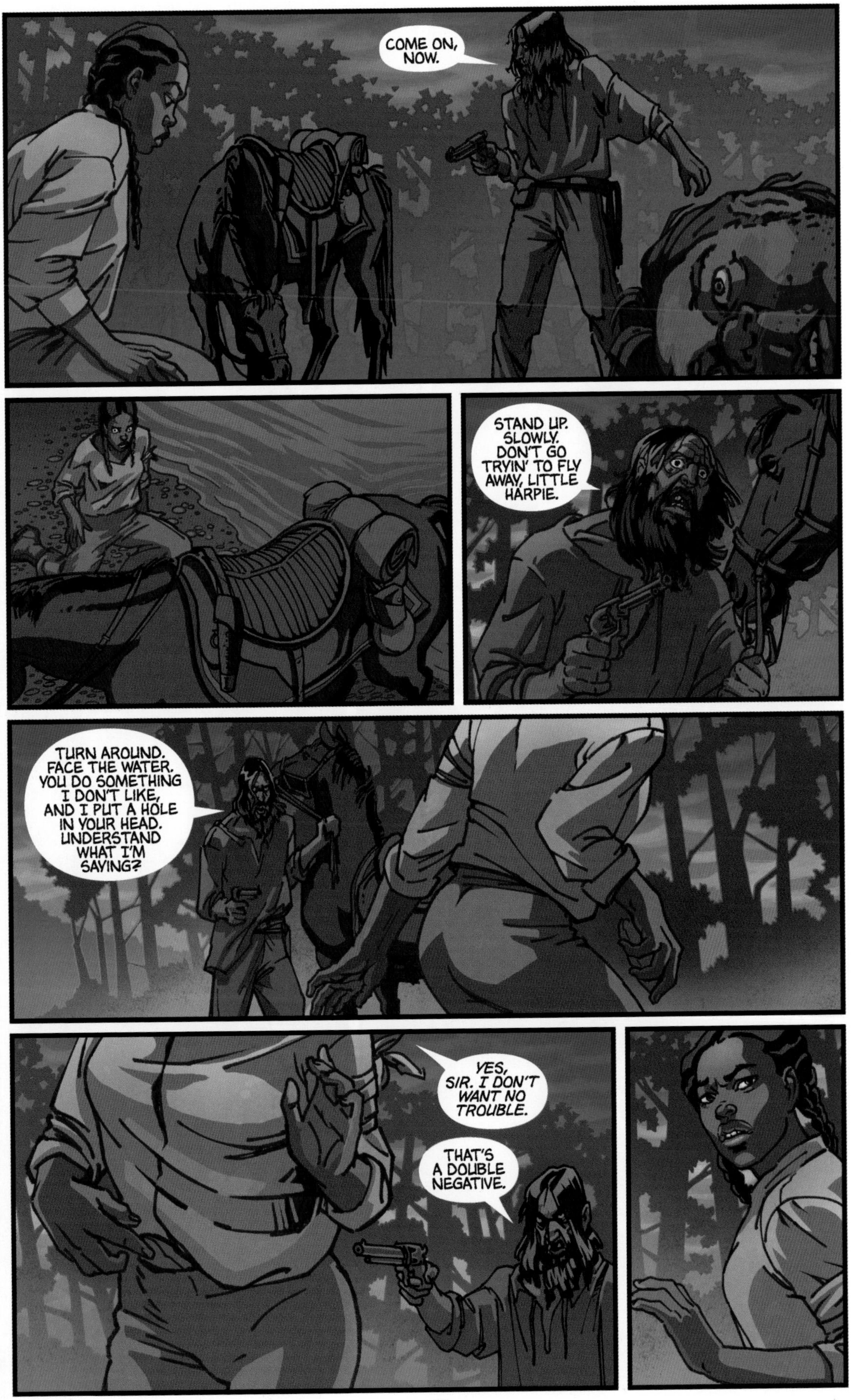
COME ON, NOW.
STAND UP. SLOWLY. DON'T GO TRYIN' TO FLY AWAY, LITTLE HARPIE.
TURN AROUND. FACE THE WATER. YOU DO SOMETHING I DON'T LIKE, AND I PUT A HOLE IN YOUR HEAD. UNDERSTAND WHAT I'M SAYING?
YES, SIR. I DON'T WANT NO TROUBLE.
THAT'S A DOUBLE NEGATIVE.

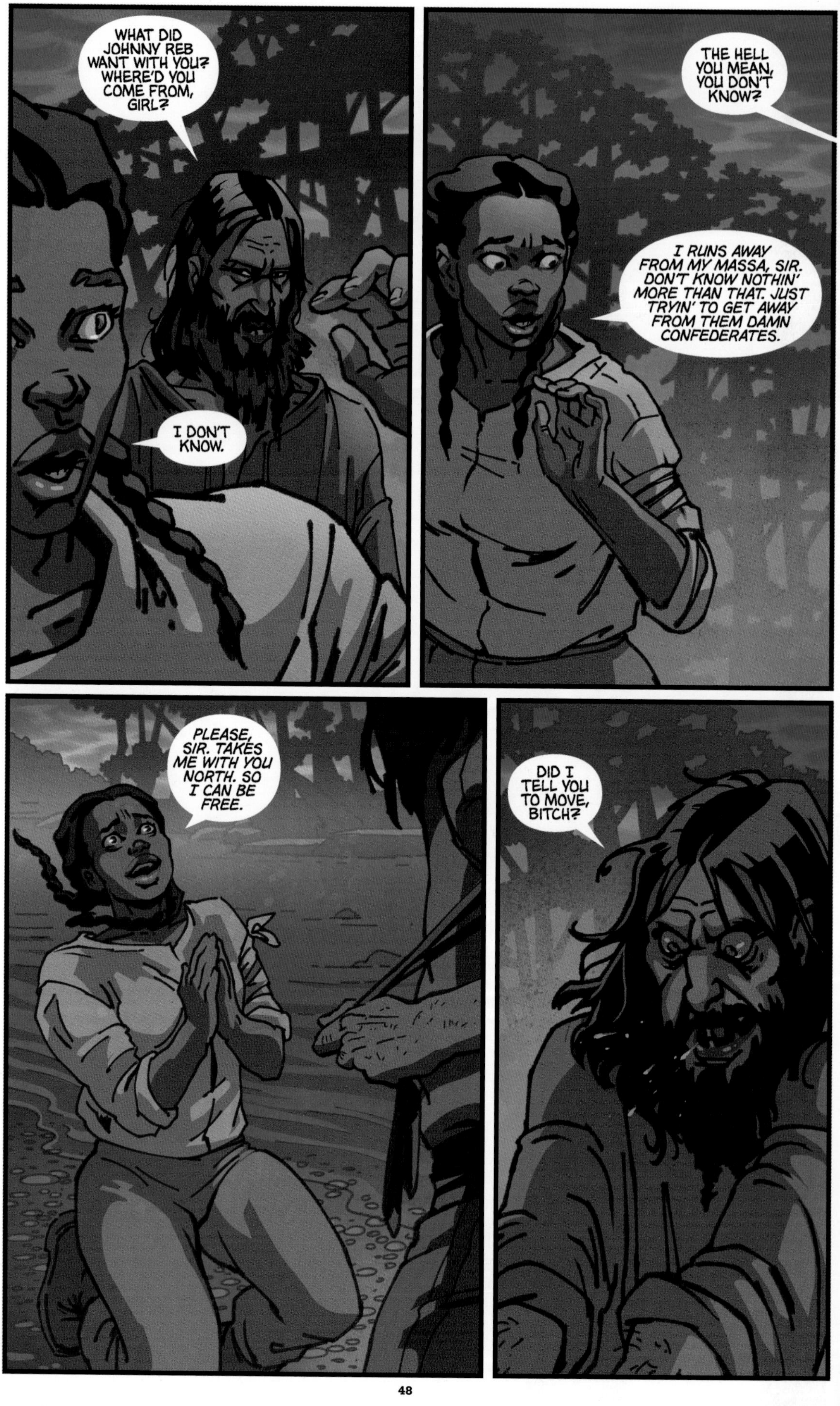
WHAT DID JOHNNY REB WANT WITH YOU? WHERE'D YOU COME FROM, GIRL?
I DON'T KNOW.
THE HELL YOU MEAN, YOU DON'T KNOW?
I RUNS AWAY FROM MY MASSA, SIR. DON'T KNOW NOTHIN' MORE THAN THAT. JUST TRYIN' TO GET AWAY FROM THEM DAMN CONFEDERATES.
PLEASE, SIR. TAKES ME WITH YOU NORTH. SO I CAN BE FREE.
DID I TELL YOU TO MOVE, BITCH?

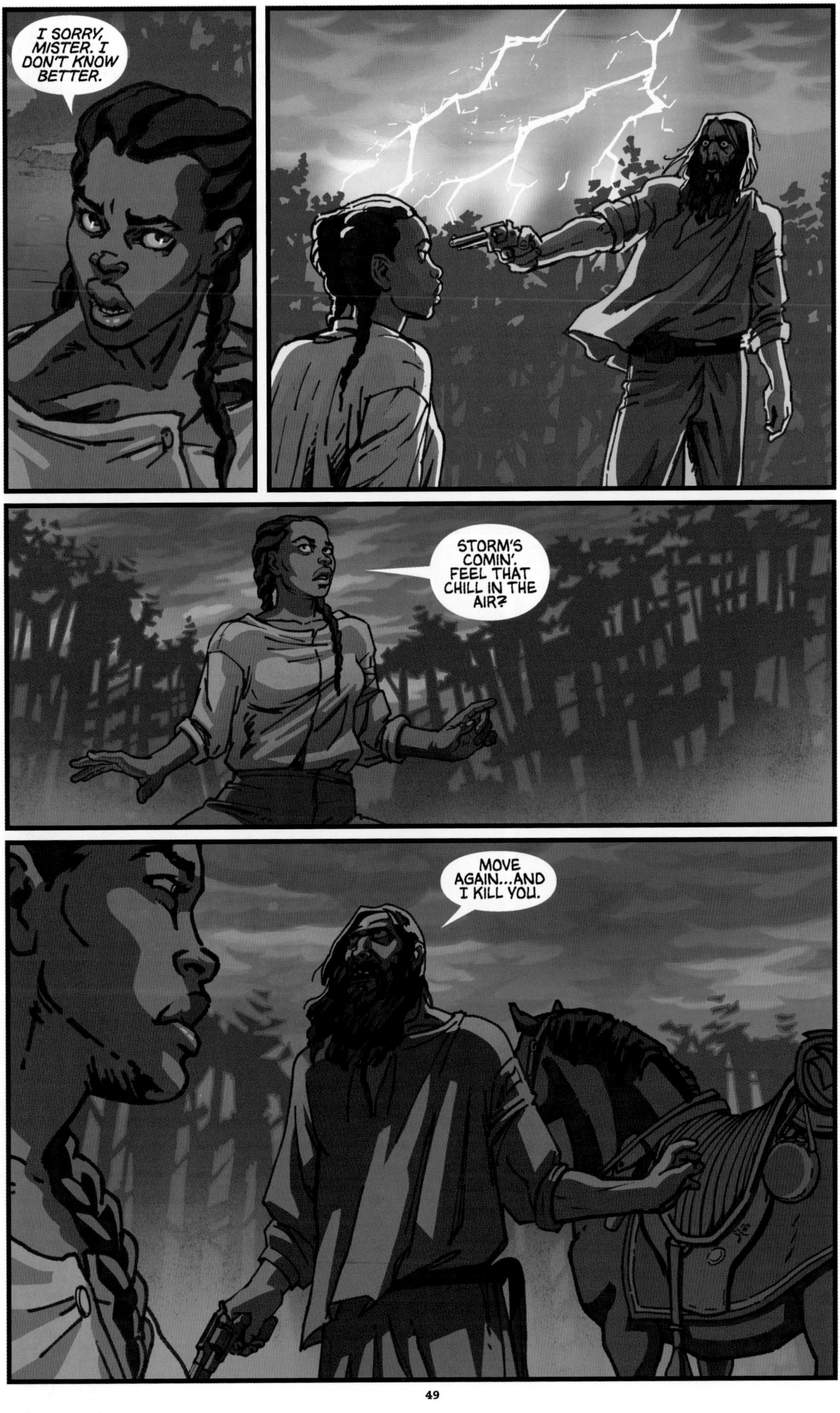
I SORRY, MISTER. I DON'T KNOW BETTER.
STORM'S COMIN'. FEEL THAT CHILL IN THE AIR?
MOVE AGAIN...AND I KILL YOU.

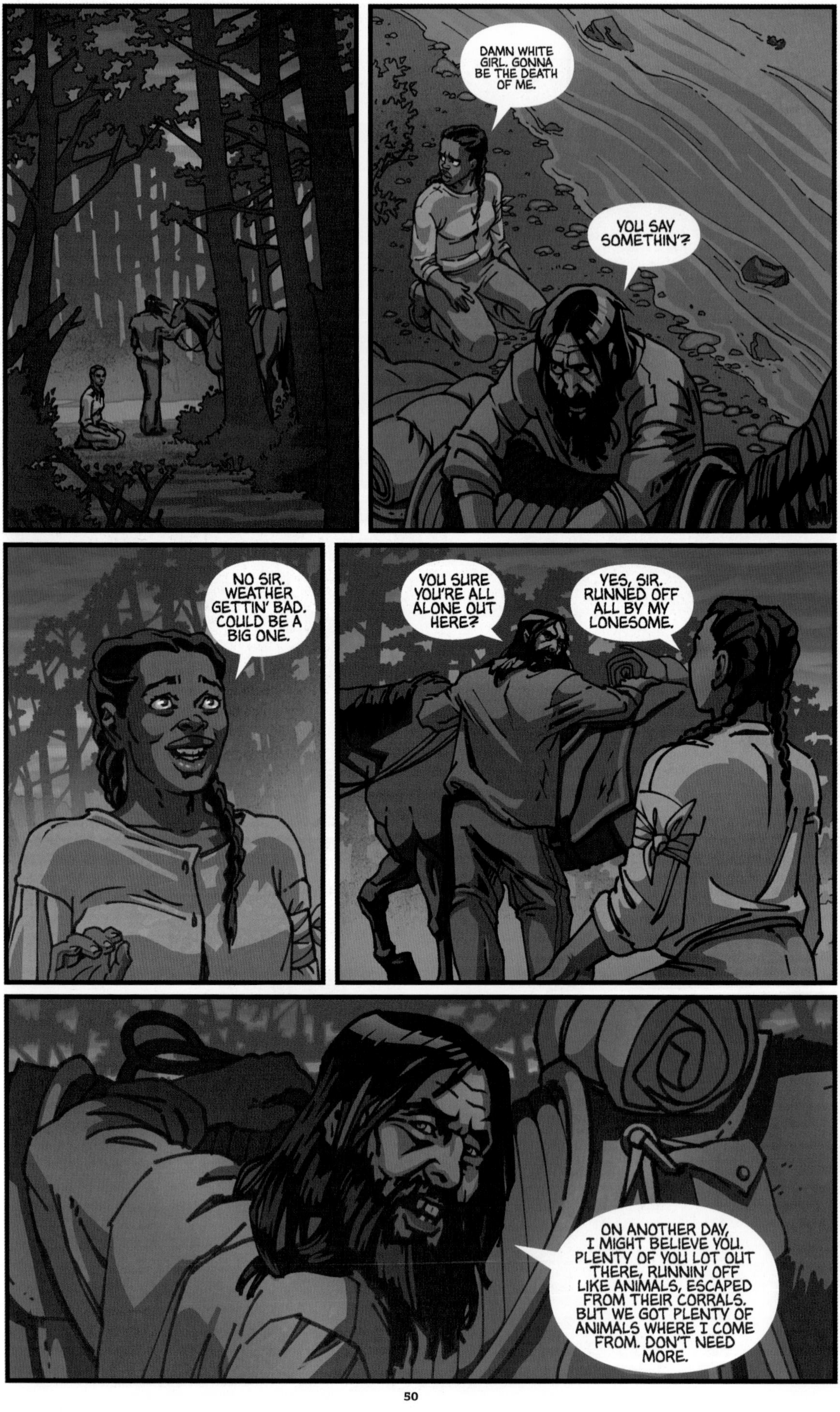
DAMN WHITE GIRL. GONNA BE THE DEATH OF ME.
YOU SAY SOMETHIN'?
NO SIR. WEATHER GETTIN' BAD. COULD BE A BIG ONE.
YOU SURE YOU'RE ALL ALONE OUT HERE?
YES, SIR. RUNNED OFF ALL BY MY LONESOME.
ON ANOTHER DAY, I MIGHT BELIEVE YOU. PLENTY OF YOU LOT OUT THERE, RUNNIN' OFF LIKE ANIMALS, ESCAPED FROM THEIR CORRALS. BUT WE GOT PLENTY OF ANIMALS WHERE I COME FROM. DON'T NEED MORE.

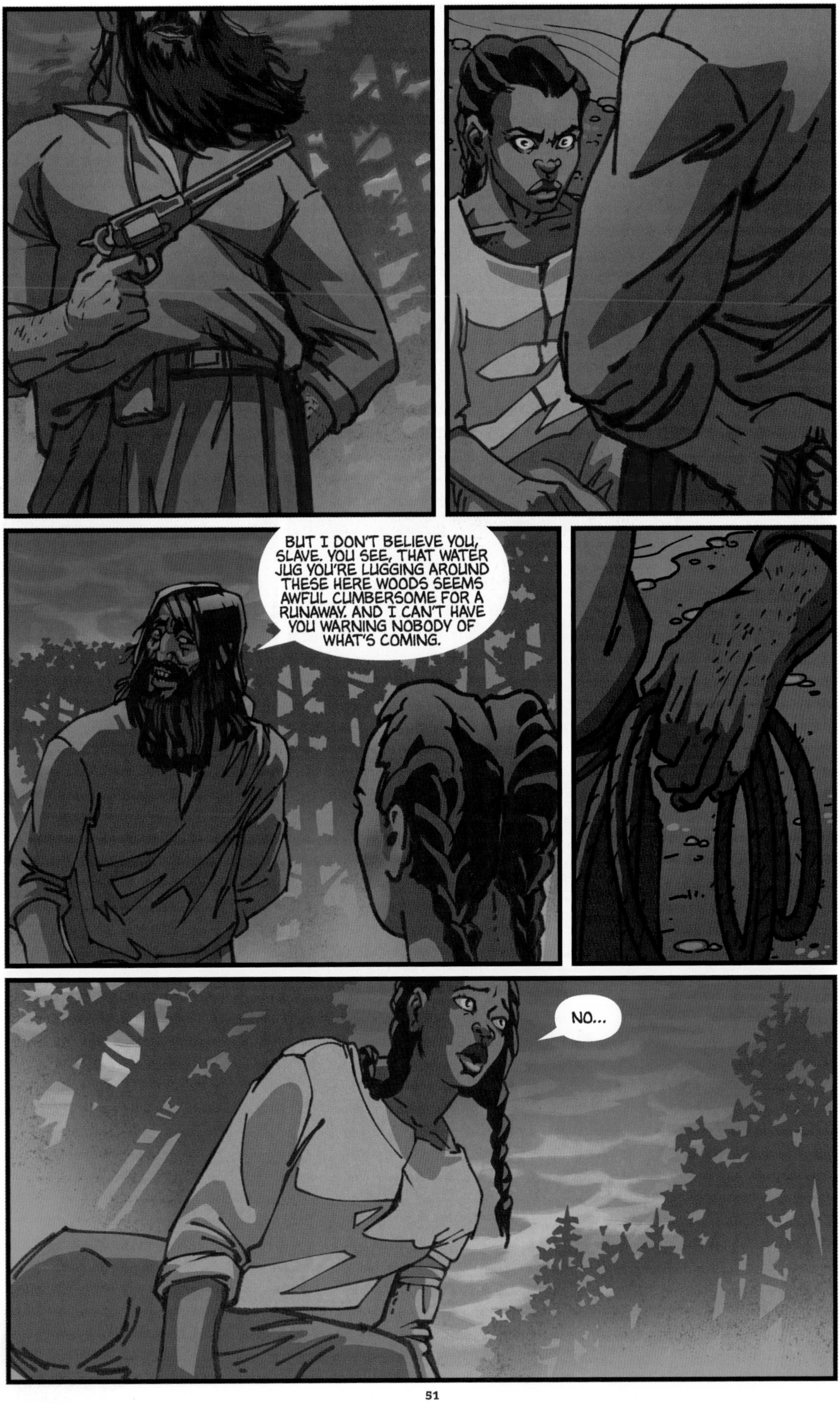
BUT I DON'T BELIEVE YOU, SLAVE. YOU SEE, THAT WATER JUG YOU'RE LUGGING AROUND THESE HERE WOODS SEEMS AWFUL CUMBERSOME FOR A RUNAWAY. AND I CAN'T HAVE YOU WARNING NOBODY OF WHAT'S COMING.
NO...

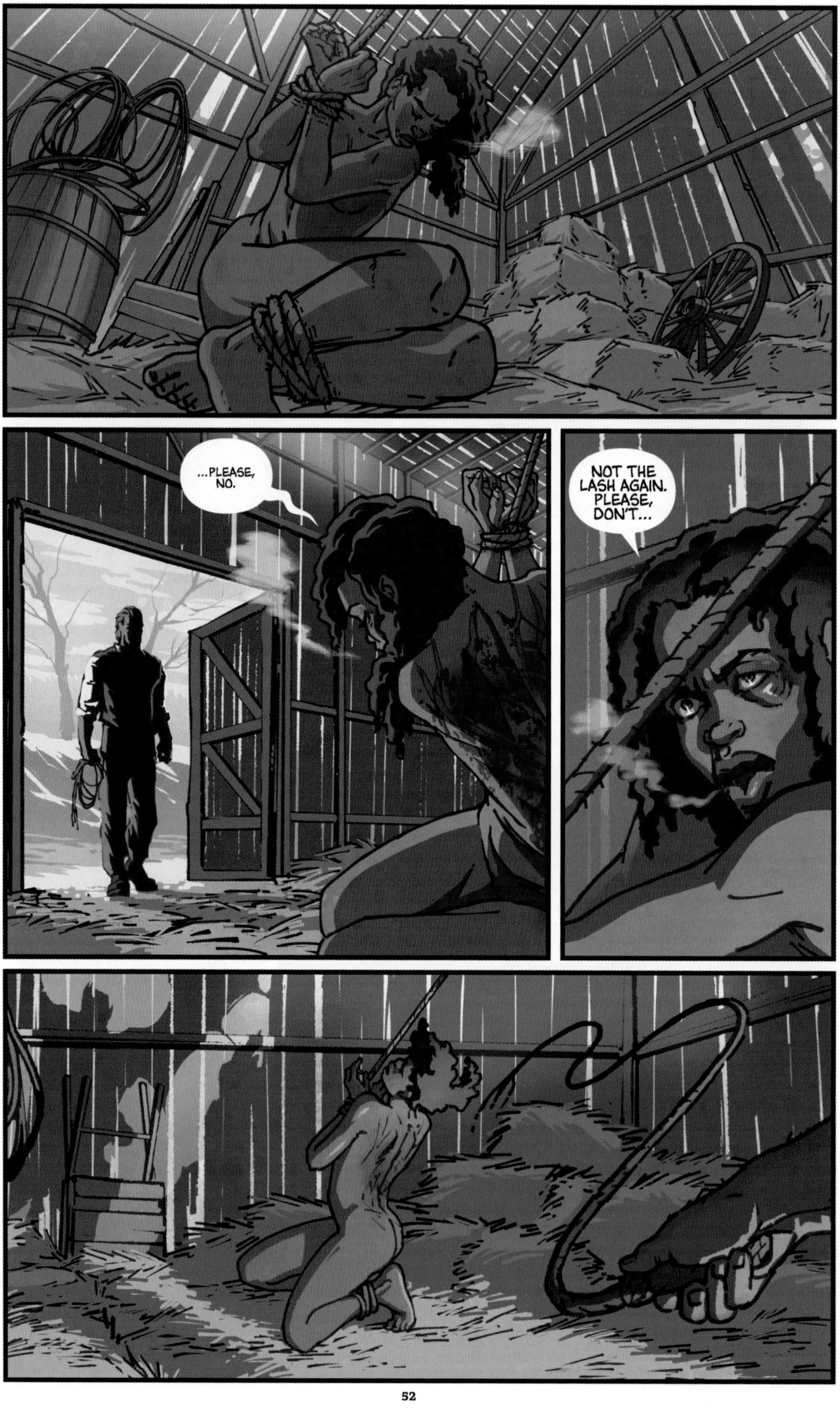
...PLEASE, NO.
NOT THE LASH AGAIN. PLEASE, DON'T...

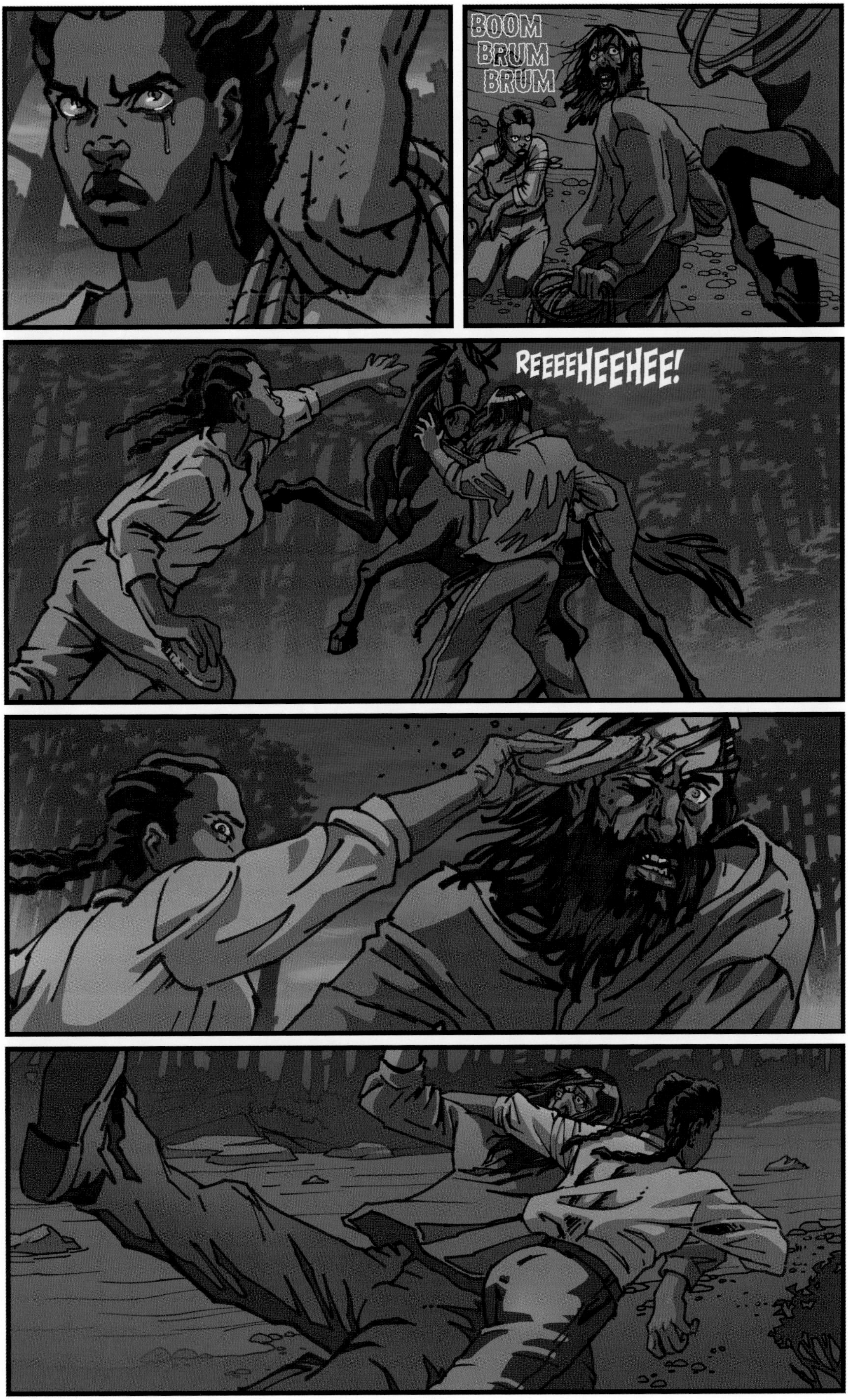
BOOM
BRUM
BRUM
REEEEHEEHEE!

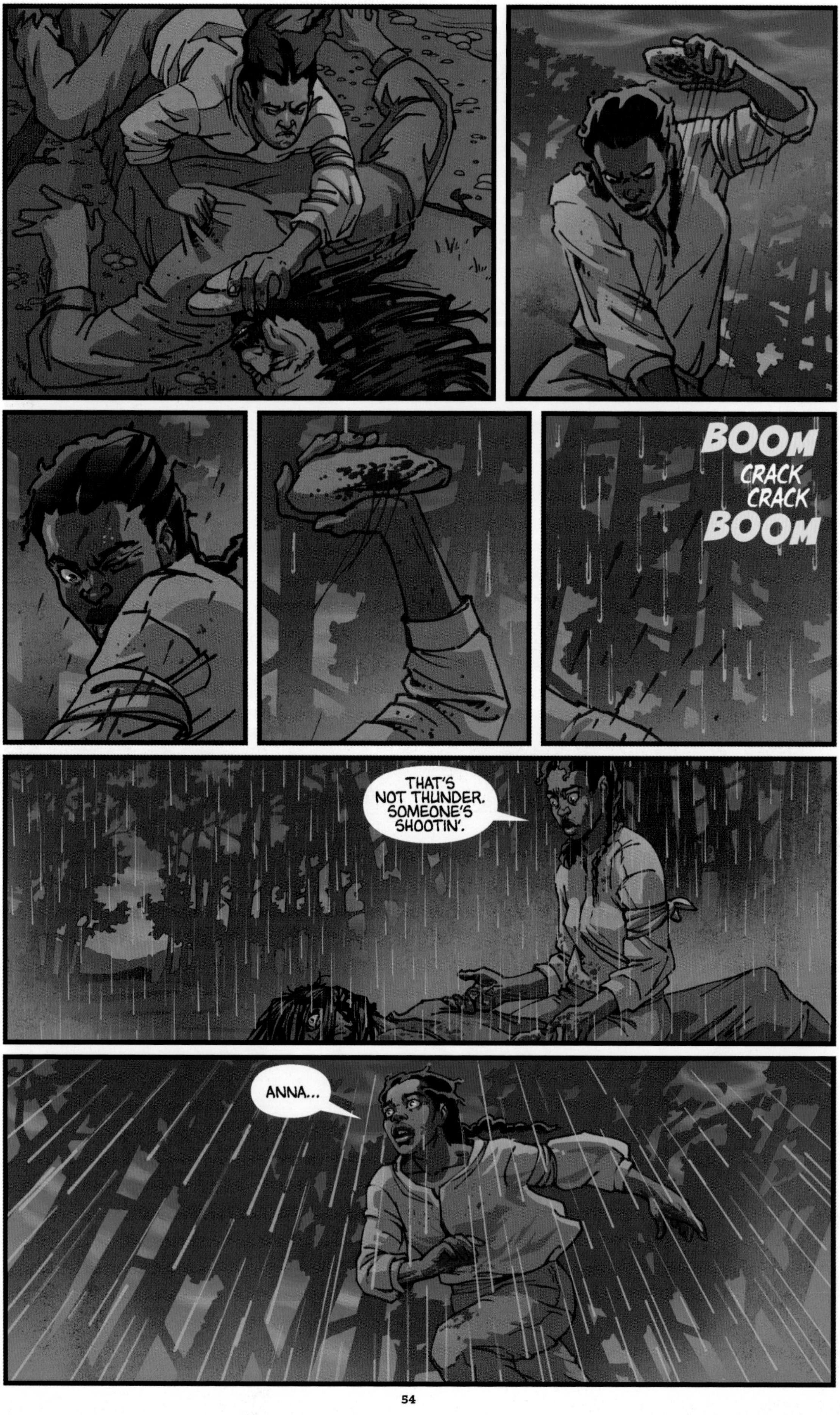
BOOM
CRACK
CRACK
BOOM
THAT'S NOT THUNDER. SOMEONE'S SHOOTIN'.
ANNA...

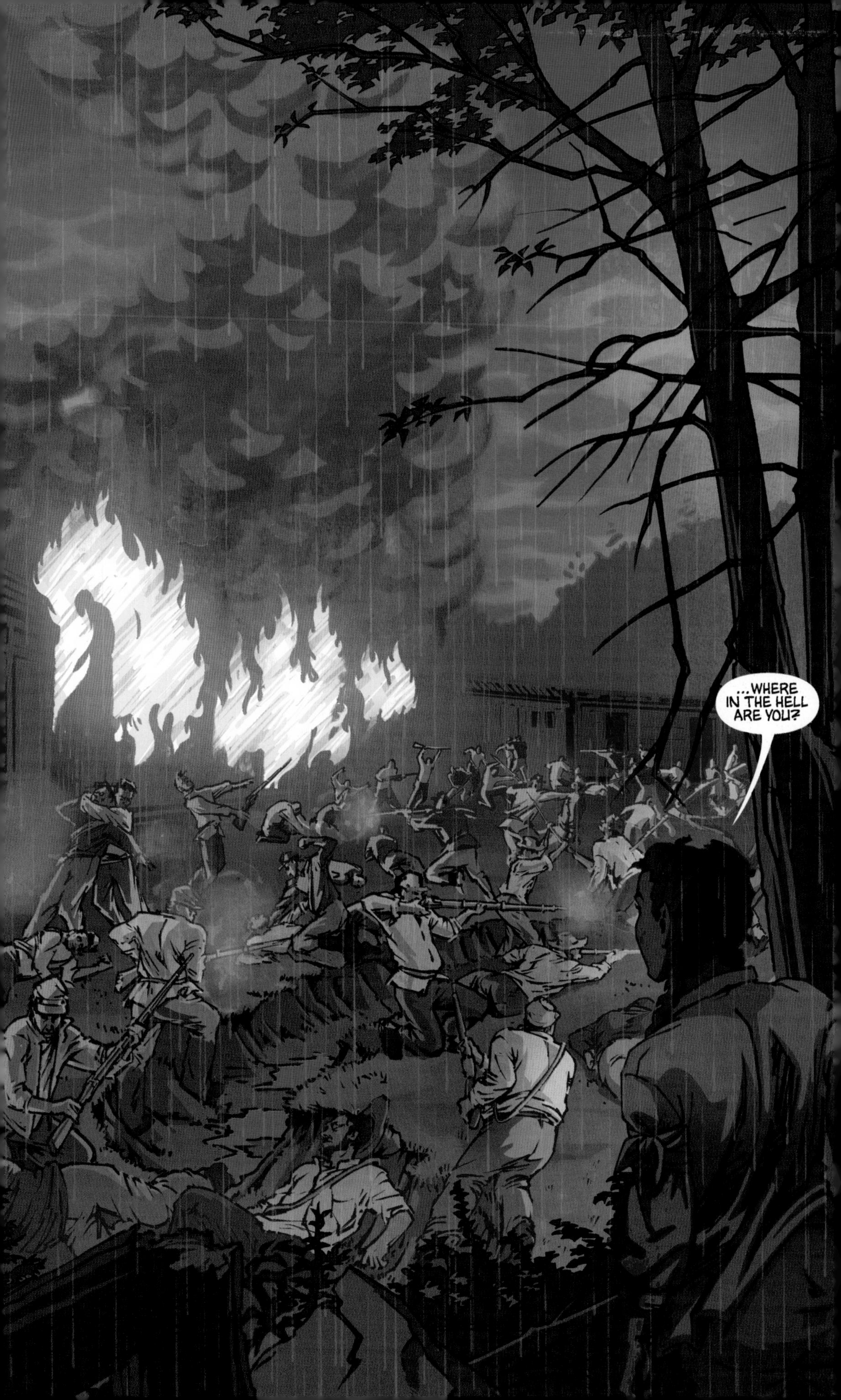
...WHERE IN THE HELL ARE YOU?

CHAPTER THREE

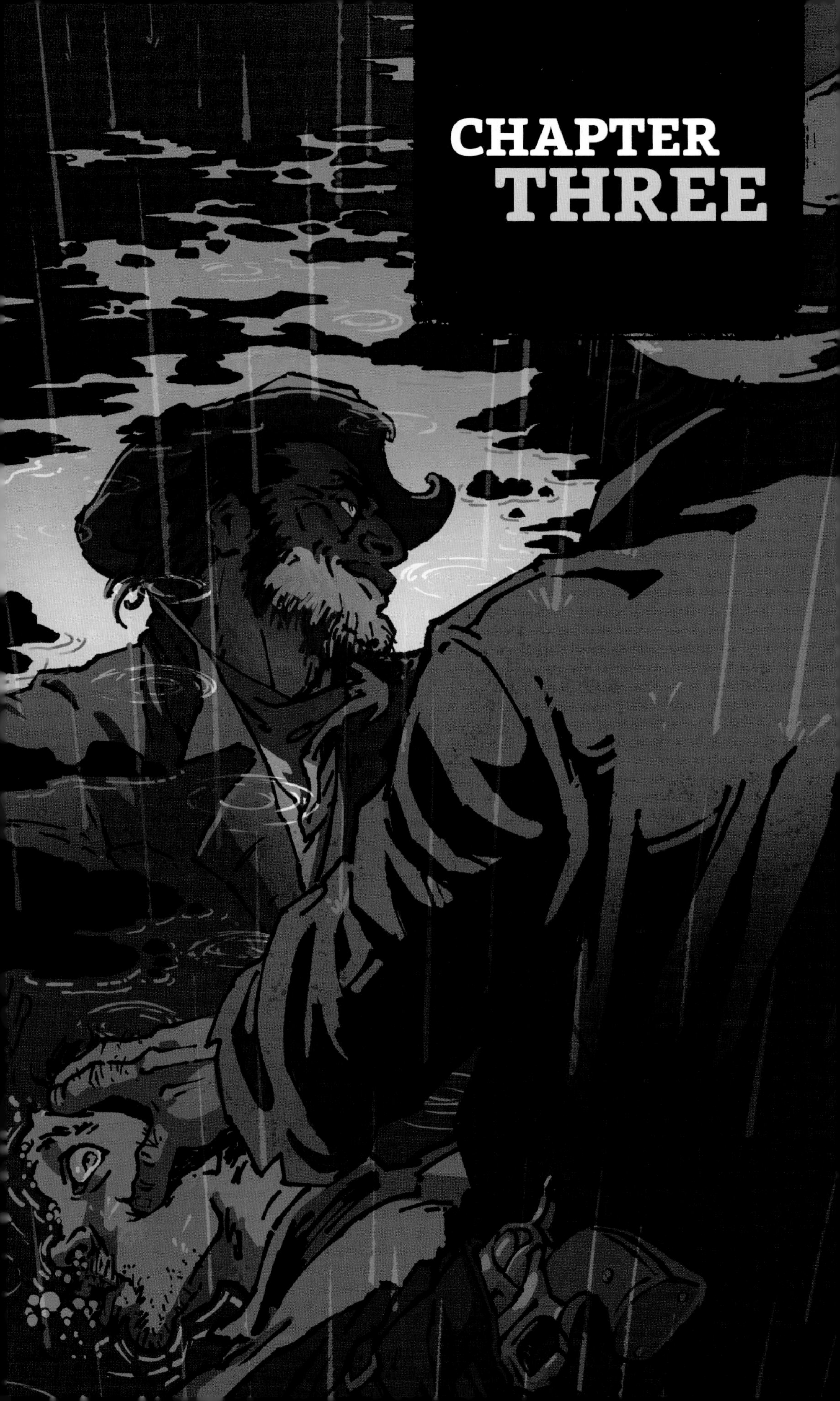

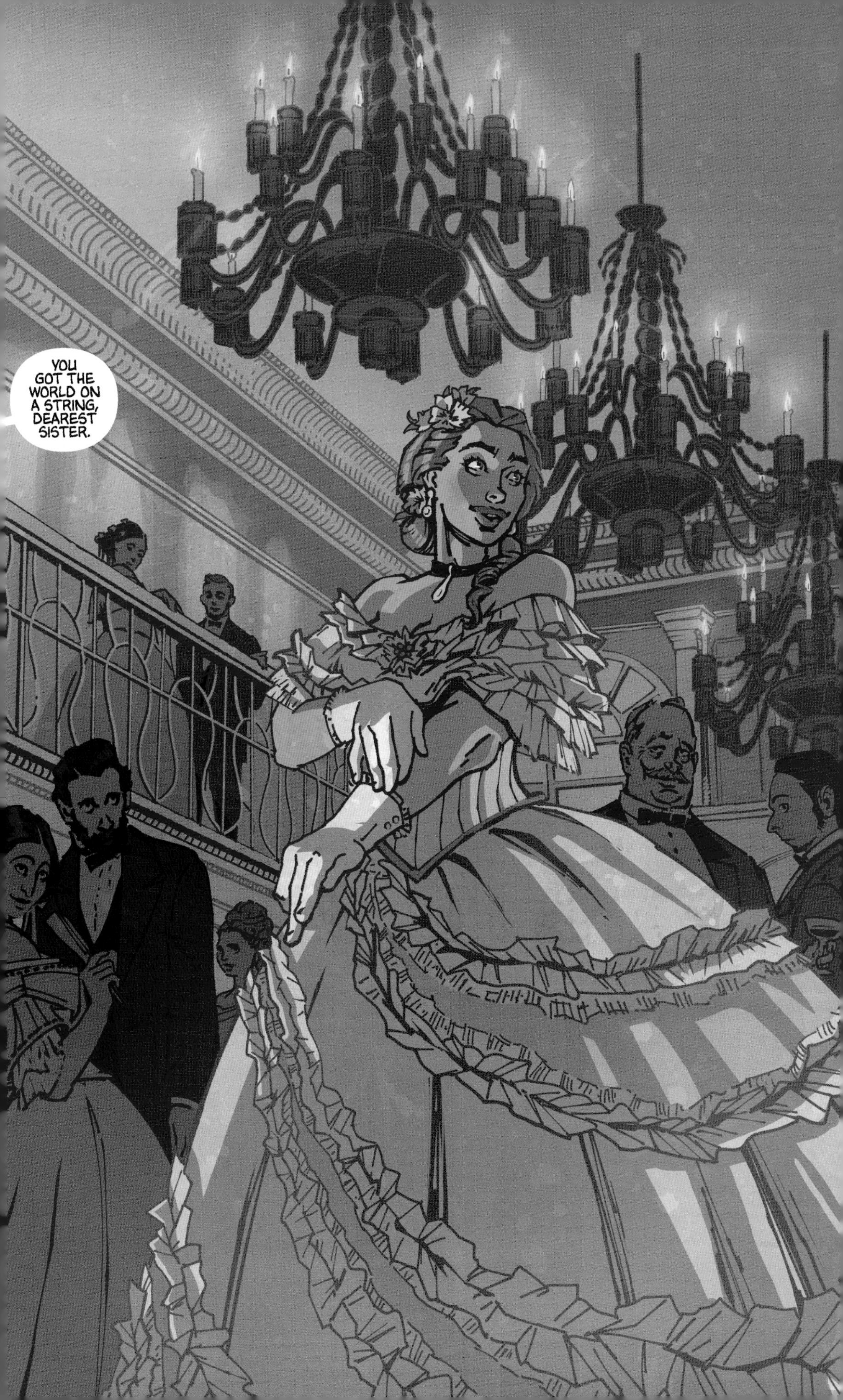
YOU GOT THE WORLD ON A STRING, DEAREST SISTER.

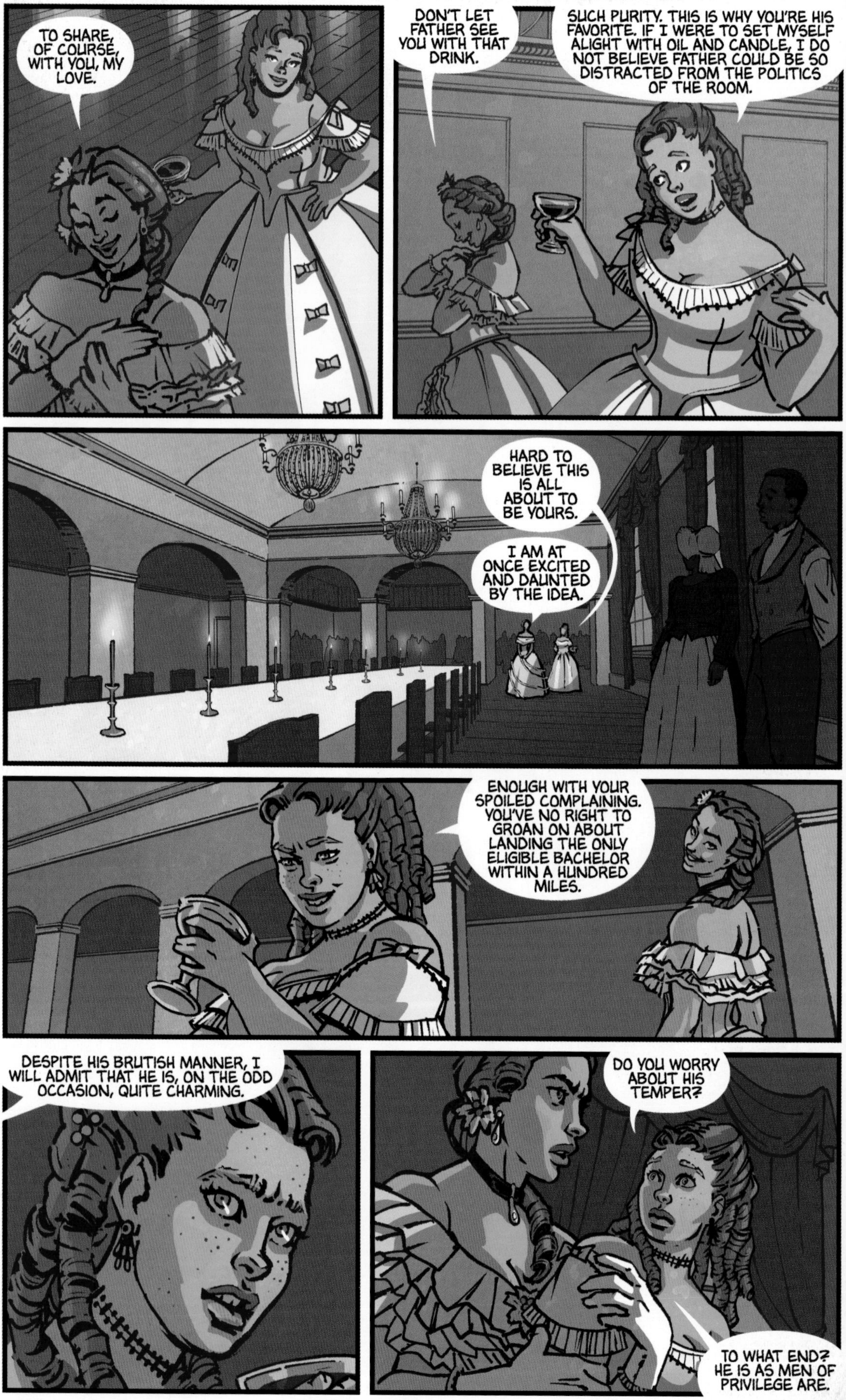

TO SHARE, OF COURSE, WITH YOU, MY LOVE.
DON'T LET FATHER SEE YOU WITH THAT DRINK.
SUCH PURITY. THIS IS WHY YOU'RE HIS FAVORITE. IF I WERE TO SET MYSELF ALIGHT WITH OIL AND CANDLE, I DO NOT BELIEVE FATHER COULD BE SO DISTRACTED FROM THE POLITICS OF THE ROOM.
HARD TO BELIEVE THIS IS ALL ABOUT TO BE YOURS.
I AM AT ONCE EXCITED AND DAUNTED BY THE IDEA.
ENOUGH WITH YOUR SPOILED COMPLAINING. YOU'VE NO RIGHT TO GROAN ON ABOUT LANDING THE ONLY ELIGIBLE BACHELOR WITHIN A HUNDRED MILES.
DESPITE HIS BRUTISH MANNER, I WILL ADMIT THAT HE IS, ON THE ODD OCCASION, QUITE CHARMING.
DO YOU WORRY ABOUT HIS TEMPER?
TO WHAT END? HE IS AS MEN OF PRIVILEGE ARE.

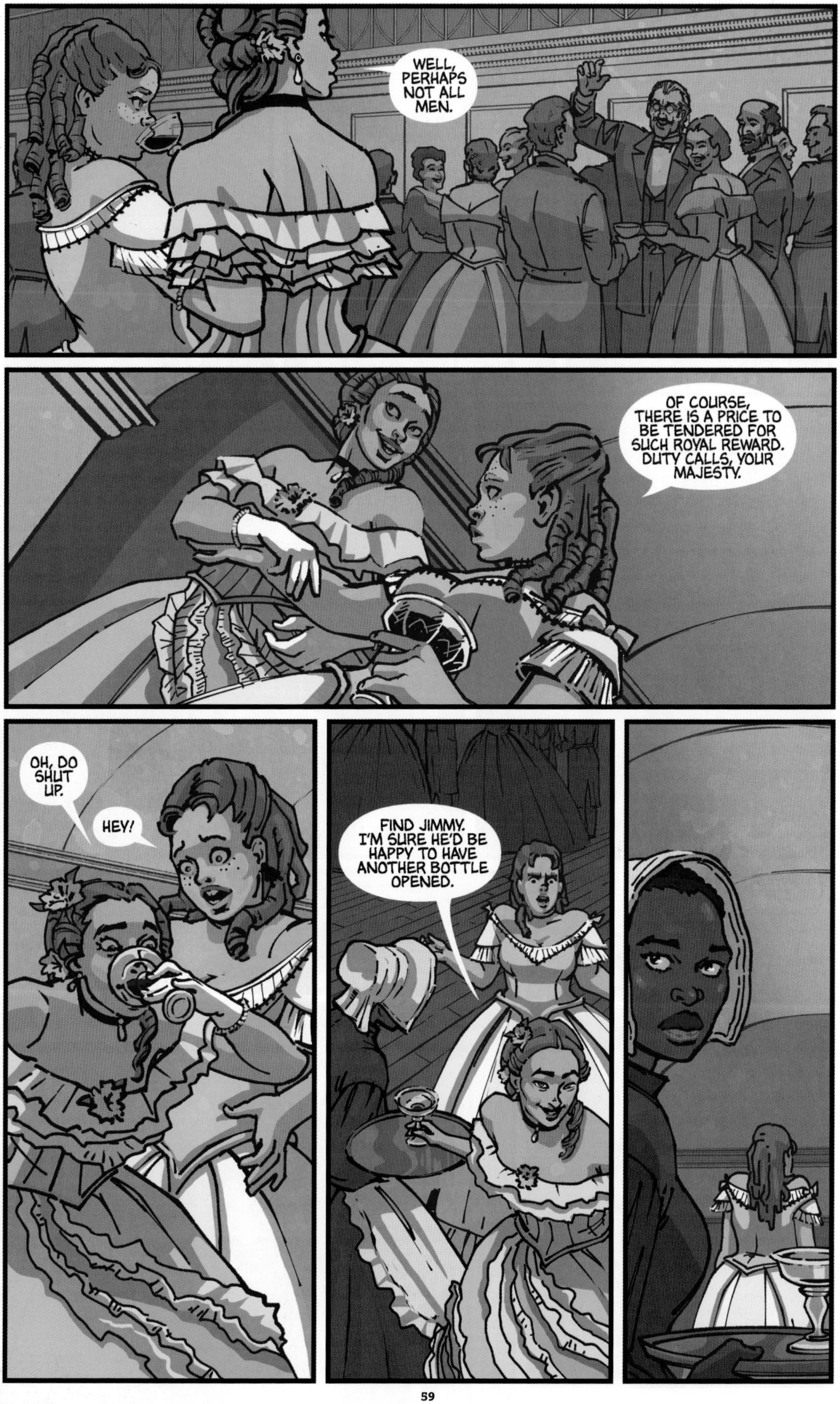
WELL, PERHAPS NOT ALL MEN.
OF COURSE, THERE IS A PRICE TO BE TENDERED FOR SUCH ROYAL REWARD. DUTY CALLS, YOUR MAJESTY.
OH, DO SHUT UP.
HEY!
FIND JIMMY. I'M SURE HE'D BE HAPPY TO HAVE ANOTHER BOTTLE OPENED.

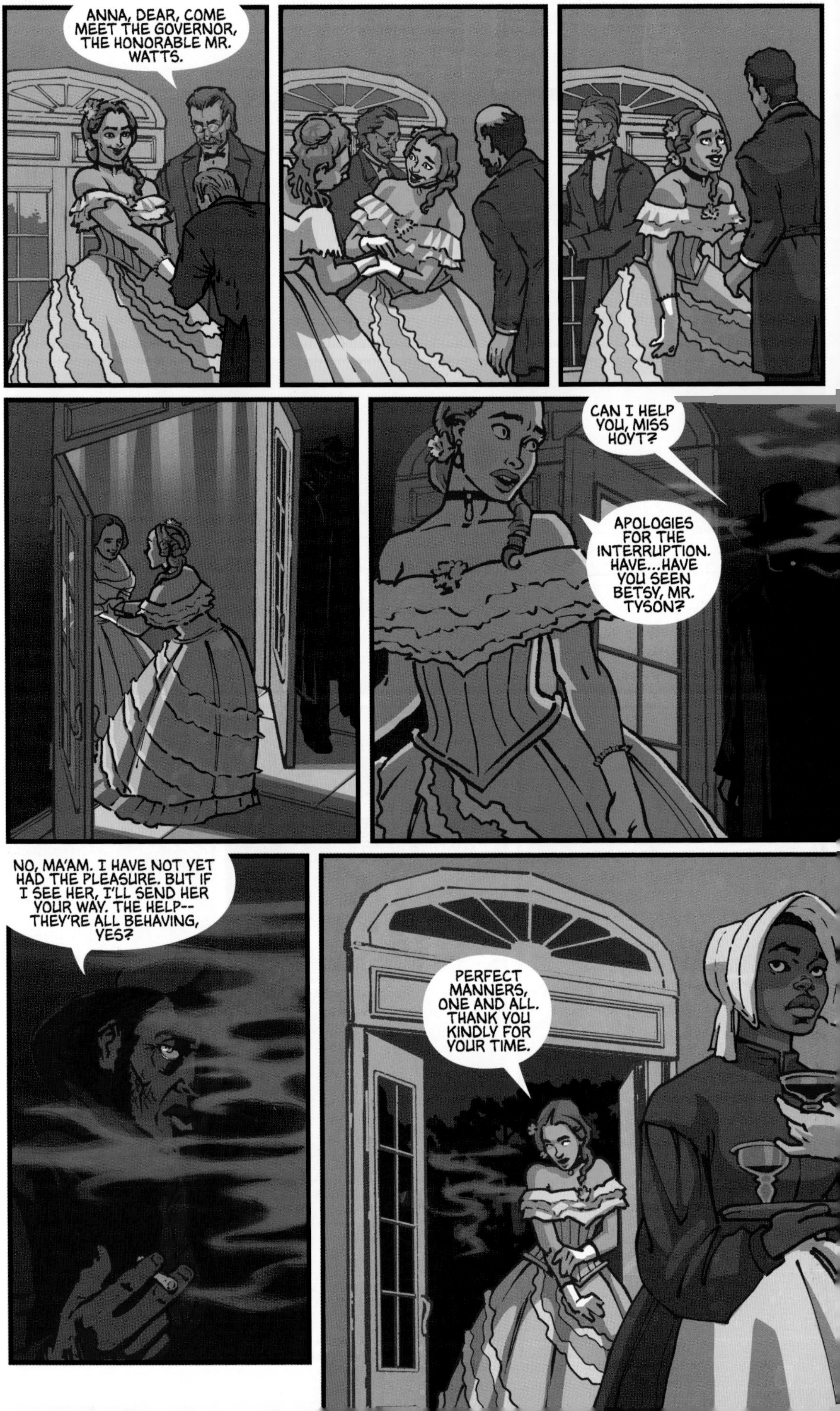
ANNA, DEAR, COME MEET THE GOVERNOR, THE HONORABLE MR. WATTS.
CAN I HELP YOU, MISS HOYT?
APOLOGIES FOR THE INTERRUPTION. HAVE...HAVE YOU SEEN BETSY, MR. TYSON?
NO, MA'AM. I HAVE NOT YET HAD THE PLEASURE. BUT IF I SEE HER, I'LL SEND HER YOUR WAY. THE HELP-- THEY'RE ALL BEHAVING, YES?
PERFECT MANNERS, ONE AND ALL. THANK YOU KINDLY FOR YOUR TIME.

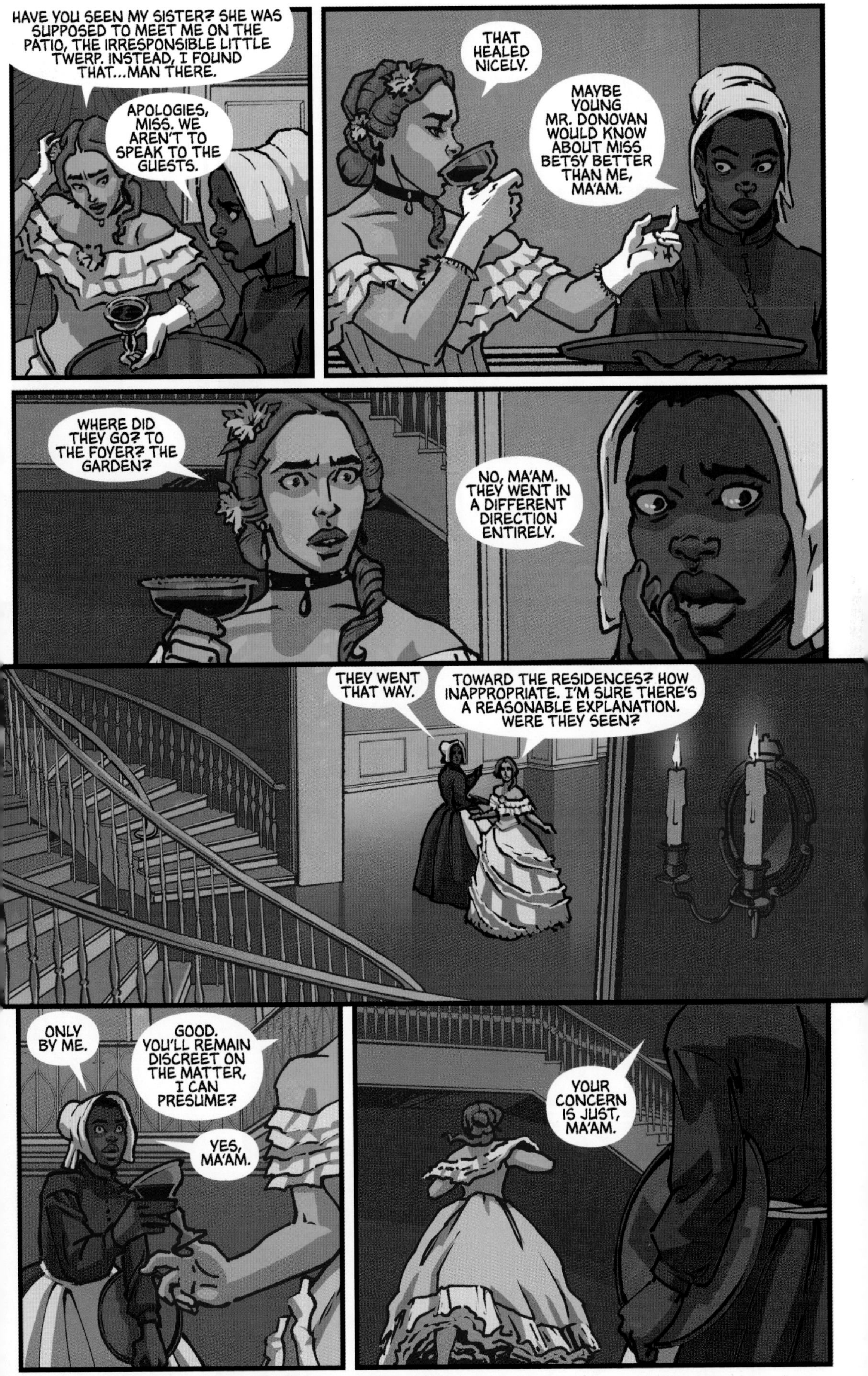
HAVE YOU SEEN MY SISTER? SHE WAS SUPPOSED TO MEET ME ON THE PATIO, THE IRRESPONSIBLE LITTLE TWERP. INSTEAD, I FOUND THAT...MAN THERE.
APOLOGIES, MISS. WE AREN'T TO SPEAK TO THE GUESTS.
THAT HEALED NICELY.
MAYBE YOUNG MR. DONOVAN WOULD KNOW ABOUT MISS BETSY BETTER THAN ME, MA'AM.
WHERE DID THEY GO? TO THE FOYER? THE GARDEN?
NO, MA'AM. THEY WENT IN A DIFFERENT DIRECTION ENTIRELY.
THEY WENT THAT WAY.
TOWARD THE RESIDENCES? HOW INAPPROPRIATE. I'M SURE THERE'S A REASONABLE EXPLANATION. WERE THEY SEEN?
ONLY BY ME.
GOOD. YOU'LL REMAIN DISCREET ON THE MATTER, I CAN PRESUME?
YES, MA'AM.
YOUR CONCERN IS JUST, MA'AM.

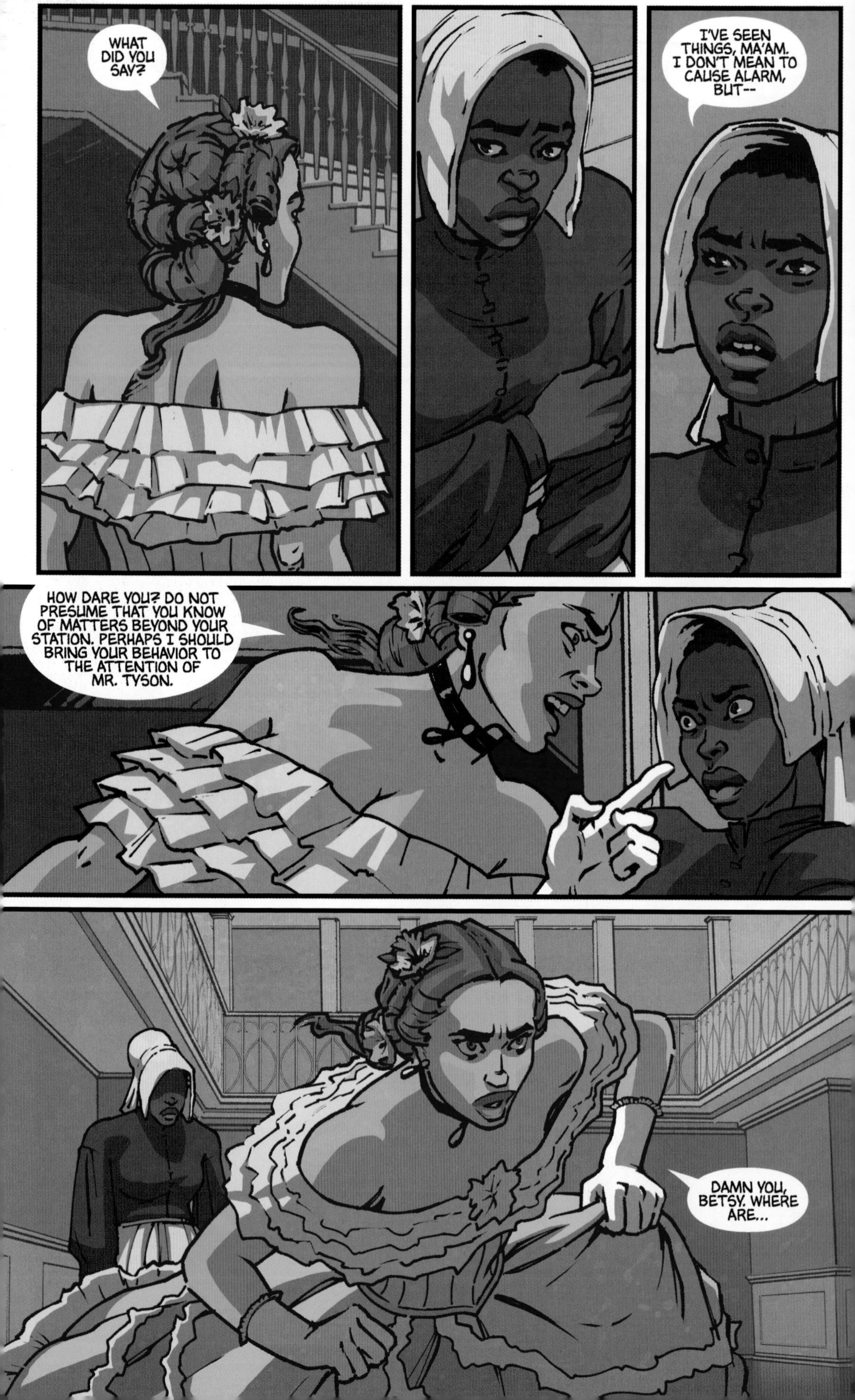
WHAT DID YOU SAY?
I'VE SEEN THINGS, MA'AM. I DON'T MEAN TO CAUSE ALARM, BUT--
HOW DARE YOU? DO NOT PRESUME THAT YOU KNOW OF MATTERS BEYOND YOUR STATION. PERHAPS I SHOULD BRING YOUR BEHAVIOR TO THE ATTENTION OF MR. TYSON.
DAMN YOU, BETSY. WHERE ARE...

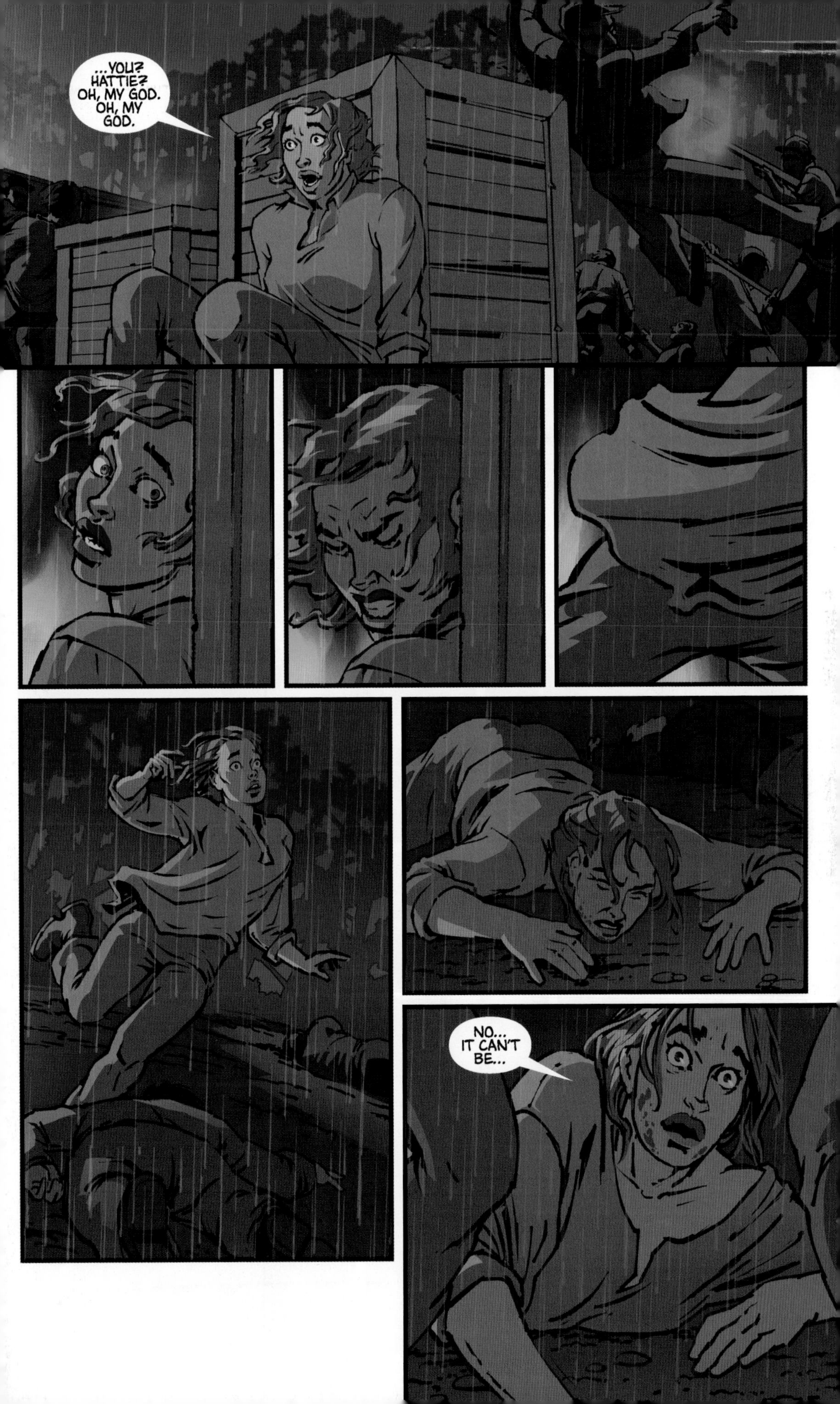
...YOU? HATTIE? OH, MY GOD. OH, MY GOD.
NO... IT CAN'T BE...

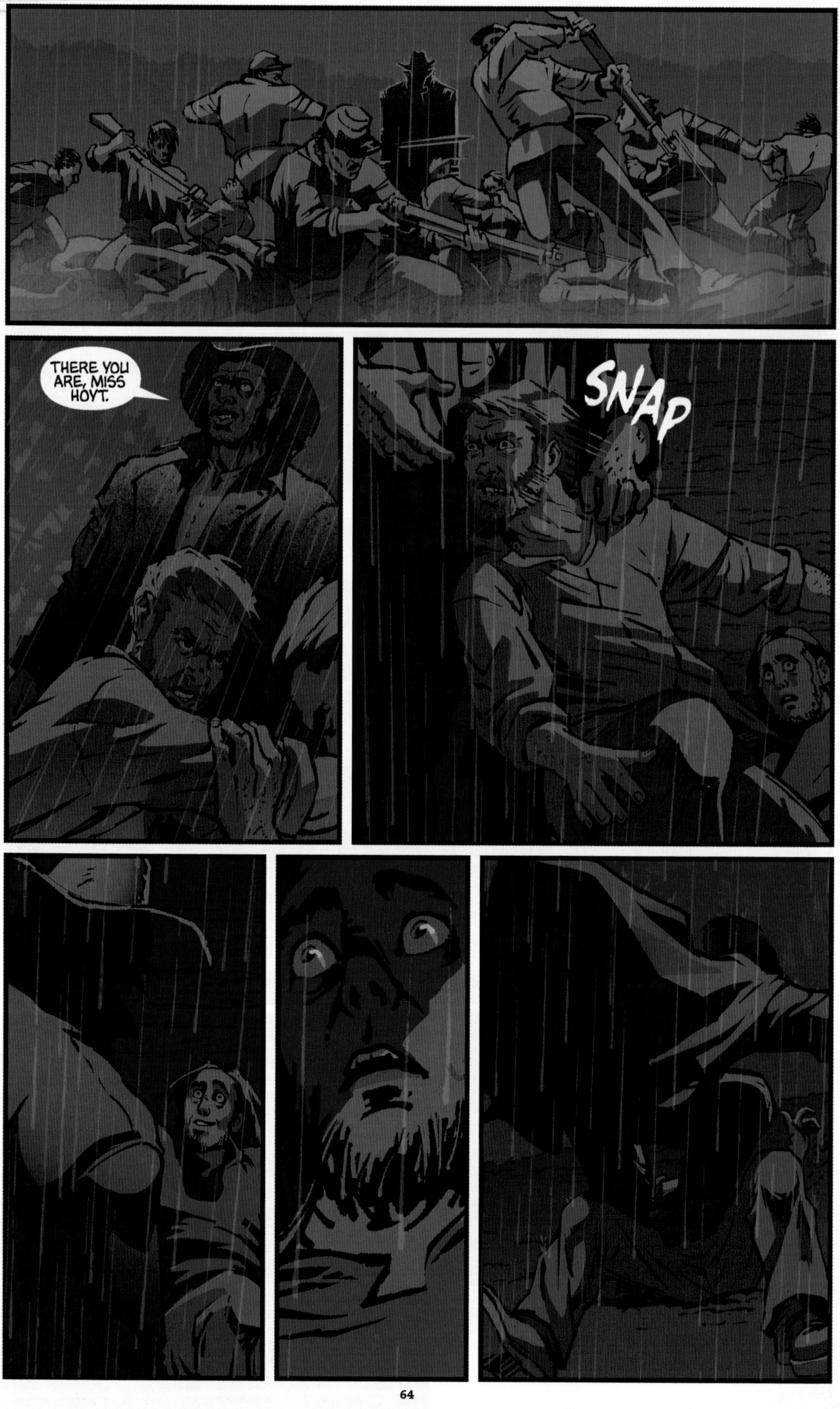
THERE YOU ARE, MISS HOYT.
SNAP

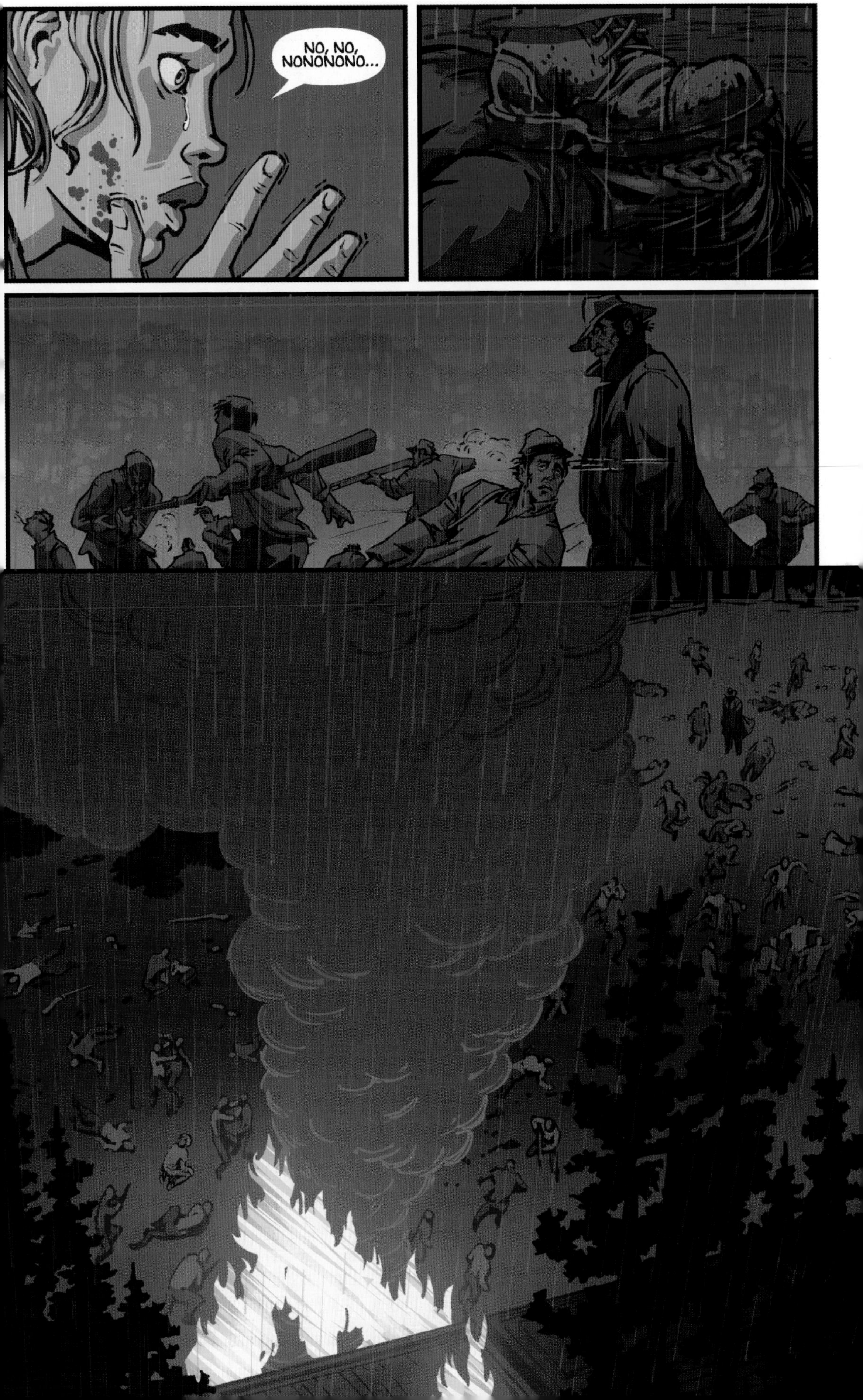
NO, NO, NONONONO...

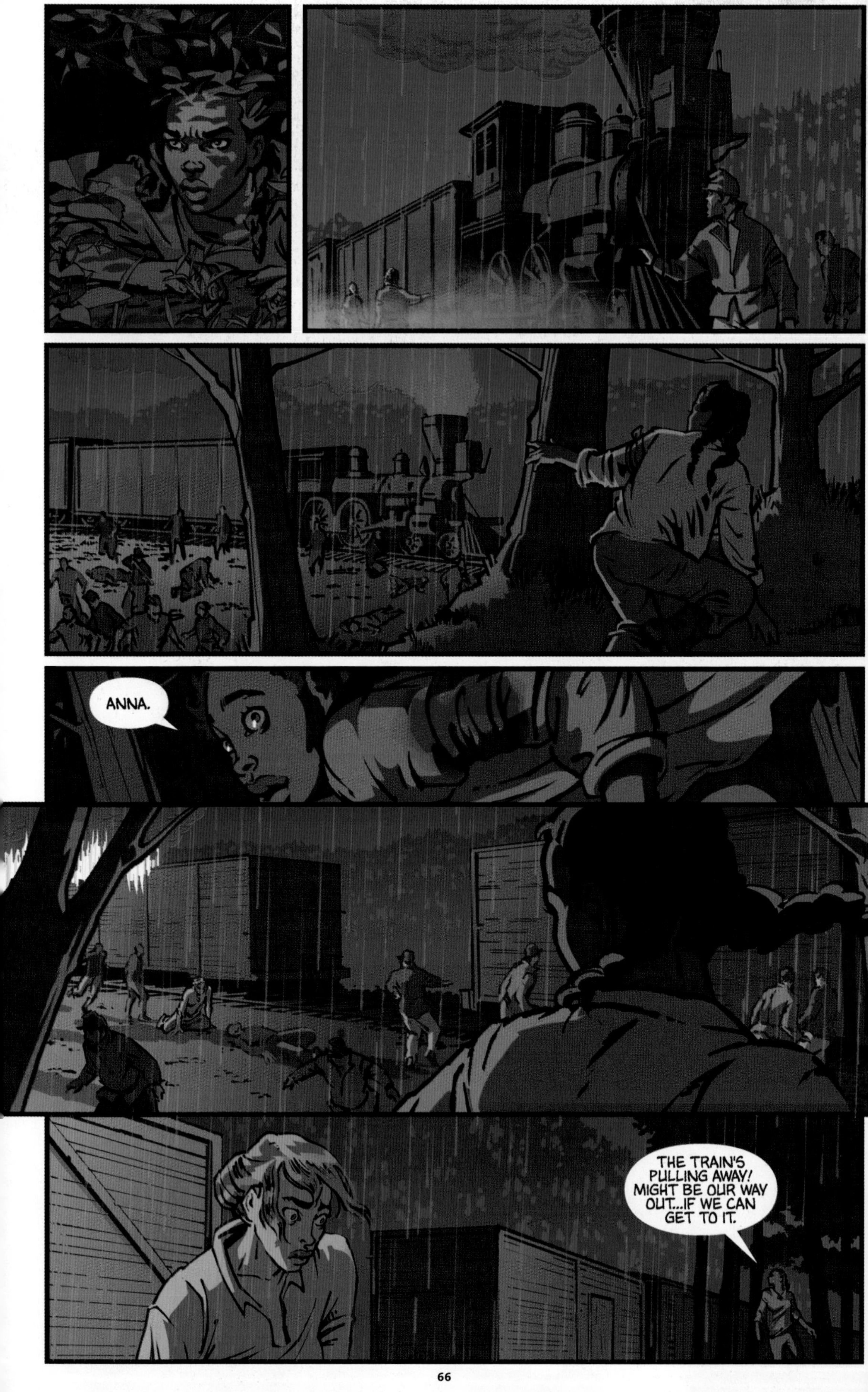
ANNA.
THE TRAIN'S PULLING AWAY! MIGHT BE OUR WAY OUT...IF WE CAN GET TO IT.

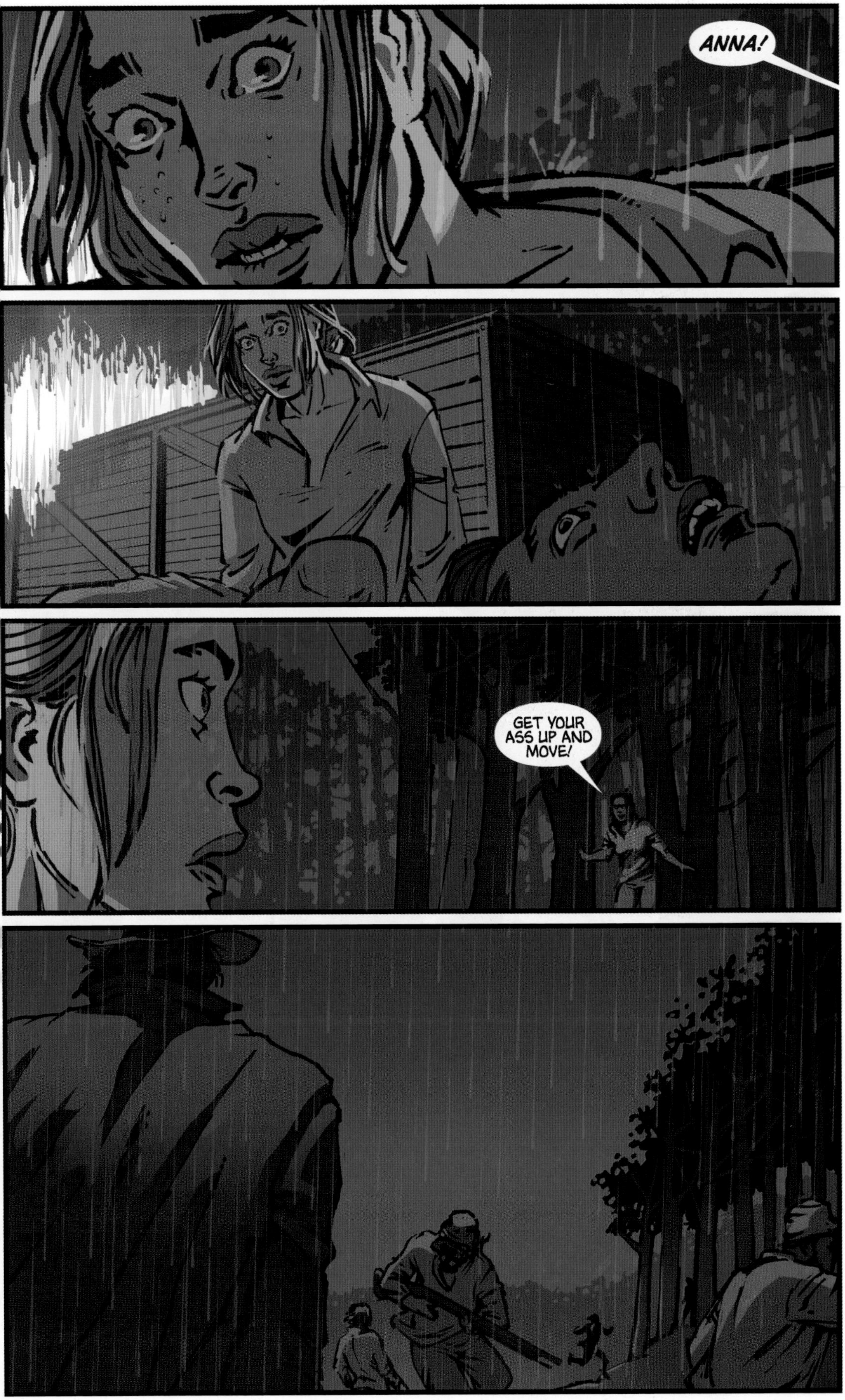
ANNA!
GET YOUR ASS UP AND MOVE!

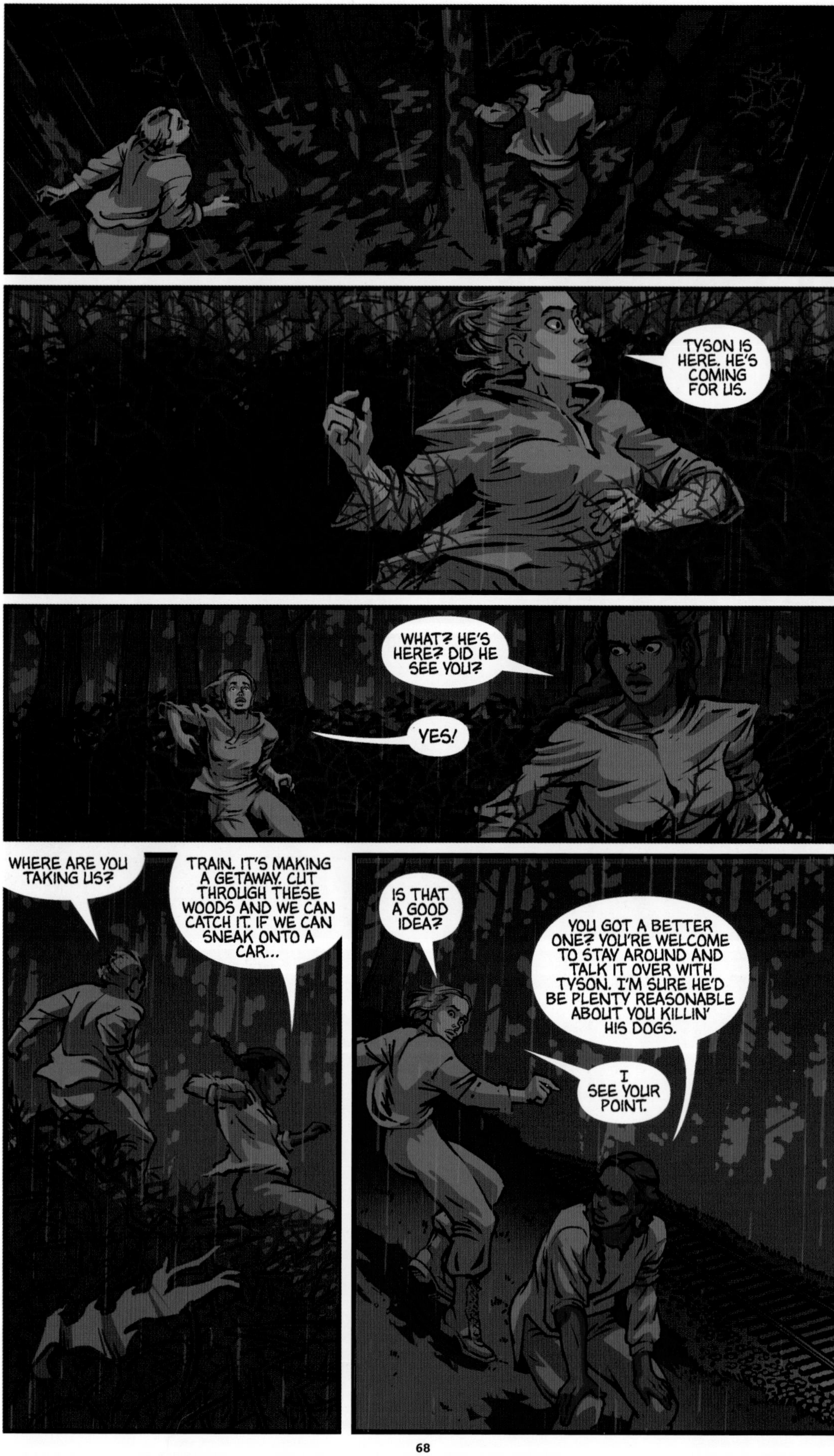

TYSON IS HERE. HE'S COMING FOR US.
WHAT? HE'S HERE? DID HE SEE YOU?
YES!
WHERE ARE YOU TAKING US?
TRAIN. IT'S MAKING A GETAWAY. CUT THROUGH THESE WOODS AND WE CAN CATCH IT. IF WE CAN SNEAK ONTO A CAR...
IS THAT A GOOD IDEA?
YOU GOT A BETTER ONE? YOU'RE WELCOME TO STAY AROUND AND TALK IT OVER WITH TYSON. I'M SURE HE'D BE PLENTY REASONABLE ABOUT YOU KILLIN' HIS DOGS.
I SEE YOUR POINT.

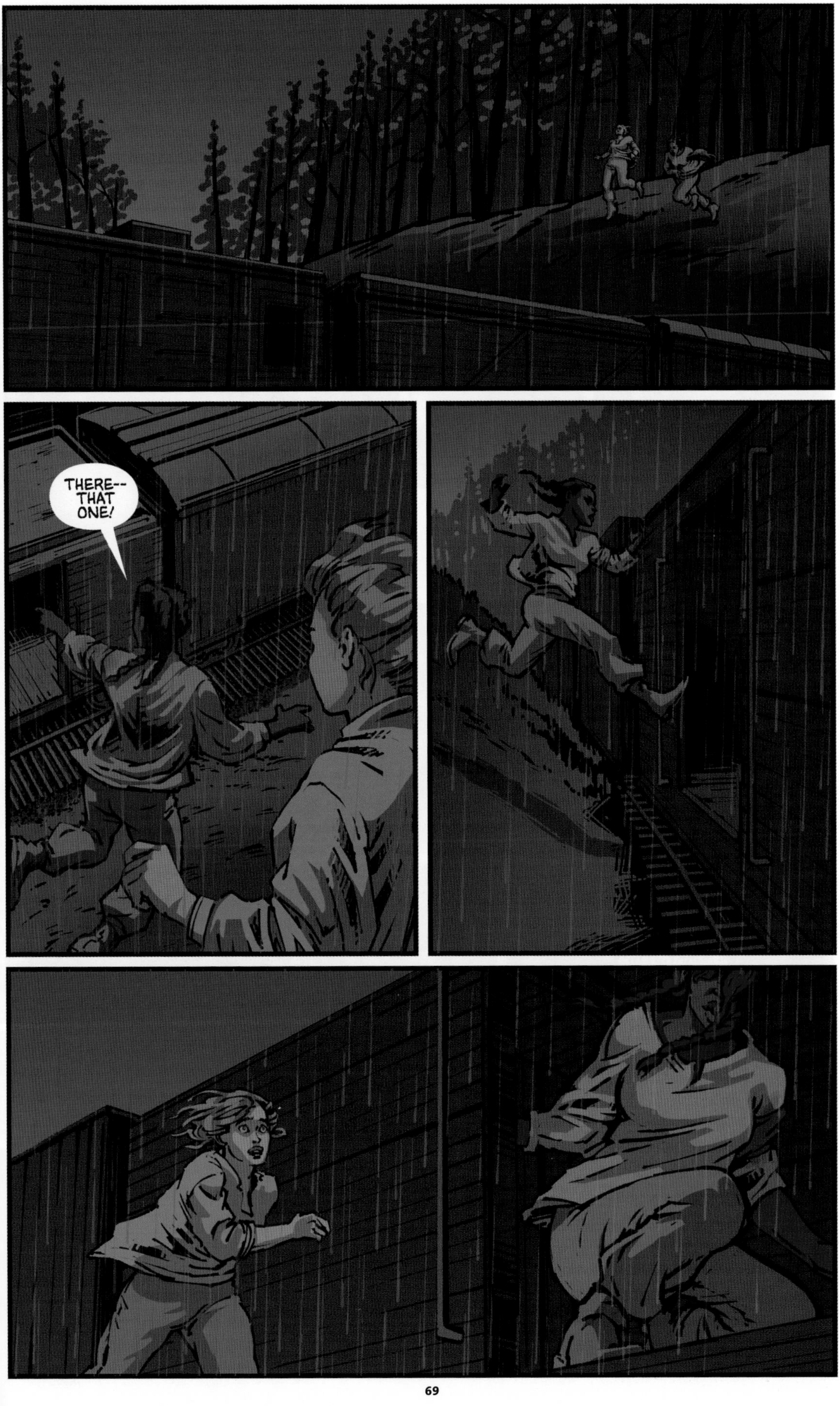
THERE-- THAT ONE!

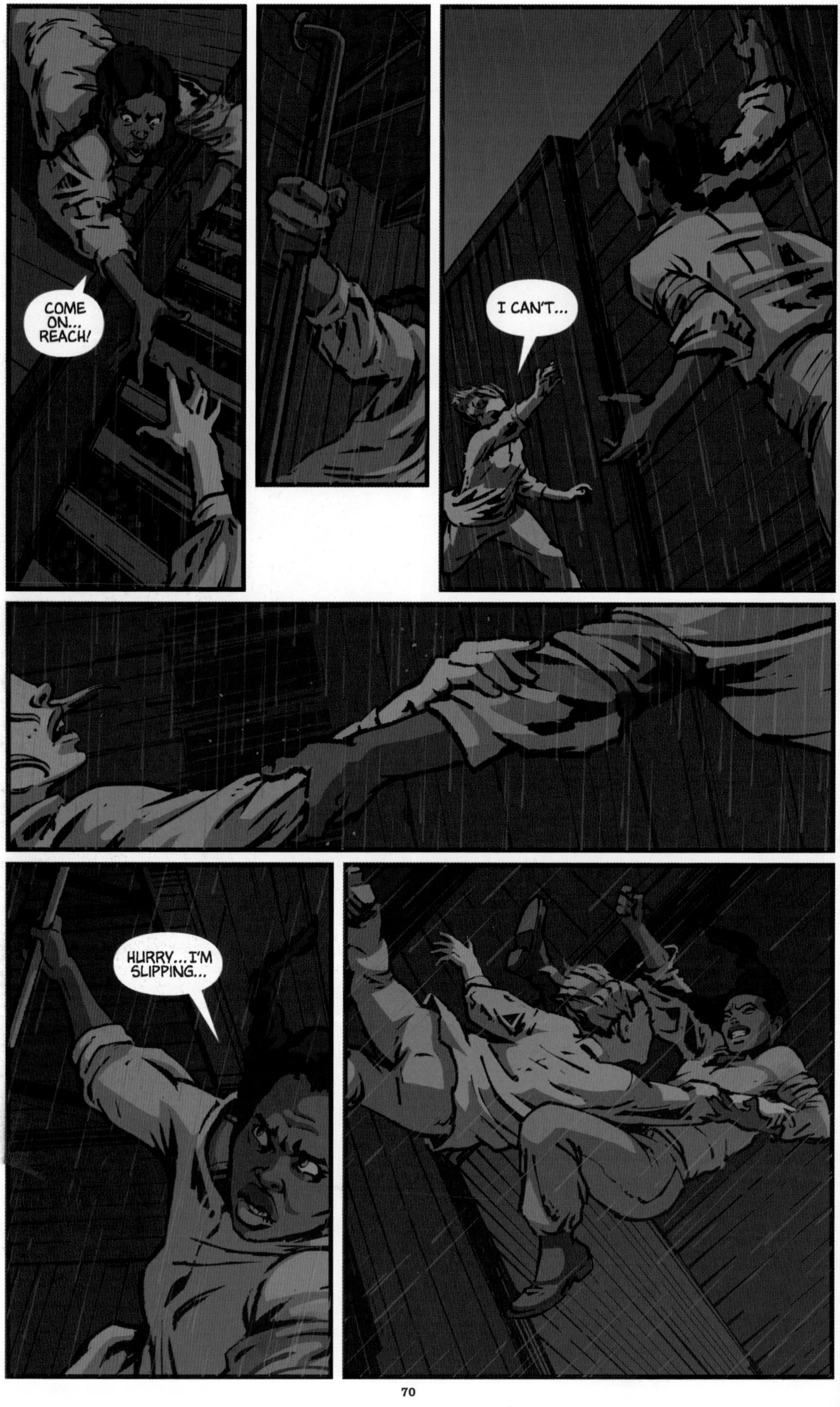
COME ON... REACH!
I CAN'T...
HURRY...I'M SLIPPING...

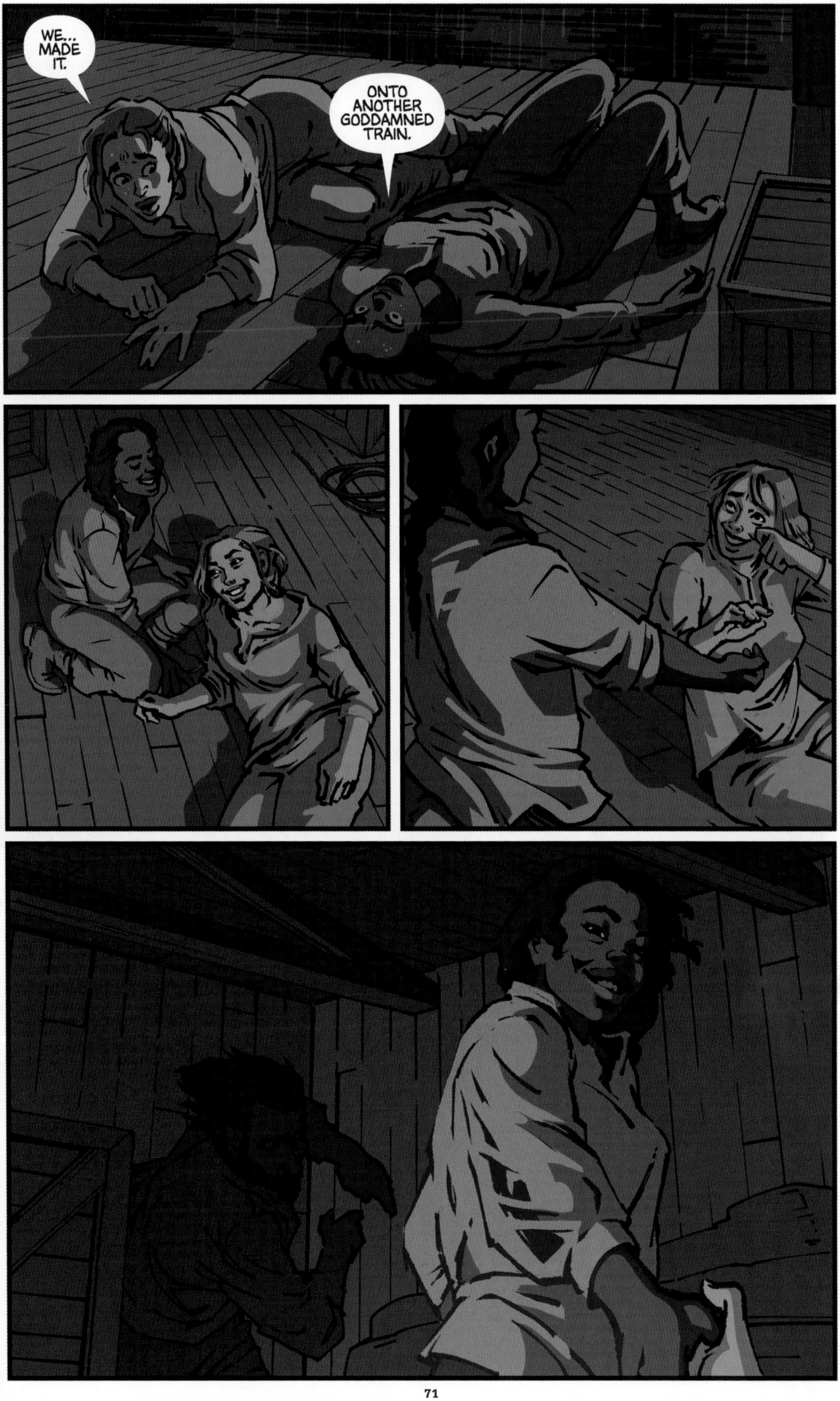
WE... MADE IT.
ONTO ANOTHER GODDAMNED TRAIN.

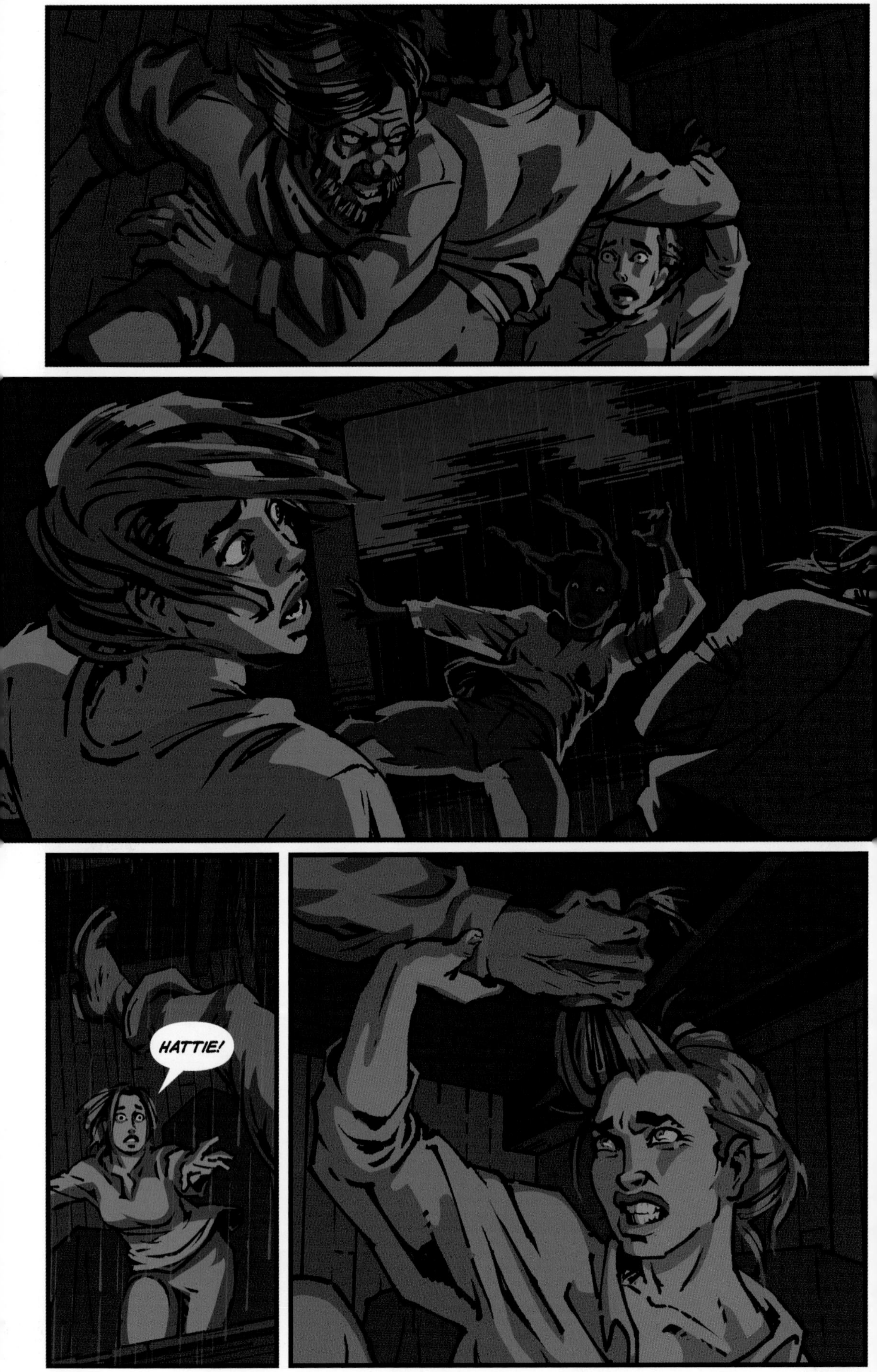
HATTIE!

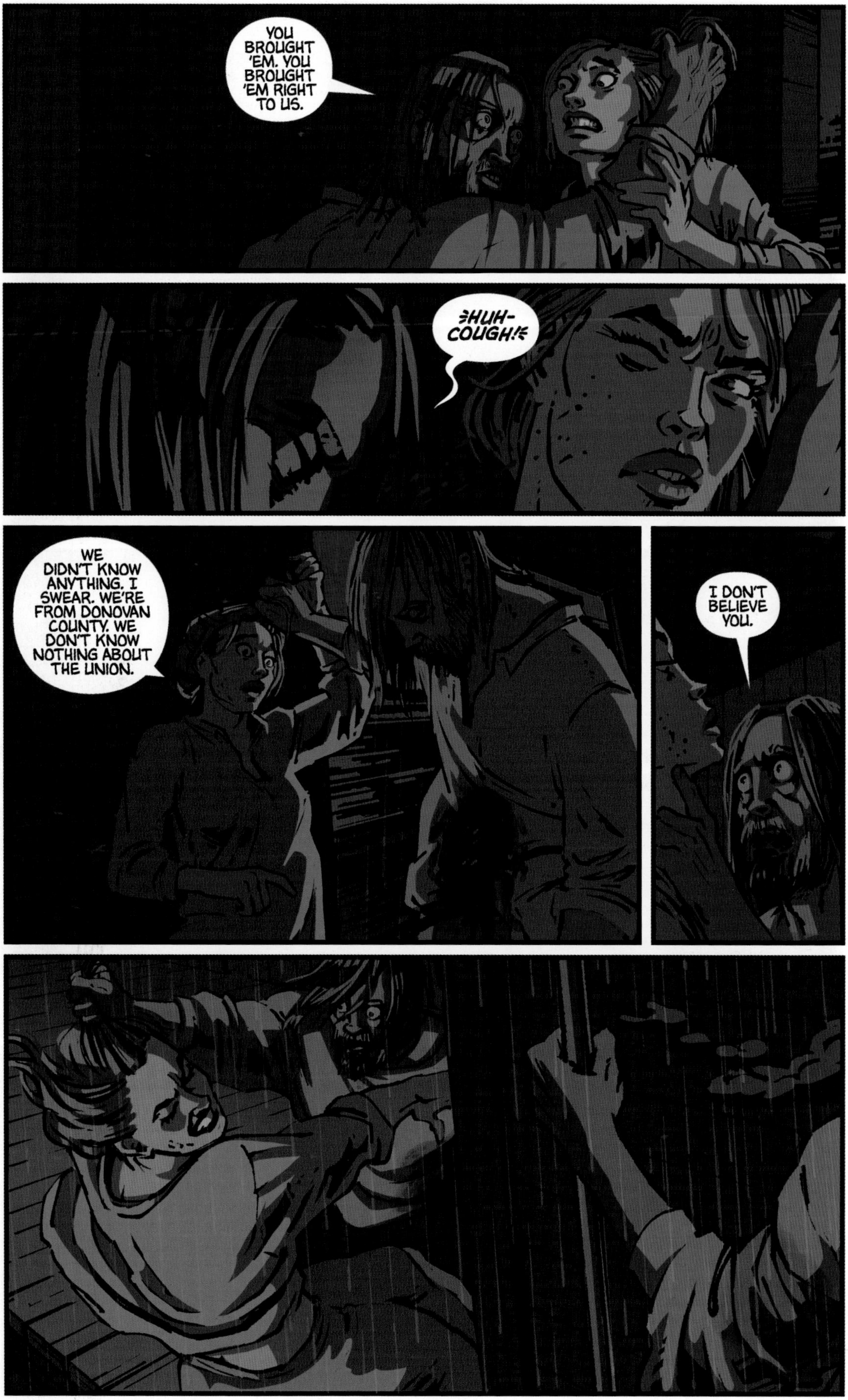
YOU BROUGHT 'EM. YOU BROUGHT 'EM RIGHT TO US.
HUH-COUGH!
WE DIDN'T KNOW ANYTHING. I SWEAR. WE'RE FROM DONOVAN COUNTY. WE DON'T KNOW NOTHING ABOUT THE UNION.
I DON'T BELIEVE YOU.

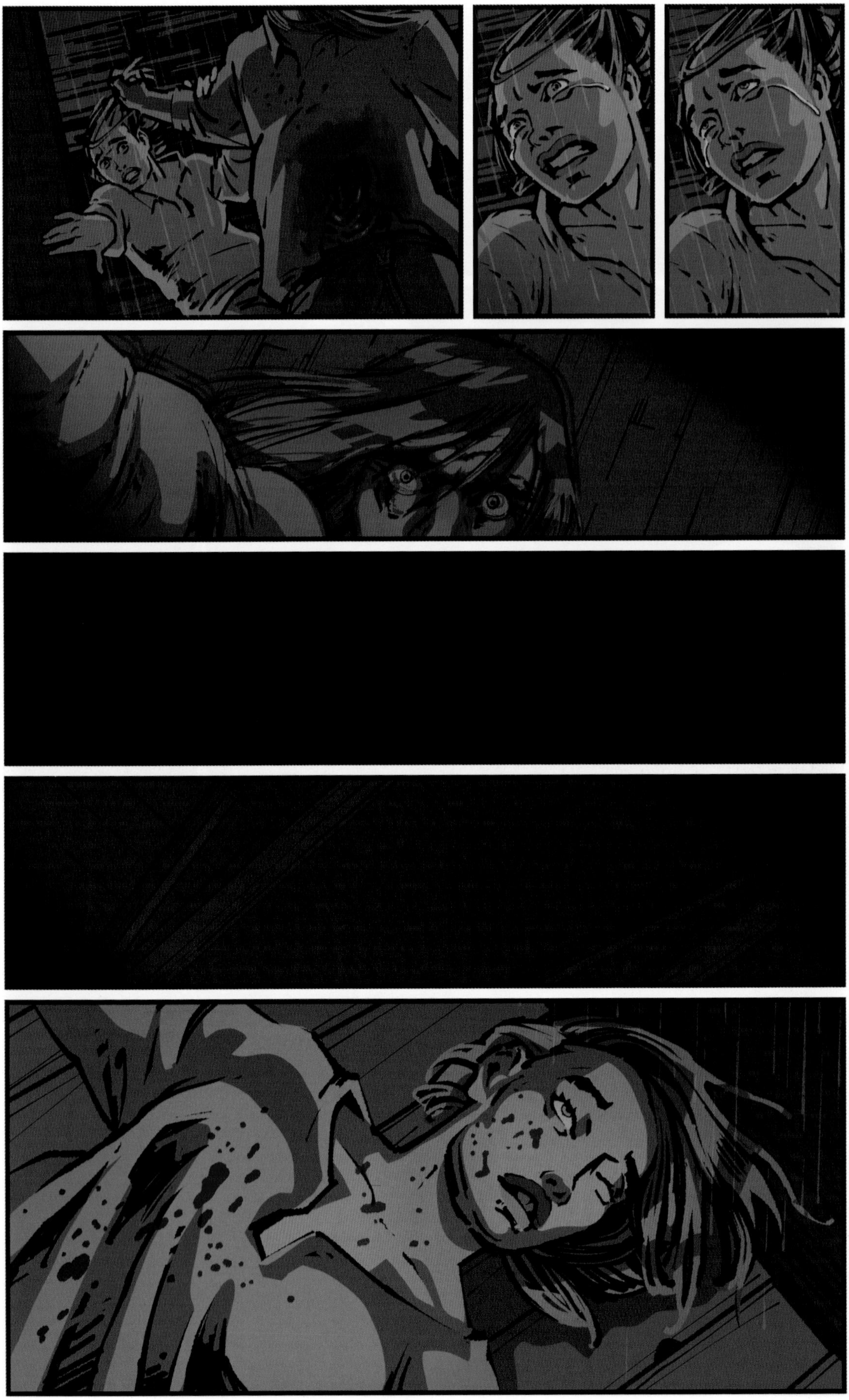

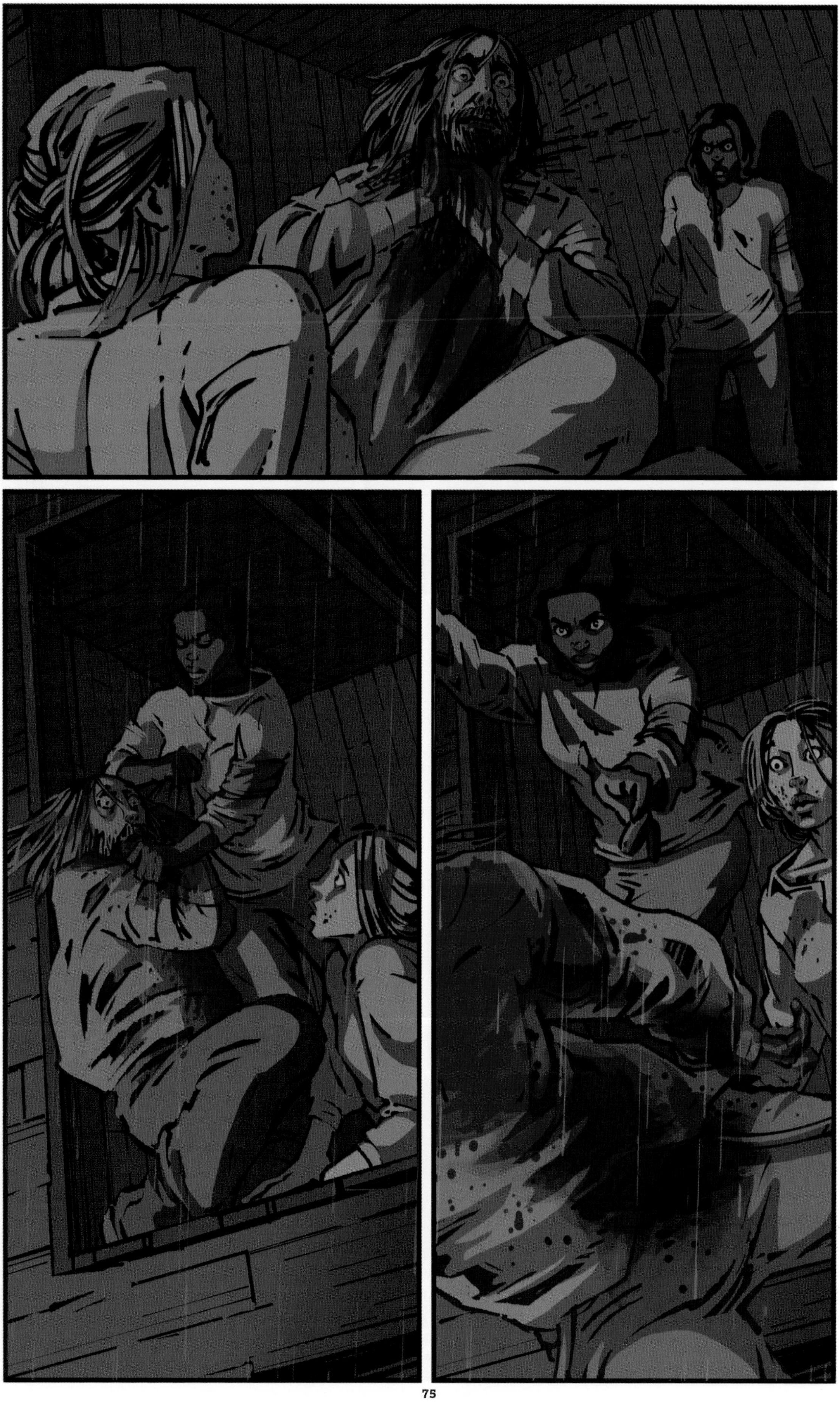

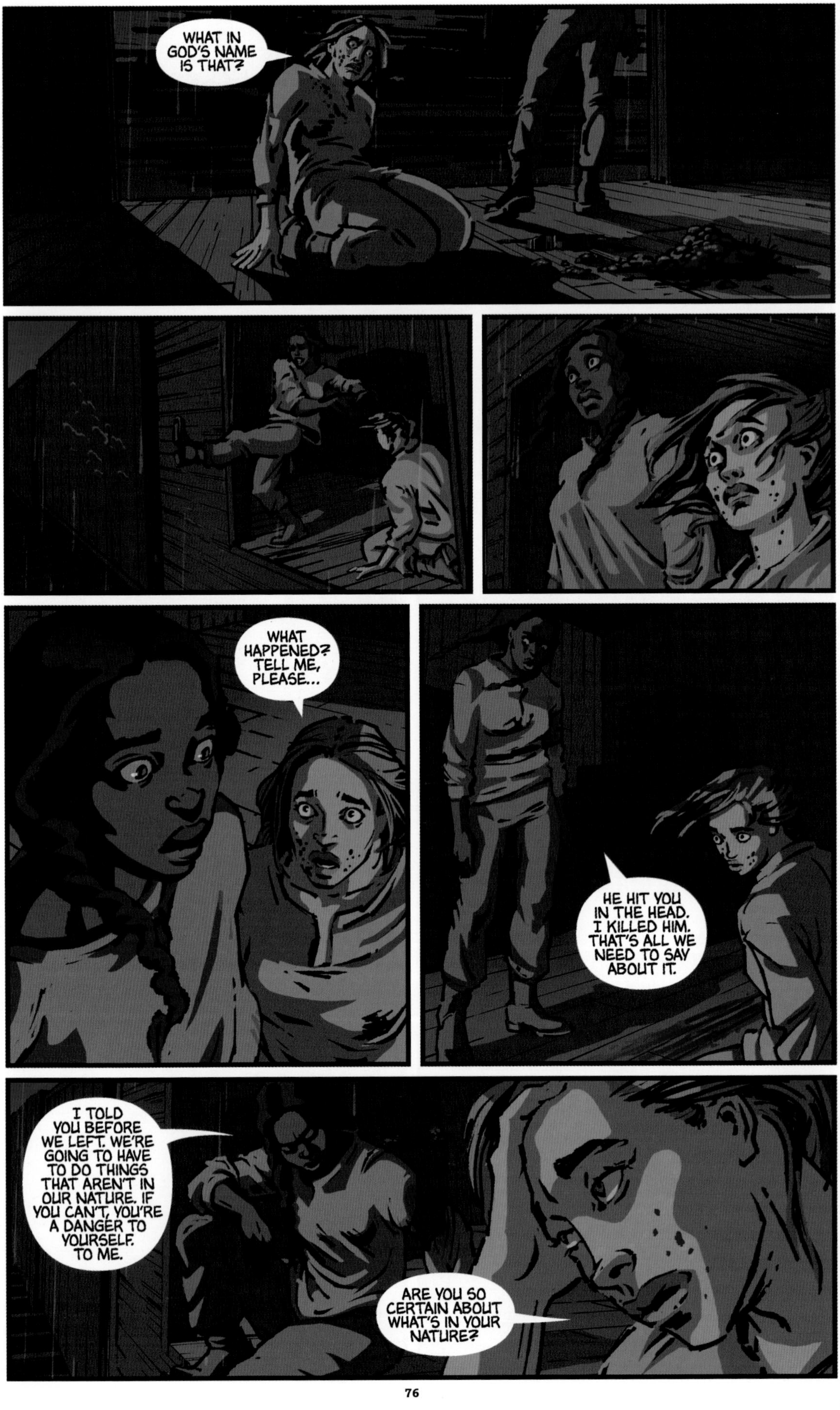

WHAT IN GOD'S NAME IS THAT?
WHAT HAPPENED? TELL ME, PLEASE...
HE HIT YOU IN THE HEAD. I KILLED HIM. THAT'S ALL WE NEED TO SAY ABOUT IT.
I TOLD YOU BEFORE WE LEFT. WE'RE GOING TO HAVE TO DO THINGS THAT AREN'T IN OUR NATURE. IF YOU CAN'T, YOU'RE A DANGER TO YOURSELF. TO ME.
ARE YOU SO CERTAIN ABOUT WHAT'S IN YOUR NATURE?

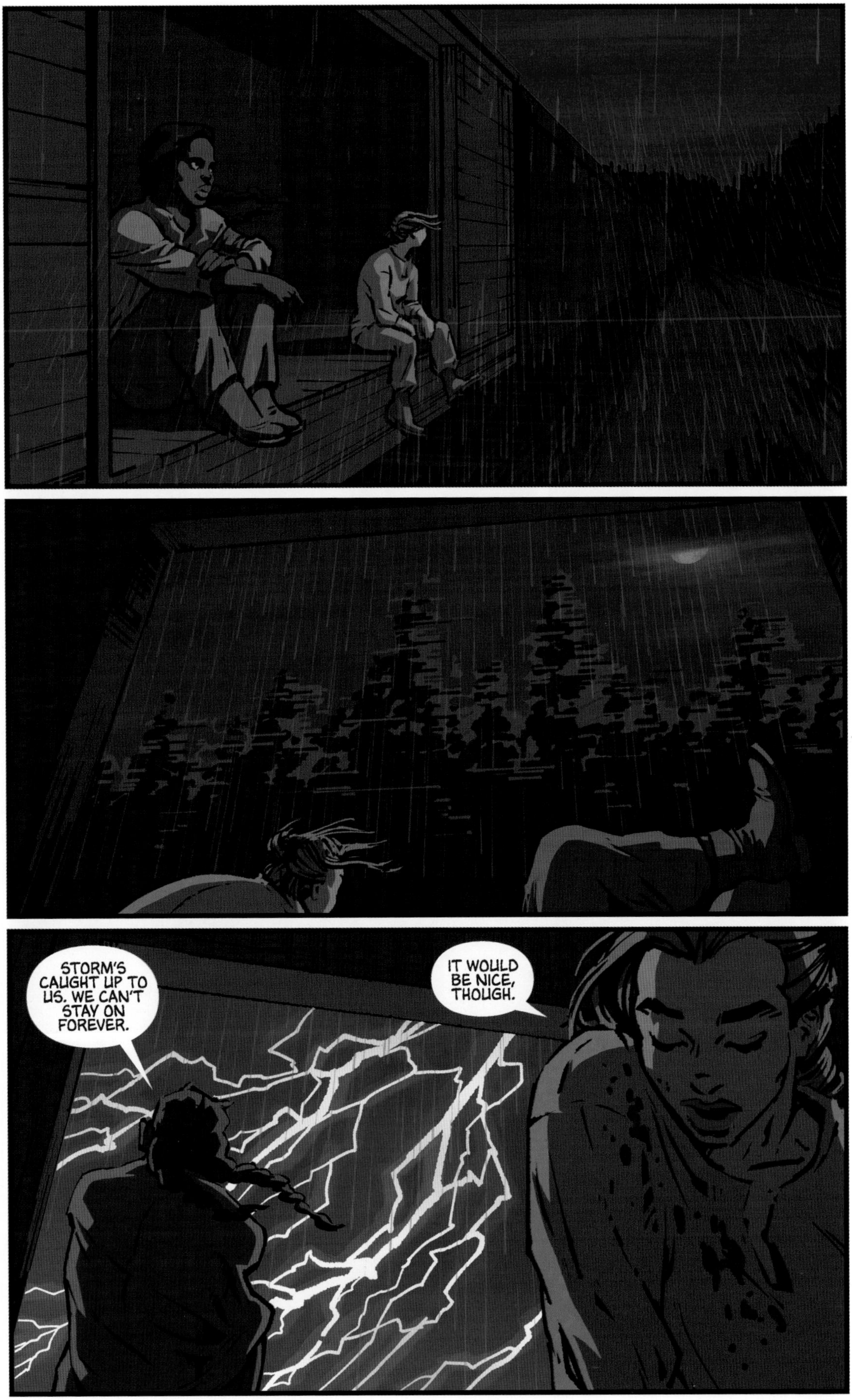
STORM'S CAUGHT UP TO US. WE CAN'T STAY ON FOREVER.
IT WOULD BE NICE, THOUGH.

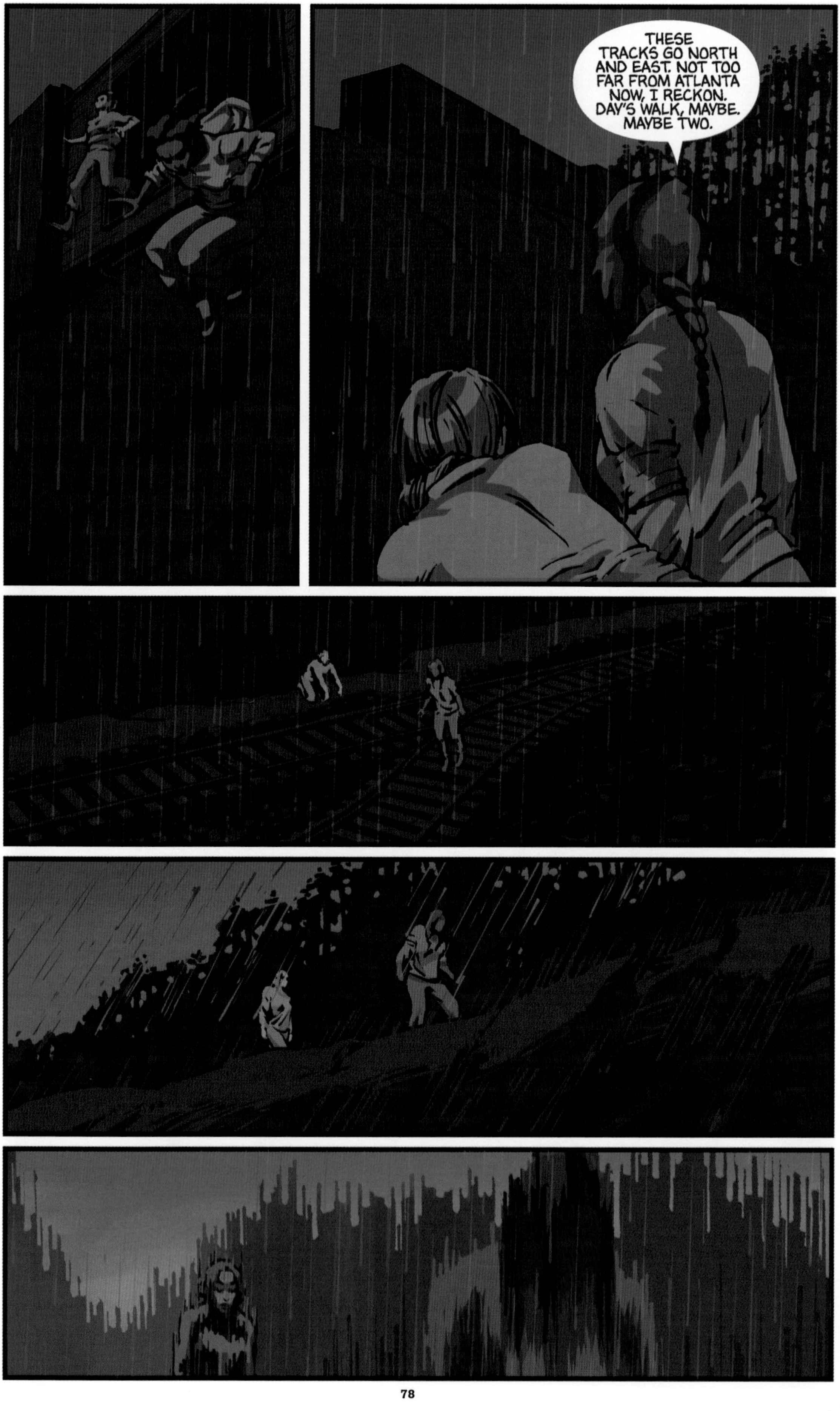
THESE TRACKS GO NORTH AND EAST. NOT TOO FAR FROM ATLANTA NOW, I RECKON. DAY'S WALK, MAYBE. MAYBE TWO.

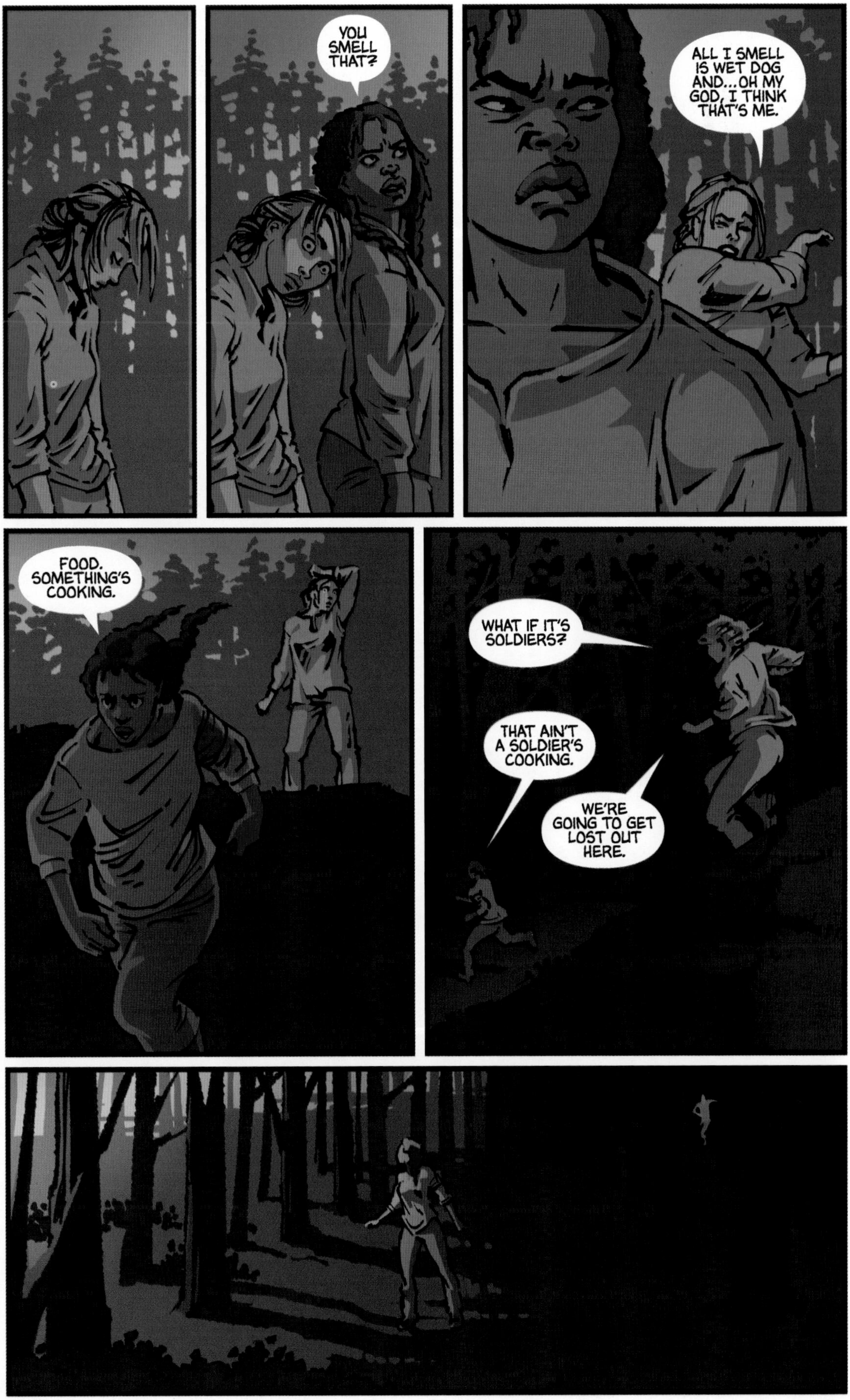
YOU SMELL THAT?
ALL I SMELL IS WET DOG AND...OH MY GOD, I THINK THAT'S ME.
FOOD. SOMETHING'S COOKING.
WHAT IF IT'S SOLDIERS?
THAT AIN'T A SOLDIER'S COOKING.
WE'RE GOING TO GET LOST OUT HERE.

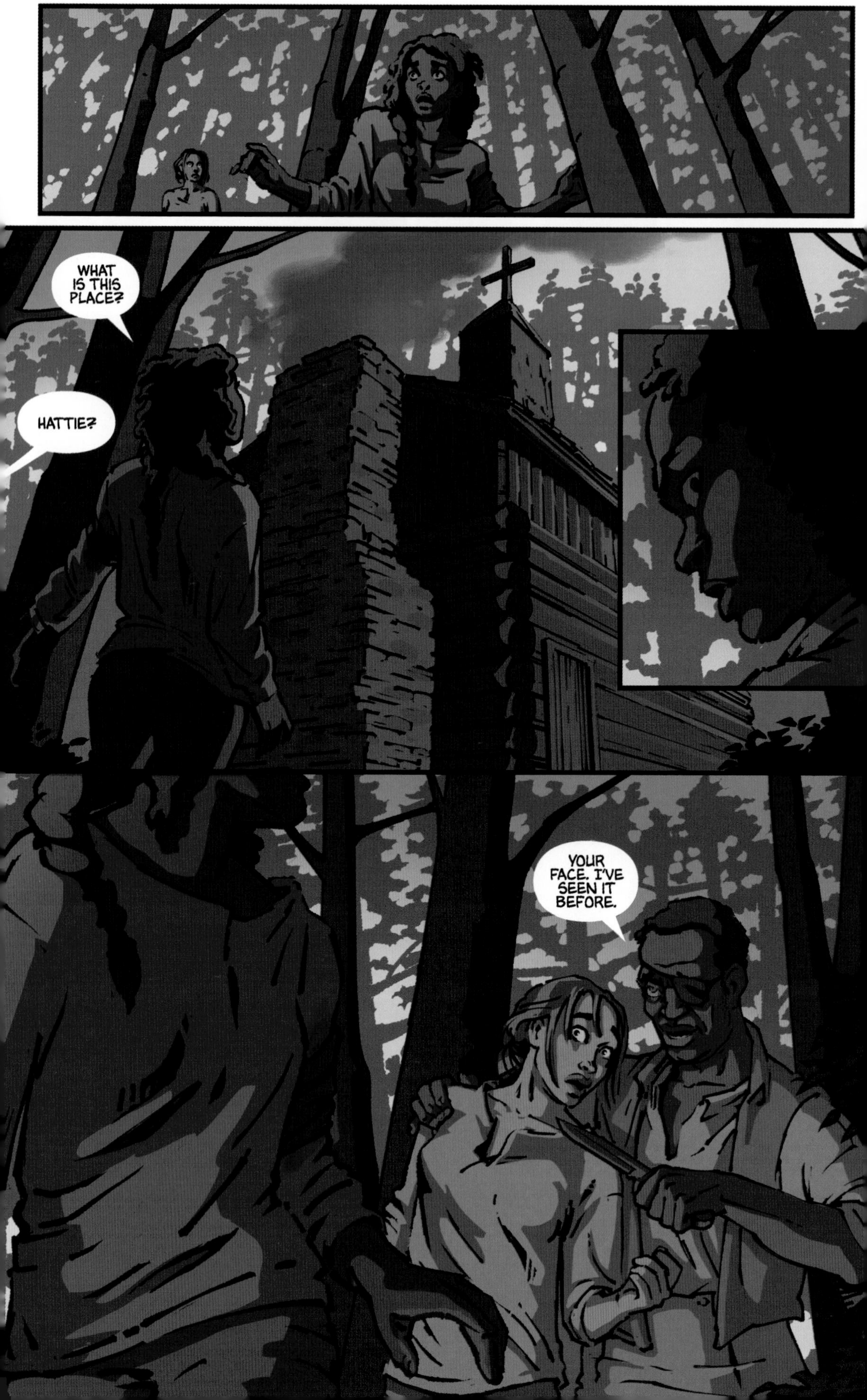
WHAT IS THIS PLACE?
HATTIE?
YOUR FACE. I'VE SEEN IT BEFORE.

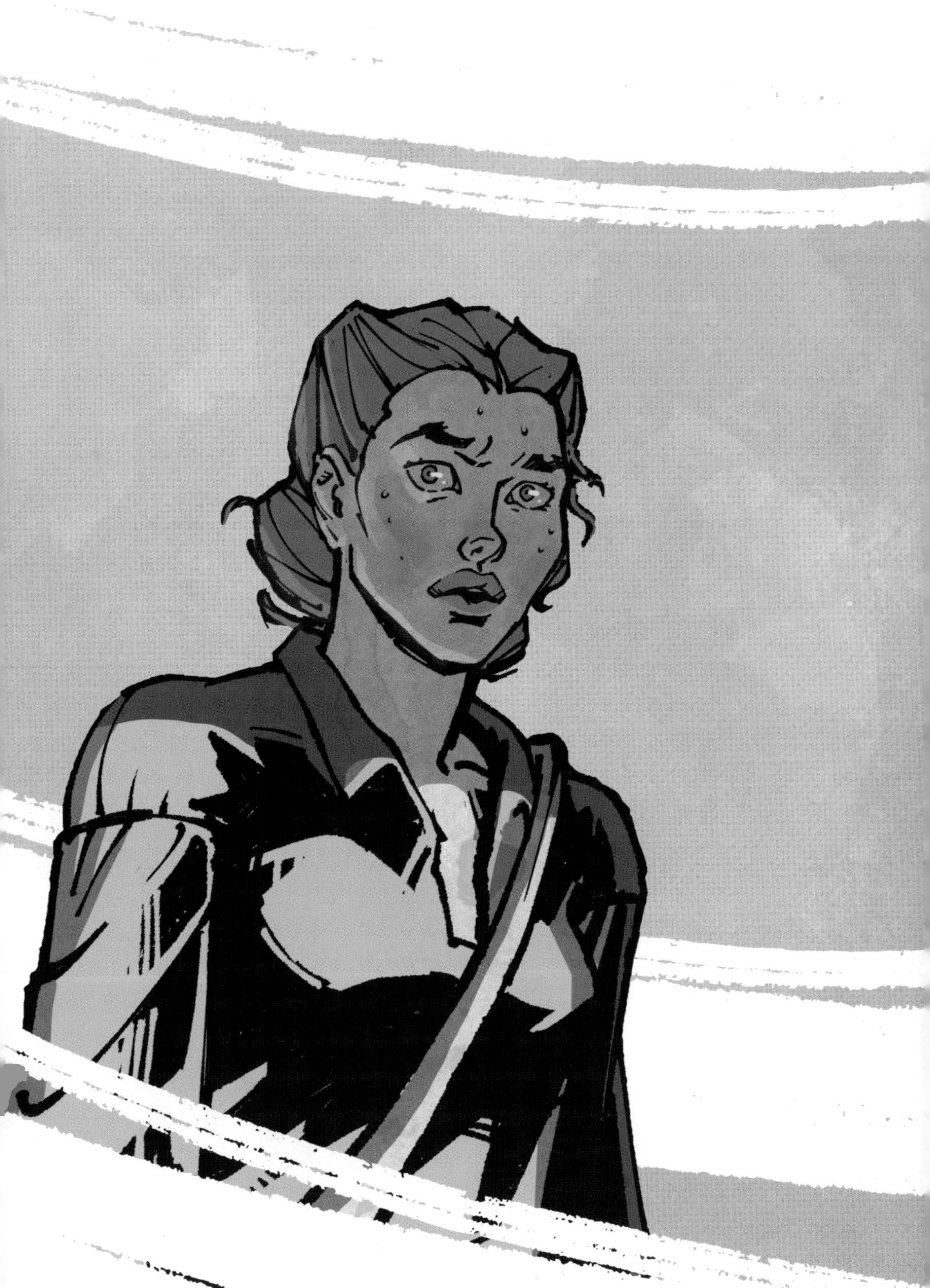

CHAPTER FOUR

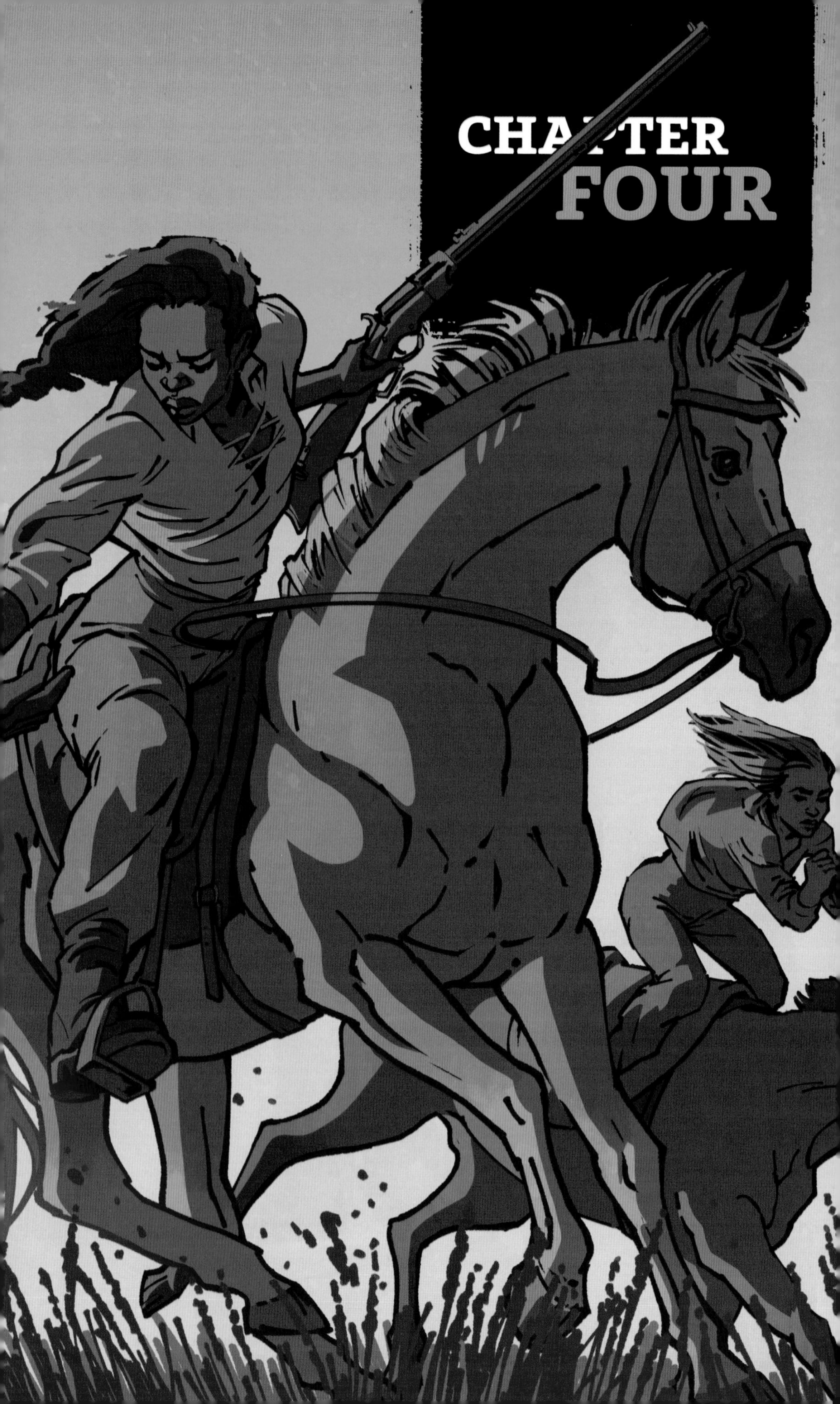

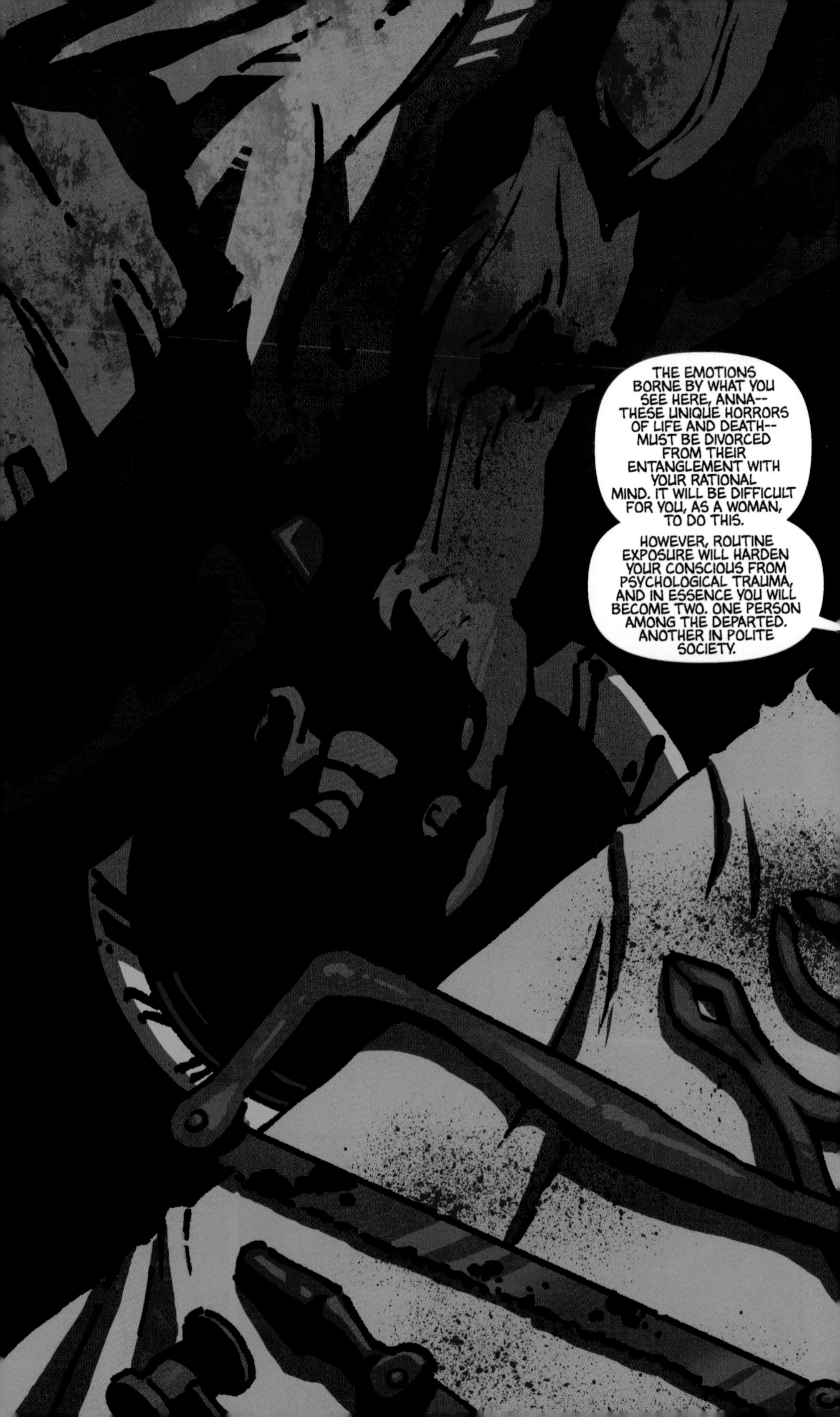
THE EMOTIONS BORNE BY WHAT YOU SEE HERE, ANNA-- THESE UNIQUE HORRORS OF LIFE AND DEATH-- MUST BE DIVORCED FROM THEIR ENTANGLEMENT WITH YOUR RATIONAL MIND. IT WILL BE DIFFICULT FOR YOU, AS A WOMAN, TO DO THIS.
HOWEVER, ROUTINE EXPOSURE WILL HARDEN YOUR CONSCIOUS FROM PSYCHOLOGICAL TRAUMA, AND IN ESSENCE YOU WILL BECOME TWO. ONE PERSON AMONG THE DEPARTED. ANOTHER IN POLITE SOCIETY.

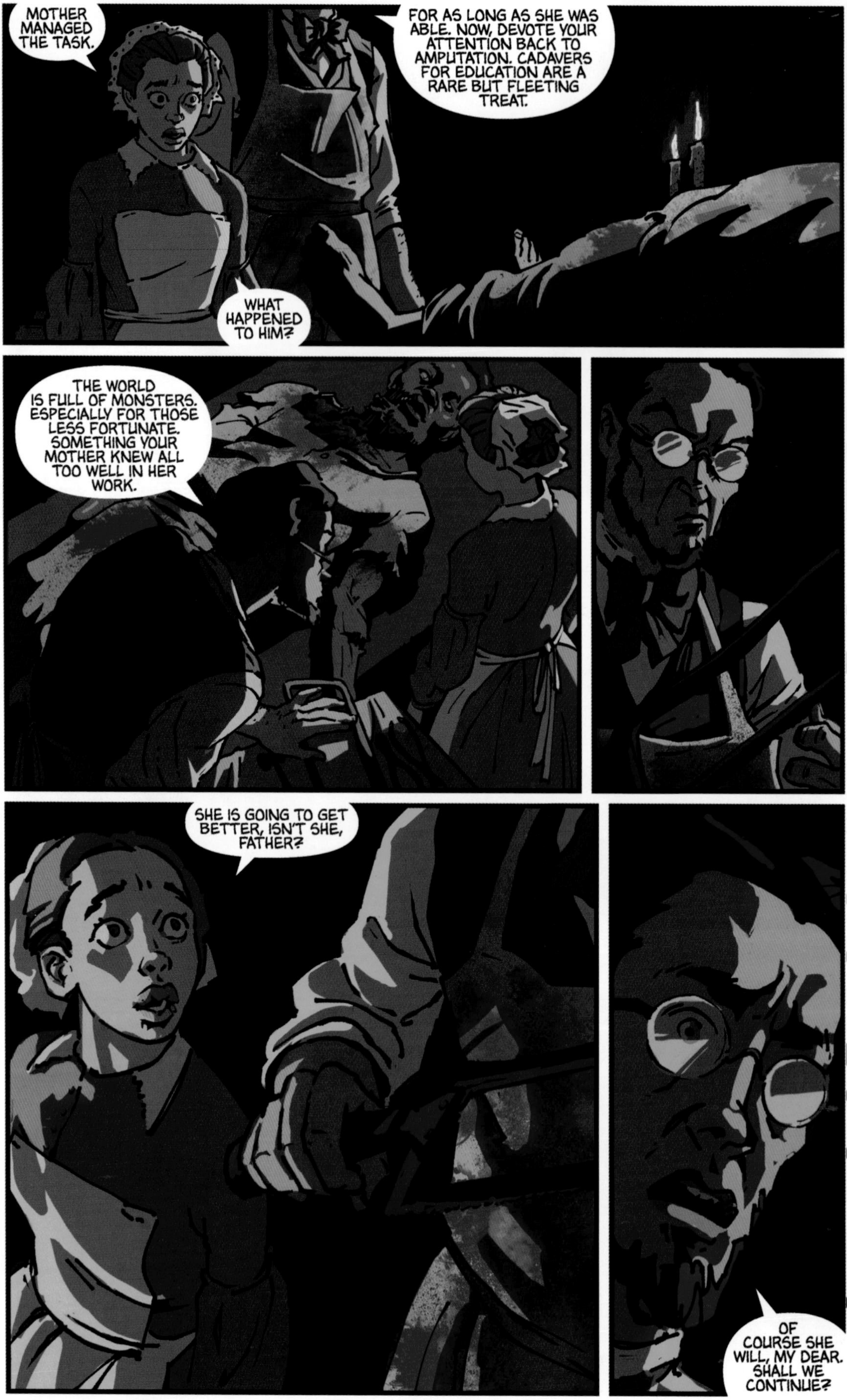
MOTHER MANAGED THE TASK.
FOR AS LONG AS SHE WAS ABLE. NOW, DEVOTE YOUR ATTENTION BACK TO AMPUTATION. CADAVERS FOR EDUCATION ARE A RARE BUT FLEETING TREAT.
WHAT HAPPENED TO HIM?
THE WORLD IS FULL OF MONSTERS. ESPECIALLY FOR THOSE LESS FORTUNATE. SOMETHING YOUR MOTHER KNEW ALL TOO WELL IN HER WORK.
SHE IS GOING TO GET BETTER, ISN'T SHE, FATHER?
OF COURSE SHE WILL, MY DEAR. SHALL WE CONTINUE?

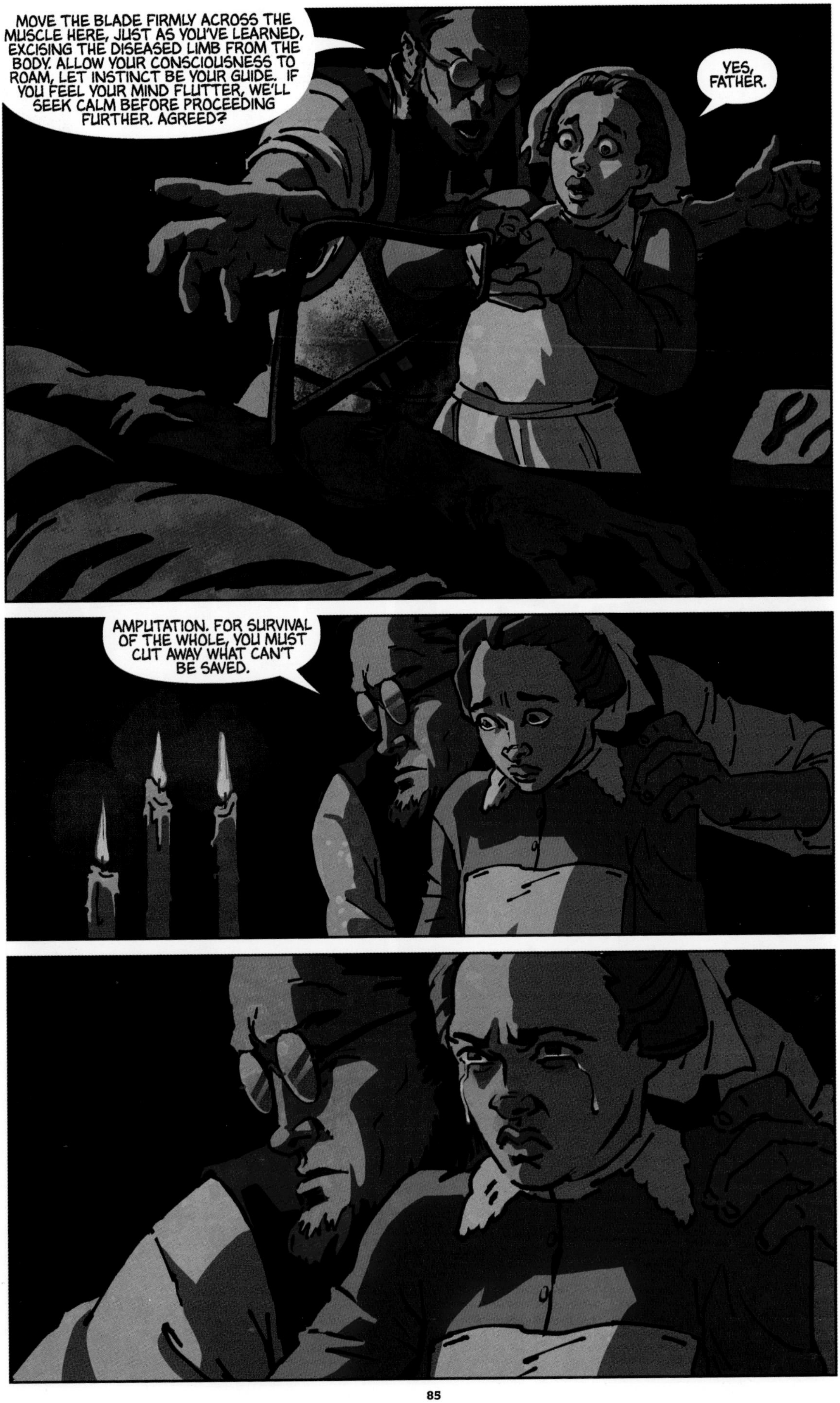
MOVE THE BLADE FIRMLY ACROSS THE MUSCLE HERE, JUST AS YOU'VE LEARNED, EXCISING THE DISEASED LIMB FROM THE BODY. ALLOW YOUR CONSCIOUSNESS TO ROAM, LET INSTINCT BE YOUR GUIDE. IF YOU FEEL YOUR MIND FLUTTER, WE'LL SEEK CALM BEFORE PROCEEDING FURTHER. AGREED?
YES, FATHER.
AMPUTATION. FOR SURVIVAL OF THE WHOLE, YOU MUST CUT AWAY WHAT CAN'T BE SAVED.

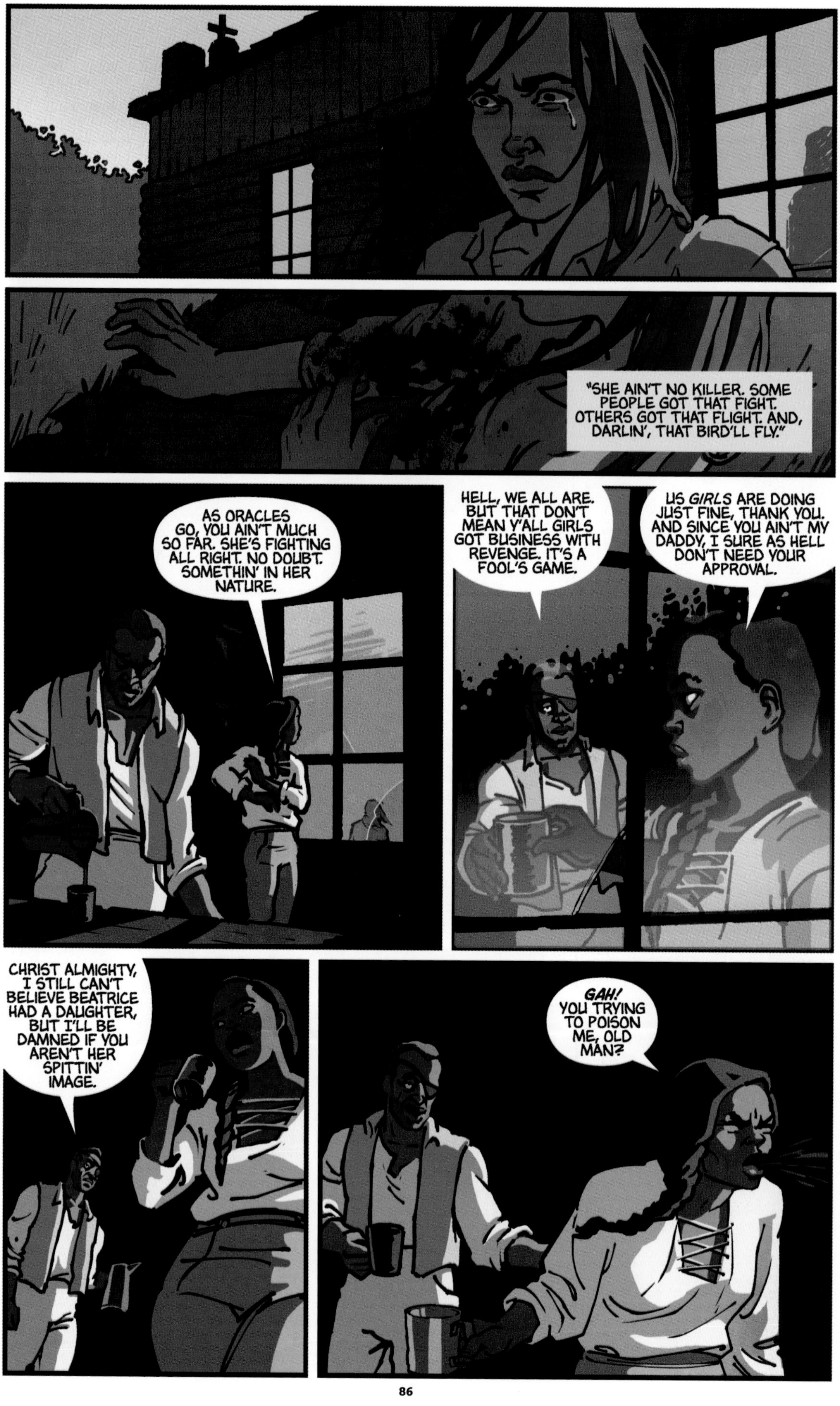
"SHE AIN'T NO KILLER. SOME PEOPLE GOT THAT FIGHT. OTHERS GOT THAT FLIGHT. AND, DARLIN', THAT BIRD'LL FLY."
AS ORACLES GO, YOU AIN'T MUCH SO FAR. SHE'S FIGHTING ALL RIGHT. NO DOUBT. SOMETHIN' IN HER NATURE.
HELL, WE ALL ARE. BUT THAT DON'T MEAN Y'ALL GIRLS GOT BUSINESS WITH REVENGE. IT'S A FOOL'S GAME.
US *GIRLS* ARE DOING JUST FINE, THANK YOU. AND SINCE YOU AIN'T MY DADDY, I SURE AS HELL DON'T NEED YOUR APPROVAL.
CHRIST ALMIGHTY, I STILL CAN'T BELIEVE BEATRICE HAD A DAUGHTER, BUT I'LL BE DAMNED IF YOU AREN'T HER SPITTIN' IMAGE.
GAH! YOU TRYING TO POISON ME, OLD MAN?

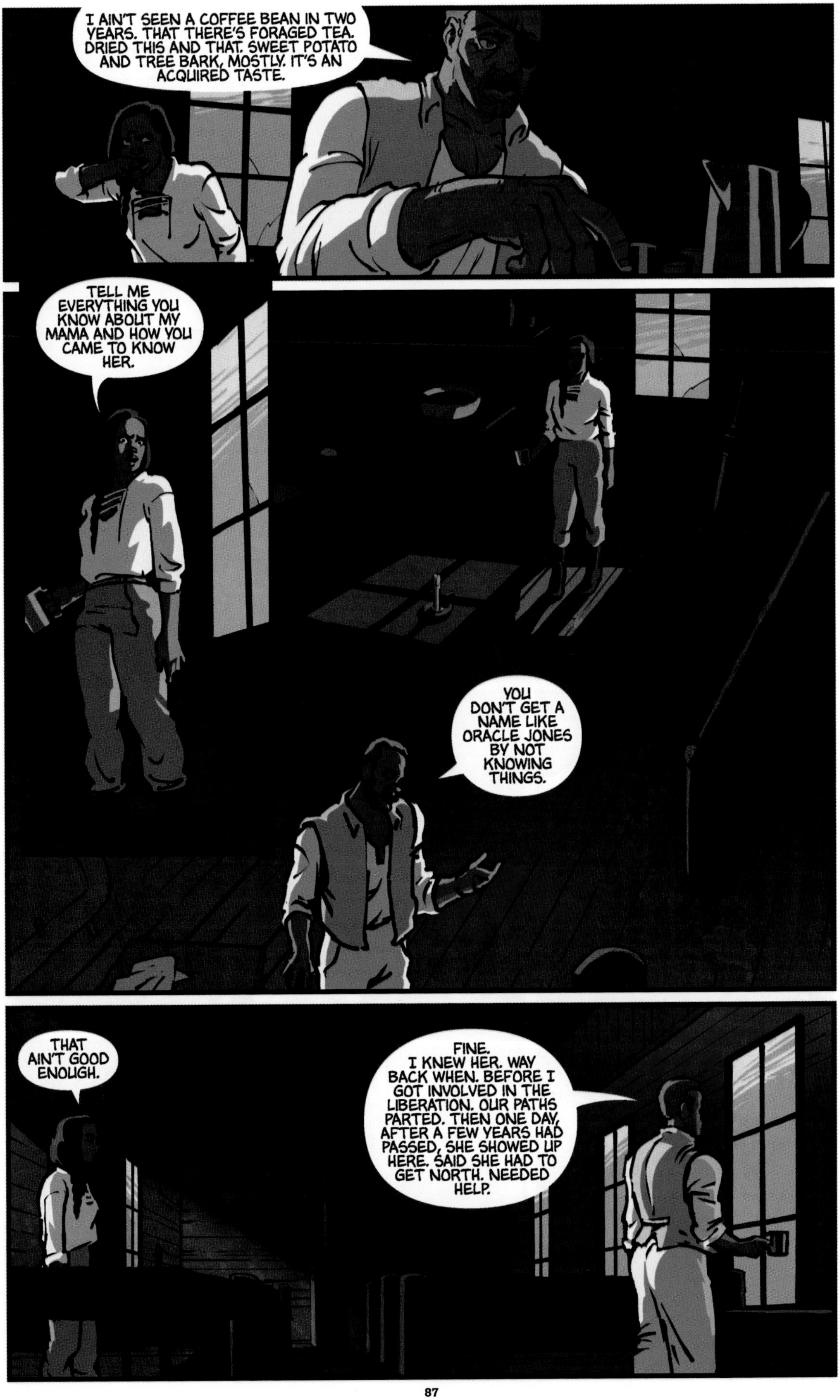
I AIN'T SEEN A COFFEE BEAN IN TWO YEARS. THAT THERE'S FORAGED TEA. DRIED THIS AND THAT. SWEET POTATO AND TREE BARK, MOSTLY. IT'S AN ACQUIRED TASTE.
TELL ME EVERYTHING YOU KNOW ABOUT MY MAMA AND HOW YOU CAME TO KNOW HER.
YOU DON'T GET A NAME LIKE ORACLE JONES BY NOT KNOWING THINGS.
THAT AIN'T GOOD ENOUGH.
FINE. I KNEW HER. WAY BACK WHEN. BEFORE I GOT INVOLVED IN THE LIBERATION. OUR PATHS PARTED. THEN ONE DAY, AFTER A FEW YEARS HAD PASSED, SHE SHOWED UP HERE. SAID SHE HAD TO GET NORTH. NEEDED HELP.

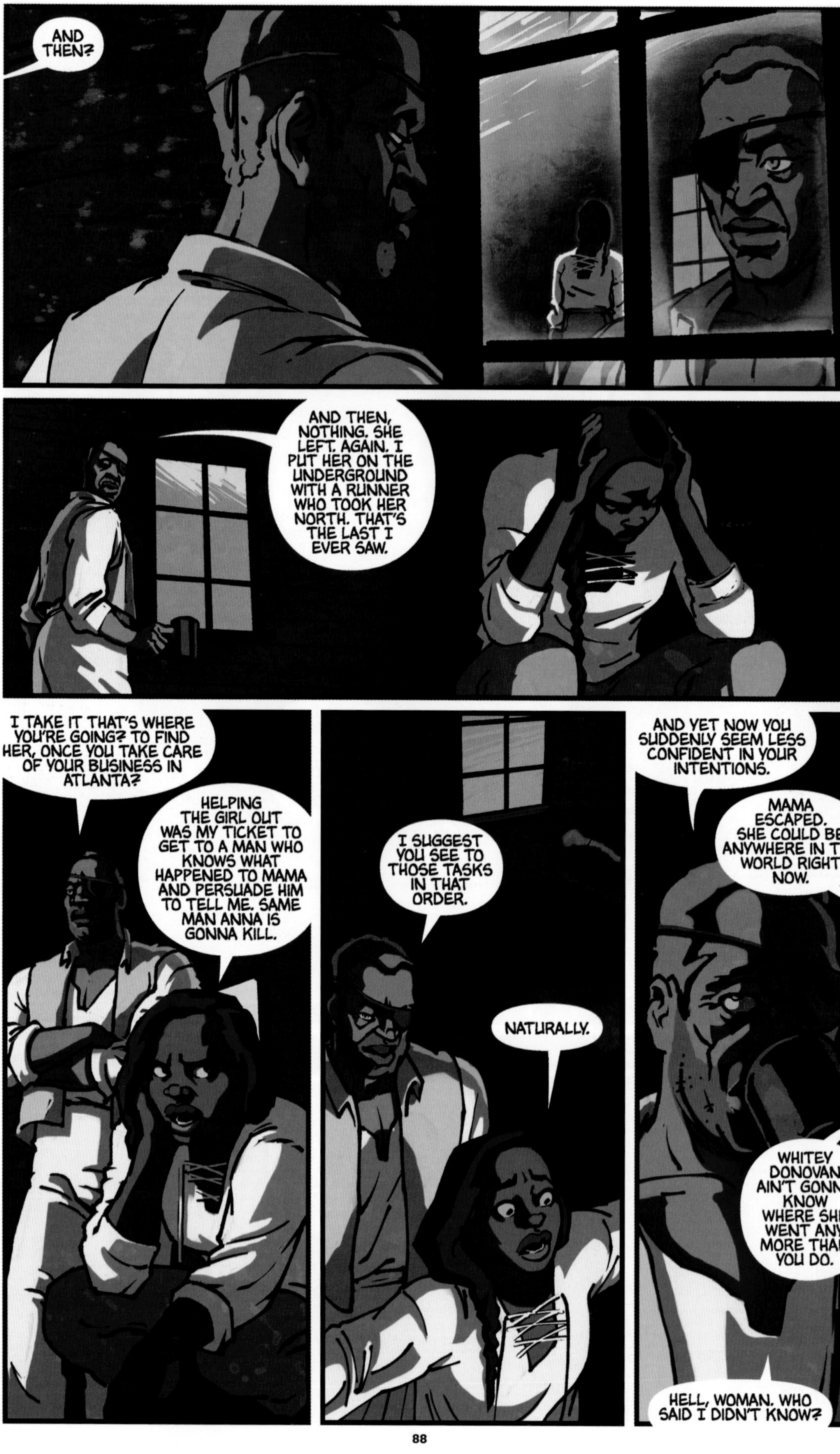
AND THEN?
AND THEN, NOTHING. SHE LEFT. AGAIN. I PUT HER ON THE UNDERGROUND WITH A RUNNER WHO TOOK HER NORTH. THAT'S THE LAST I EVER SAW.
I TAKE IT THAT'S WHERE YOU'RE GOING? TO FIND HER, ONCE YOU TAKE CARE OF YOUR BUSINESS IN ATLANTA?
HELPING THE GIRL OUT WAS MY TICKET TO GET TO A MAN WHO KNOWS WHAT HAPPENED TO MAMA AND PERSUADE HIM TO TELL ME. SAME MAN ANNA IS GONNA KILL.
I SUGGEST YOU SEE TO THOSE TASKS IN THAT ORDER.
NATURALLY.
AND YET NOW YOU SUDDENLY SEEM LESS CONFIDENT IN YOUR INTENTIONS.
MAMA ESCAPED. SHE COULD BE ANYWHERE IN THE WORLD RIGHT NOW.
WHITEY DONOVAN AIN'T GONNA KNOW WHERE SHE WENT ANY MORE THAN YOU DO.
HELL, WOMAN. WHO SAID I DIDN'T KNOW?

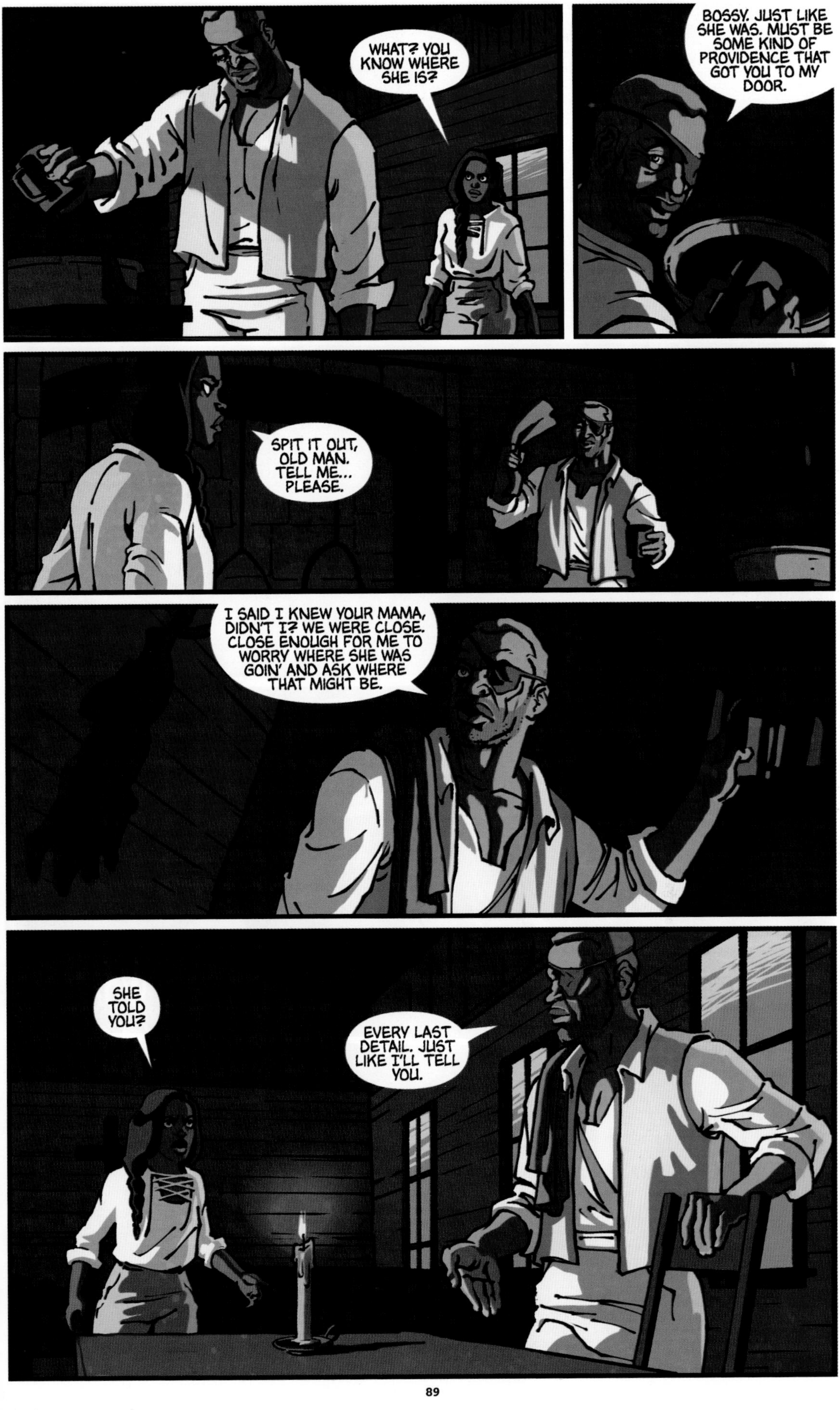
WHAT? YOU KNOW WHERE SHE IS?
BOSSY. JUST LIKE SHE WAS. MUST BE SOME KIND OF PROVIDENCE THAT GOT YOU TO MY DOOR.
SPIT IT OUT, OLD MAN. TELL ME... PLEASE.
I SAID I KNEW YOUR MAMA, DIDN'T I? WE WERE CLOSE. CLOSE ENOUGH FOR ME TO WORRY WHERE SHE WAS GOIN' AND ASK WHERE THAT MIGHT BE.
SHE TOLD YOU?
EVERY LAST DETAIL. JUST LIKE I'LL TELL YOU.

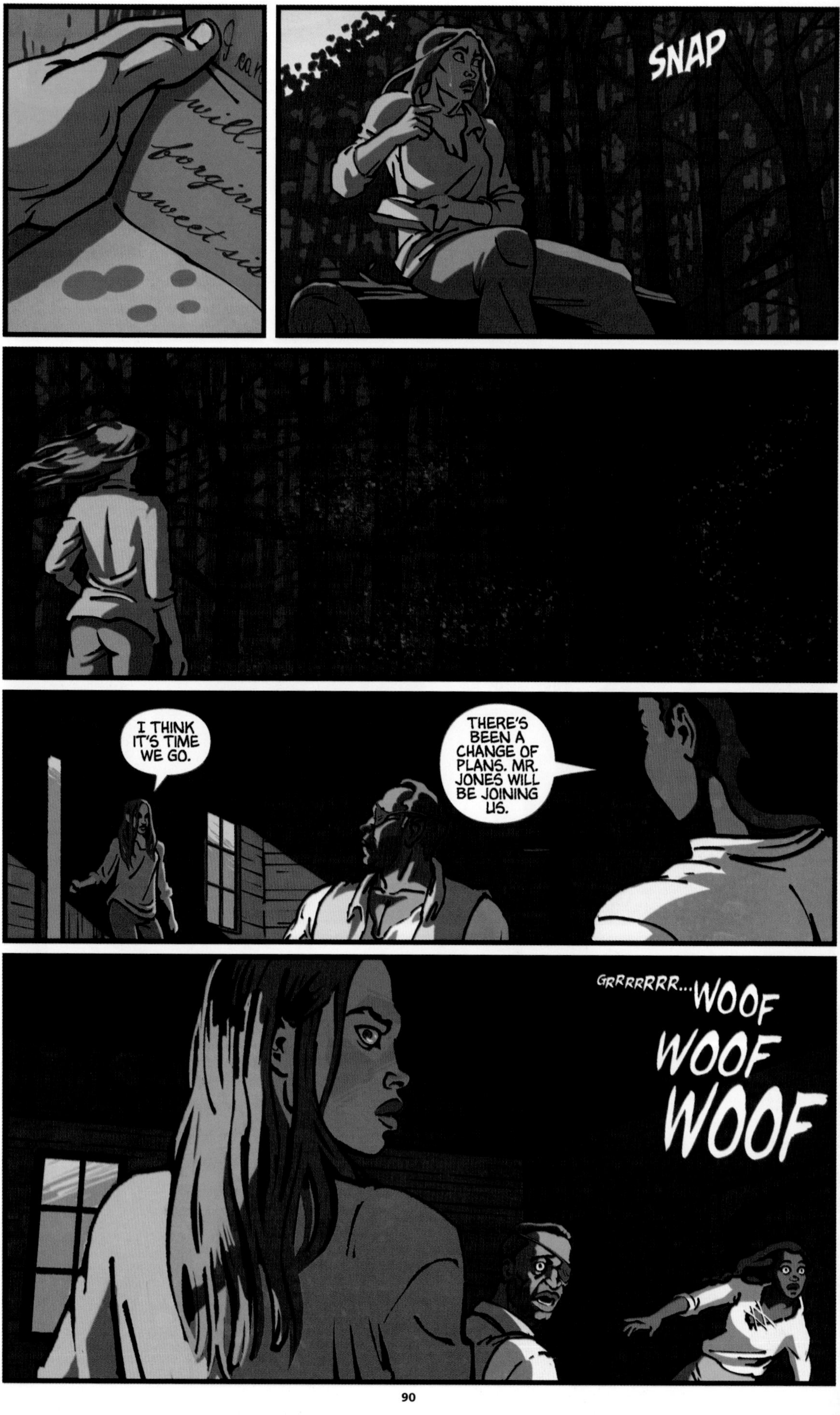
SNAP
I THINK IT'S TIME WE GO.
THERE'S BEEN A CHANGE OF PLANS. MR. JONES WILL BE JOINING US.
GRRRRRRR...WOOF
WOOF
WOOF

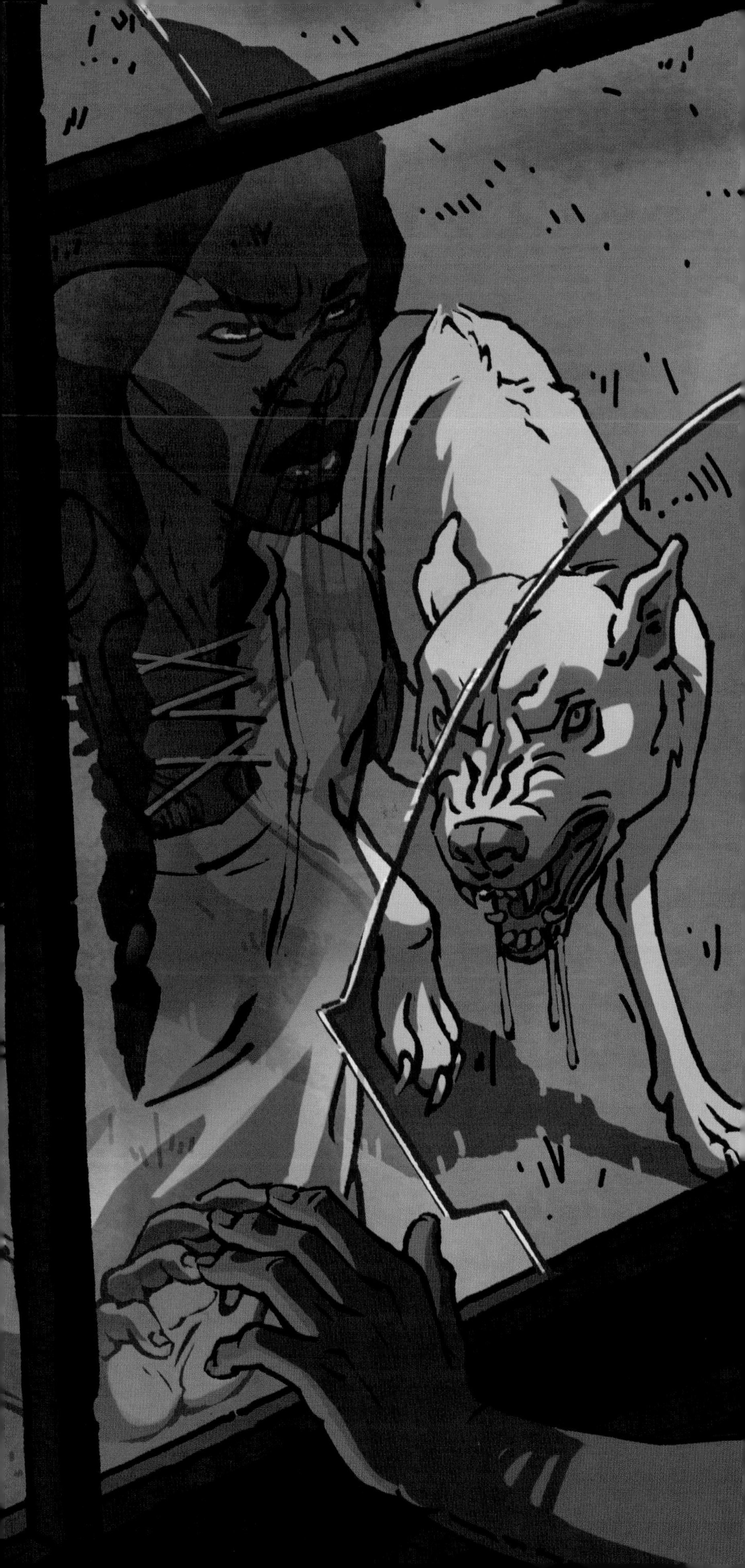

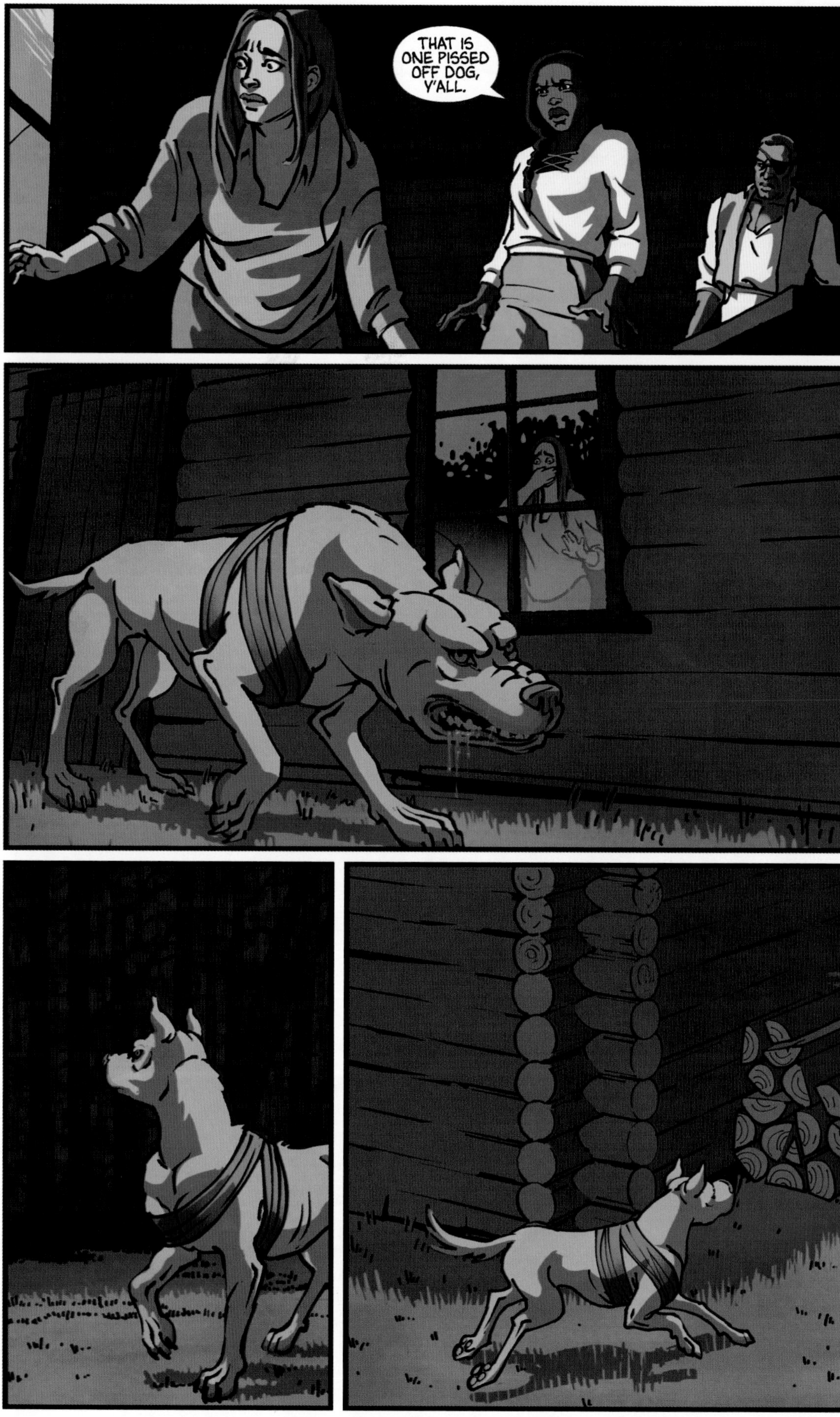
THAT IS ONE PISSED OFF DOG, Y'ALL.

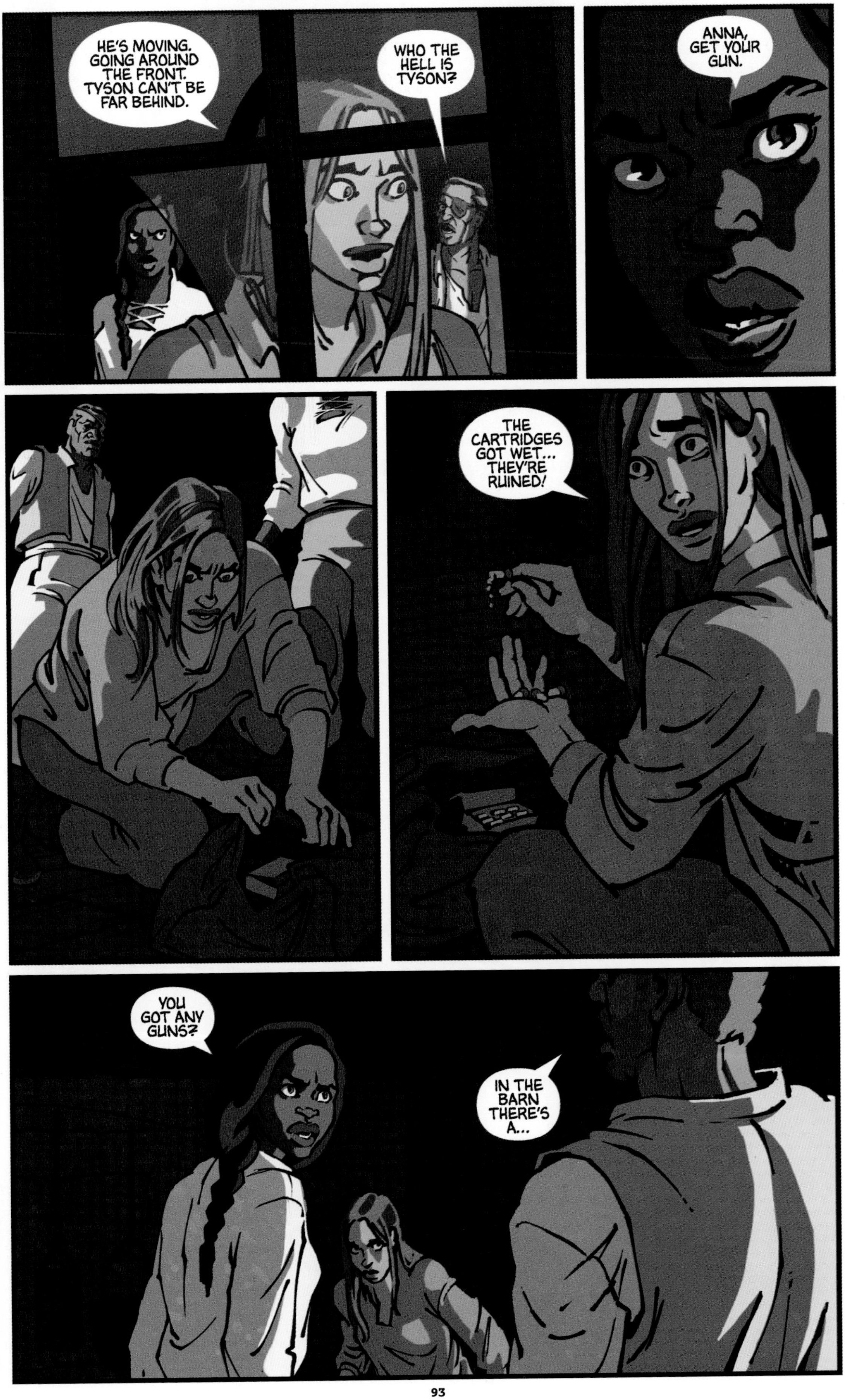
HE'S MOVING. GOING AROUND THE FRONT. TYSON CAN'T BE FAR BEHIND.
WHO THE HELL IS TYSON?
ANNA, GET YOUR GUN.
THE CARTRIDGES GOT WET... THEY'RE RUINED!
YOU GOT ANY GUNS?
IN THE BARN THERE'S A...

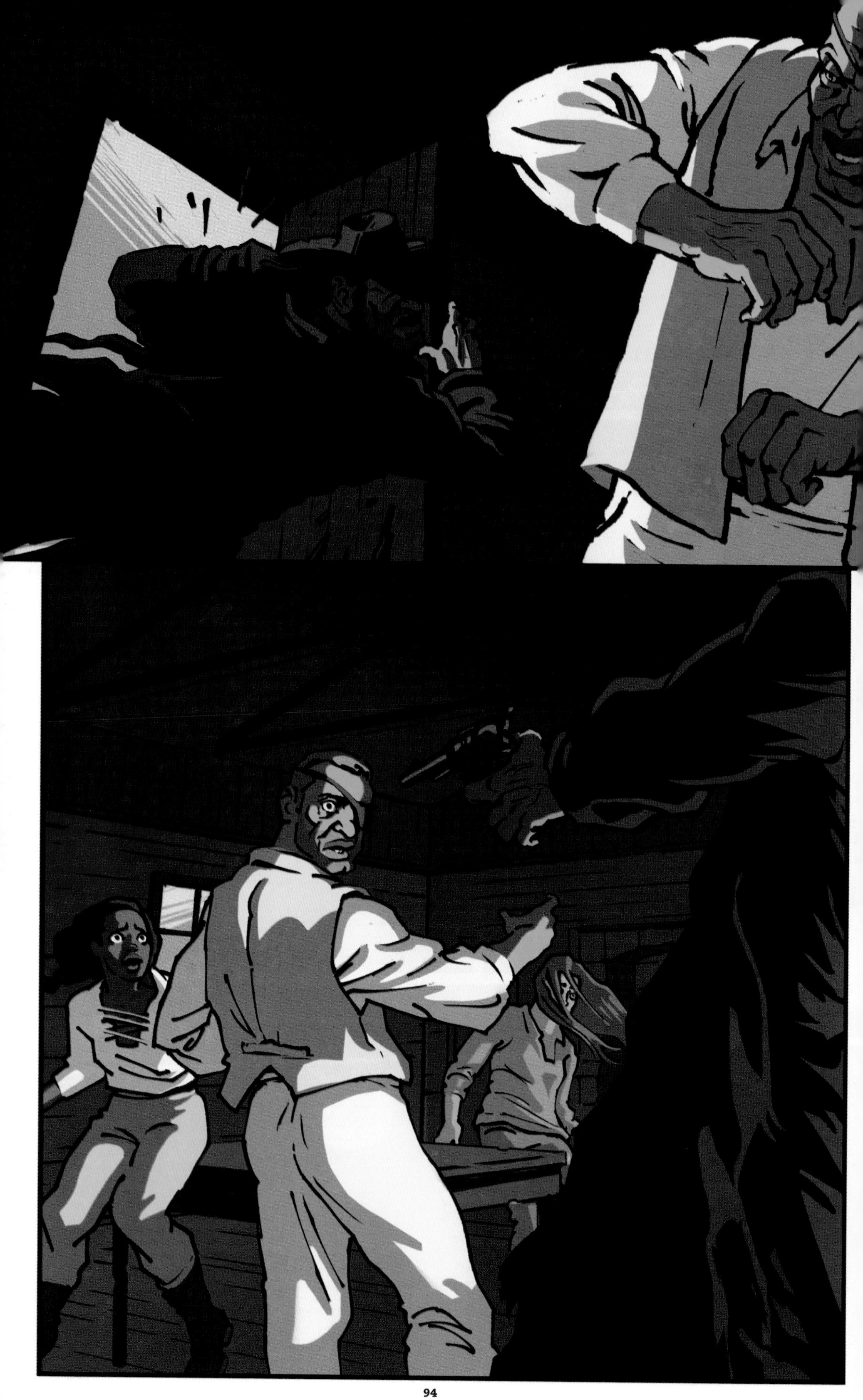

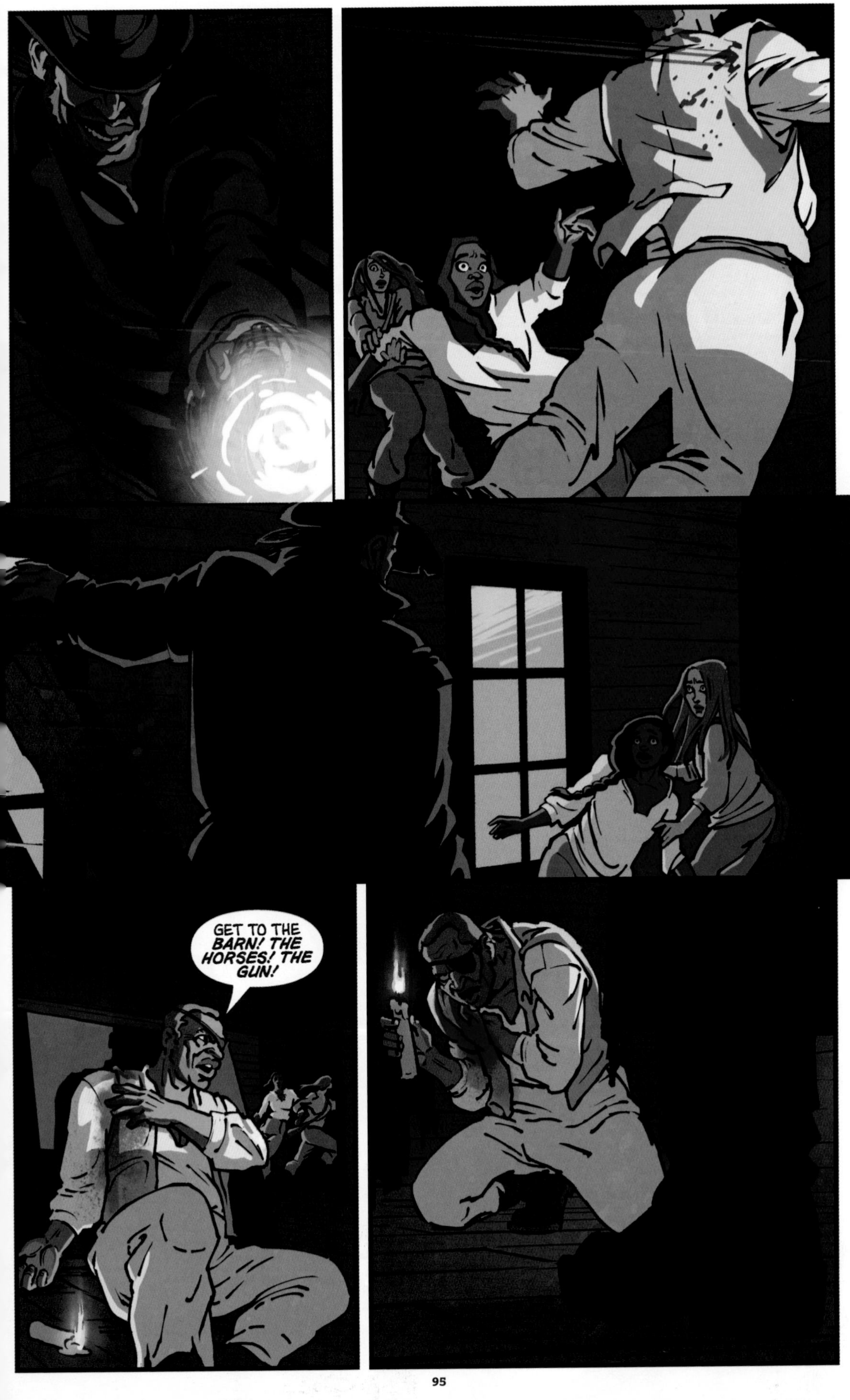
GET TO THE *BARN! THE HORSES! THE GUN!*

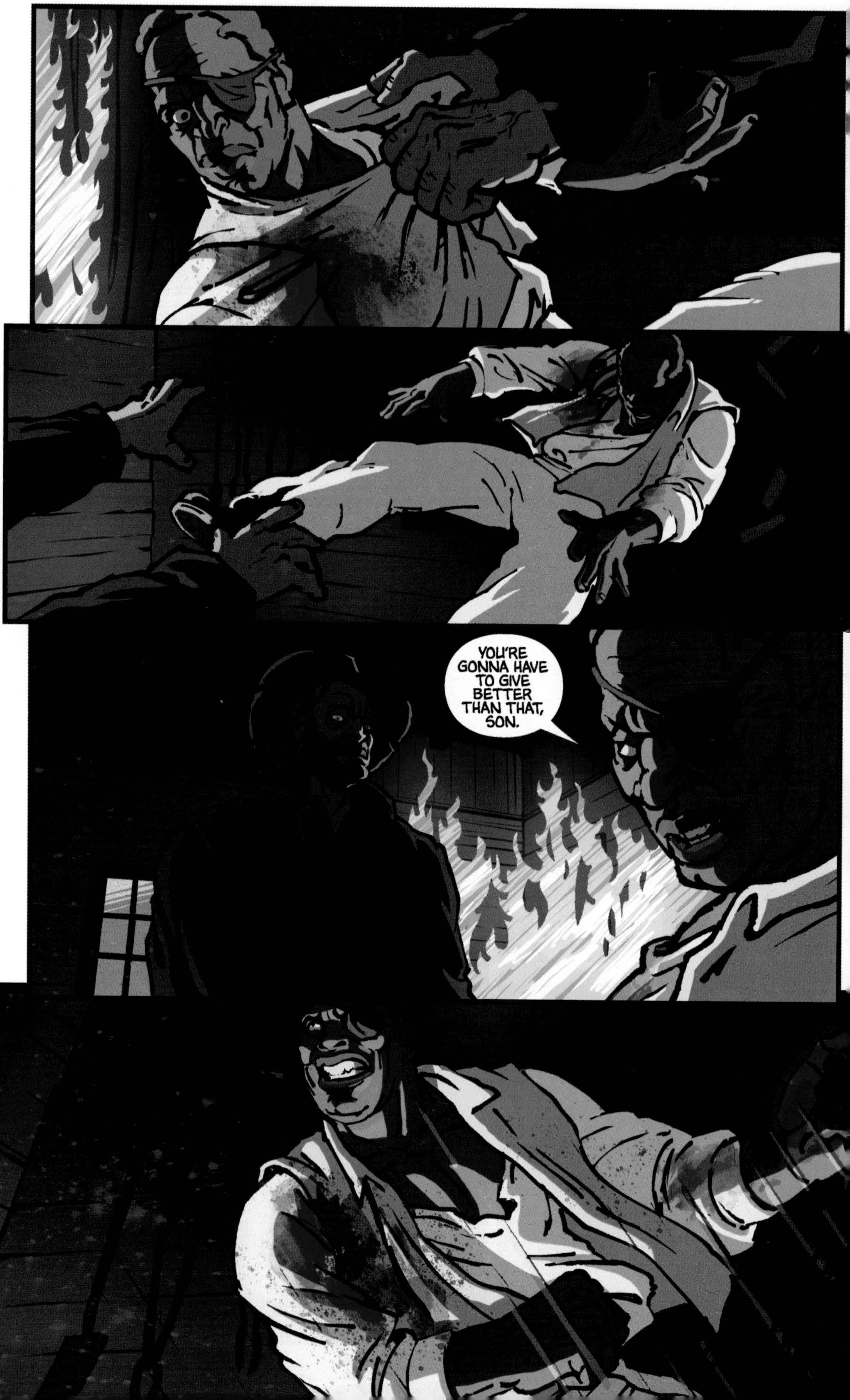
YOU'RE GONNA HAVE TO GIVE BETTER THAN THAT, SON.

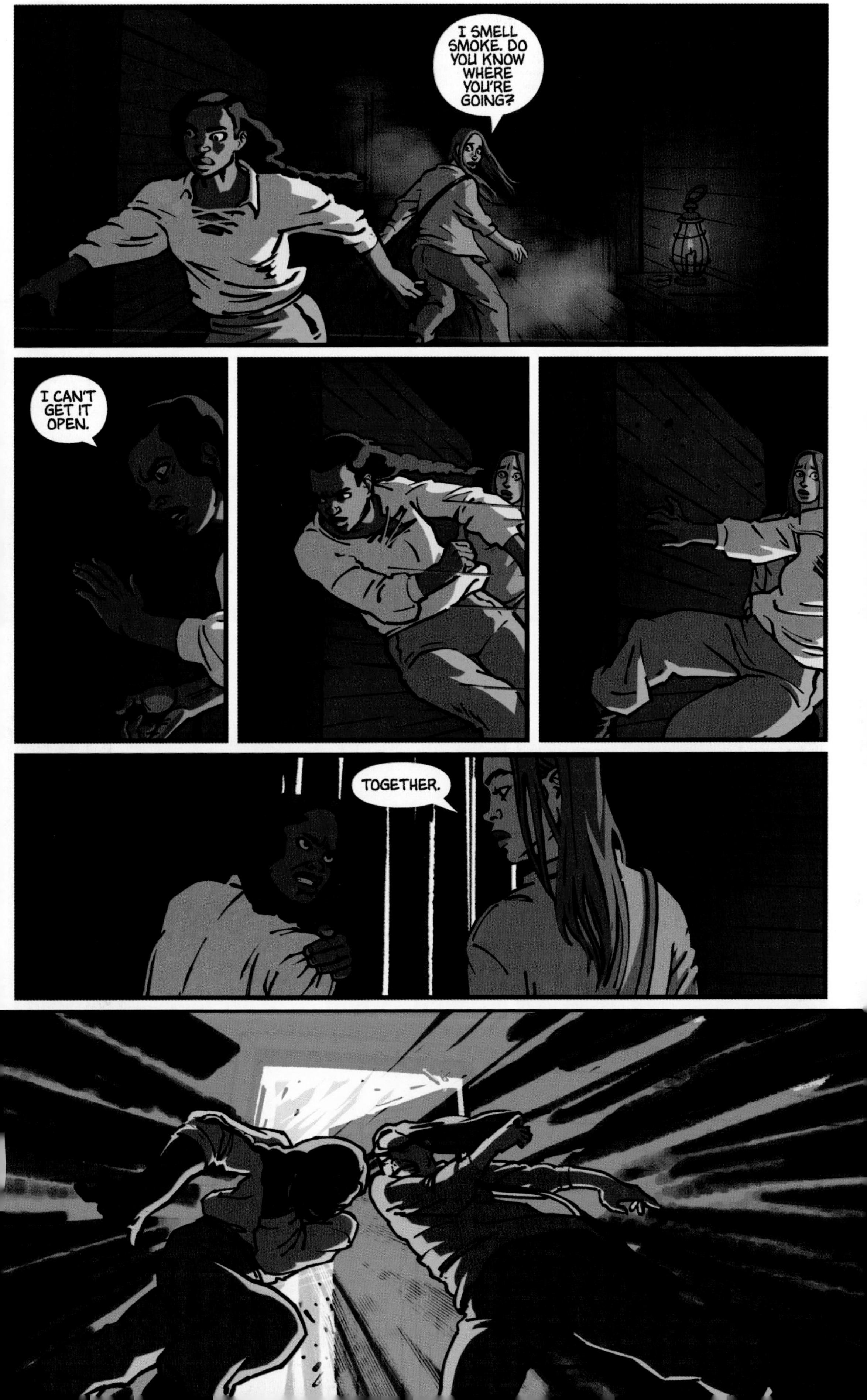
I SMELL SMOKE. DO YOU KNOW WHERE YOU'RE GOING?
I CAN'T GET IT OPEN.
TOGETHER.

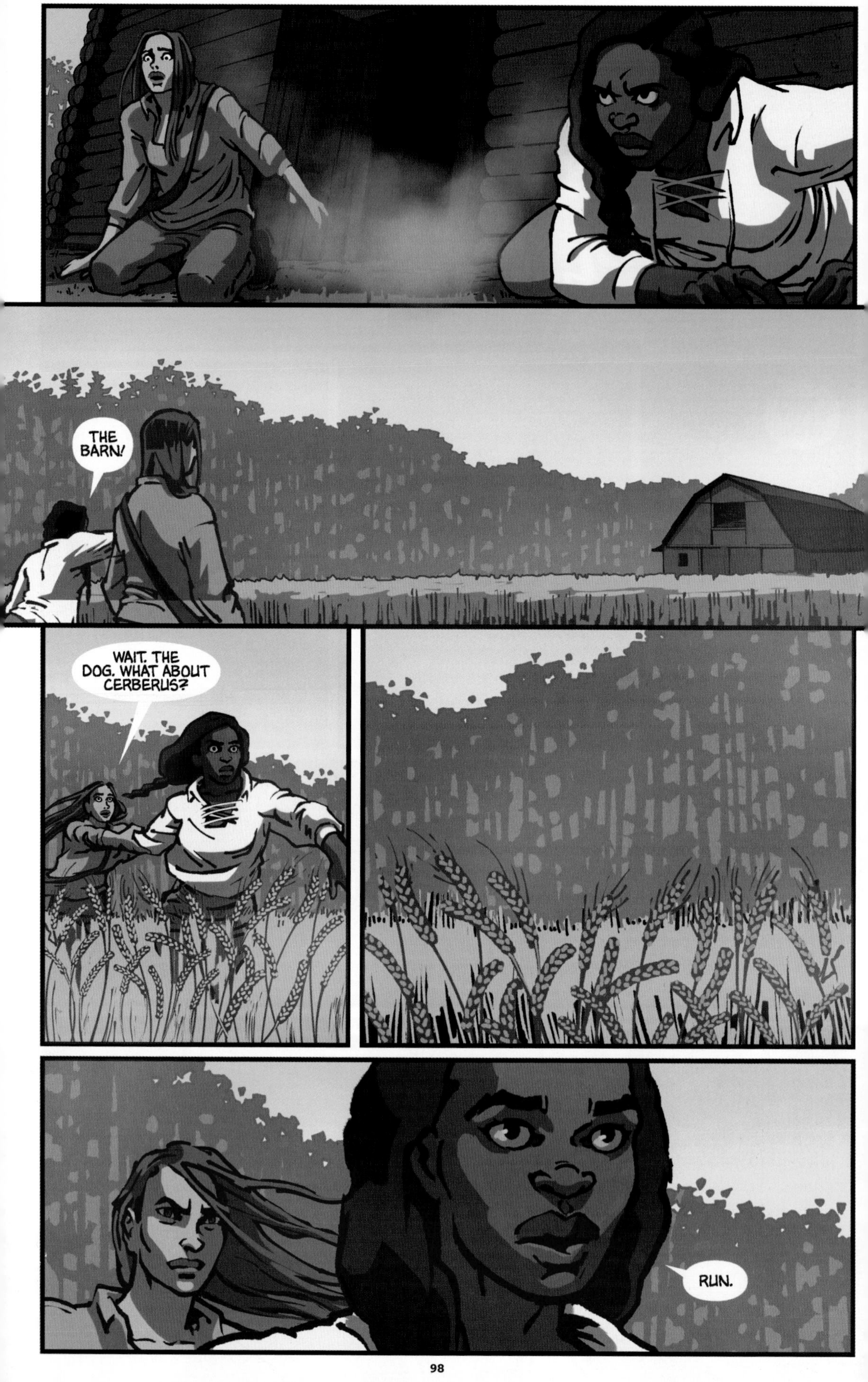
THE BARN!
WAIT. THE DOG. WHAT ABOUT CERBERUS?
RUN.

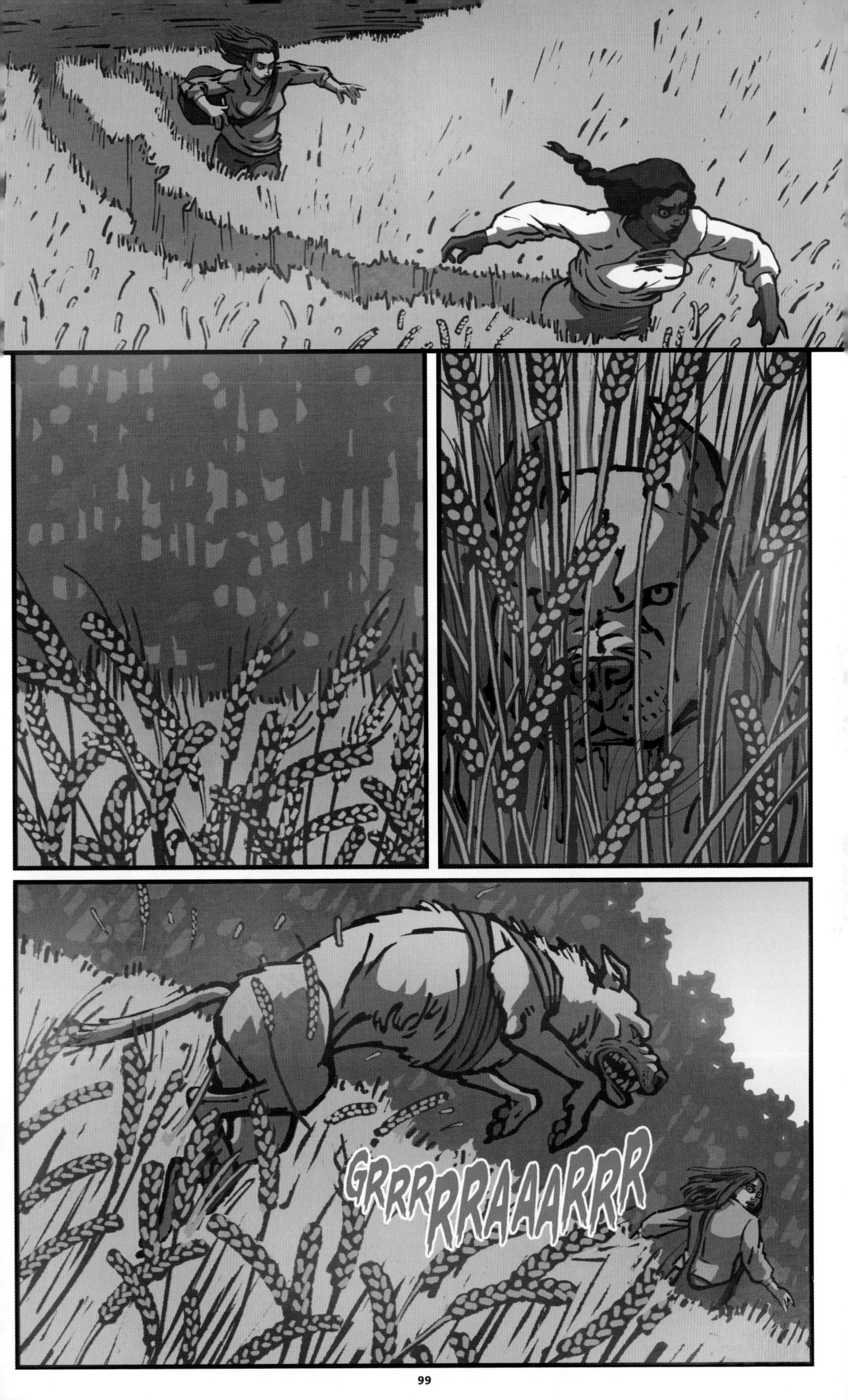
GRRRRRAAARRR

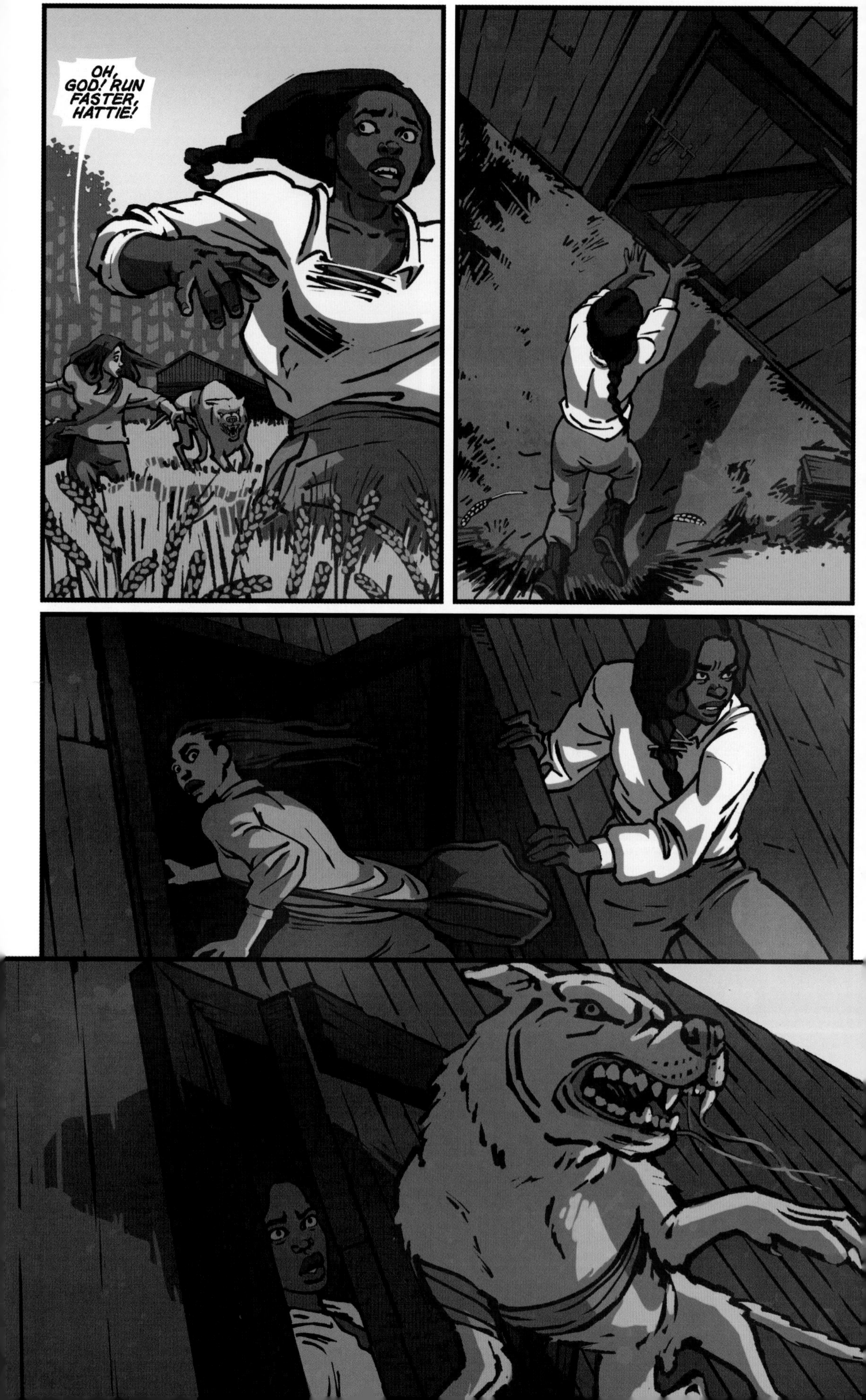
OH, GOD! RUN FASTER, HATTIE!

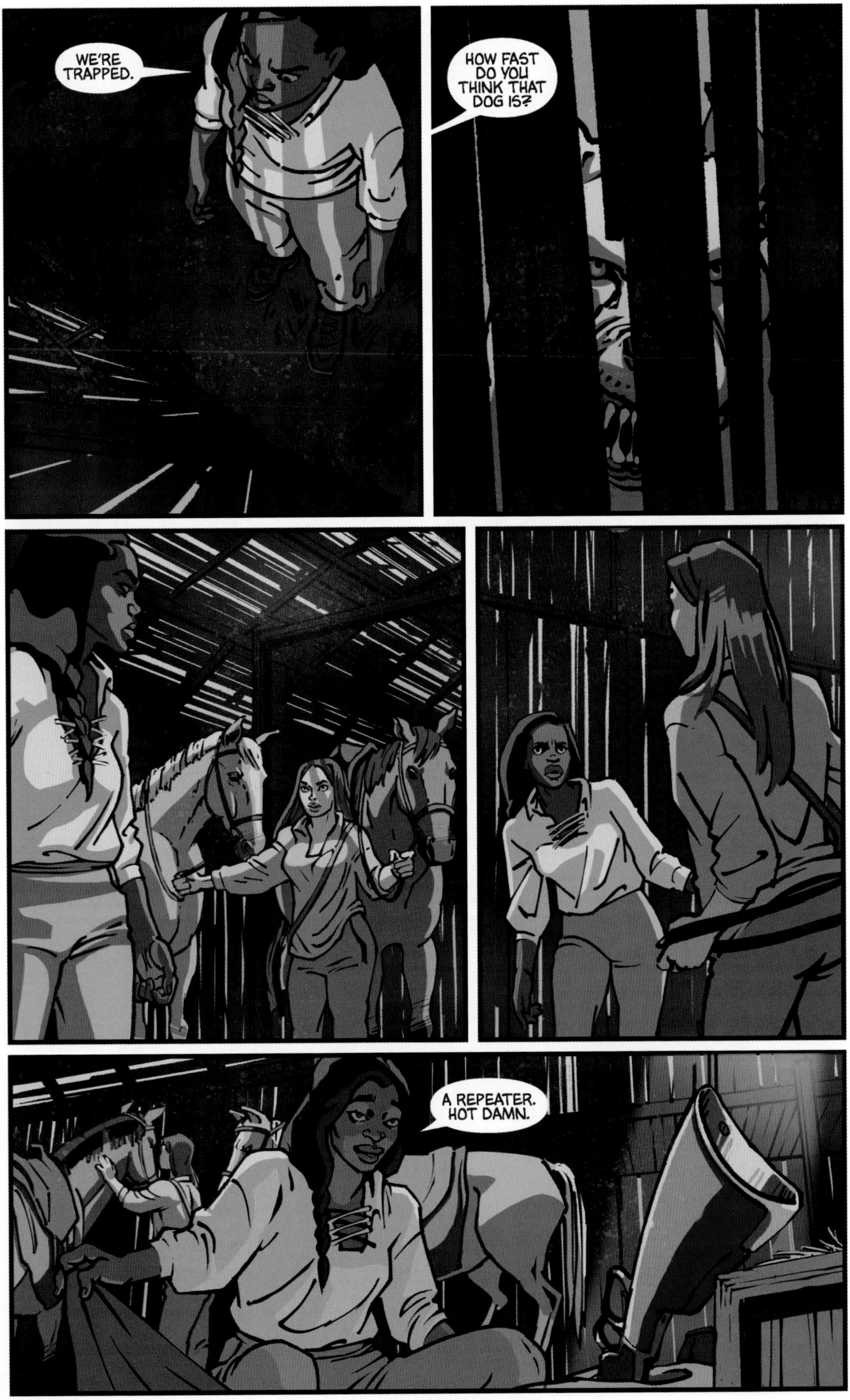
WE'RE TRAPPED.
HOW FAST DO YOU THINK THAT DOG IS?
A REPEATER. HOT DAMN.

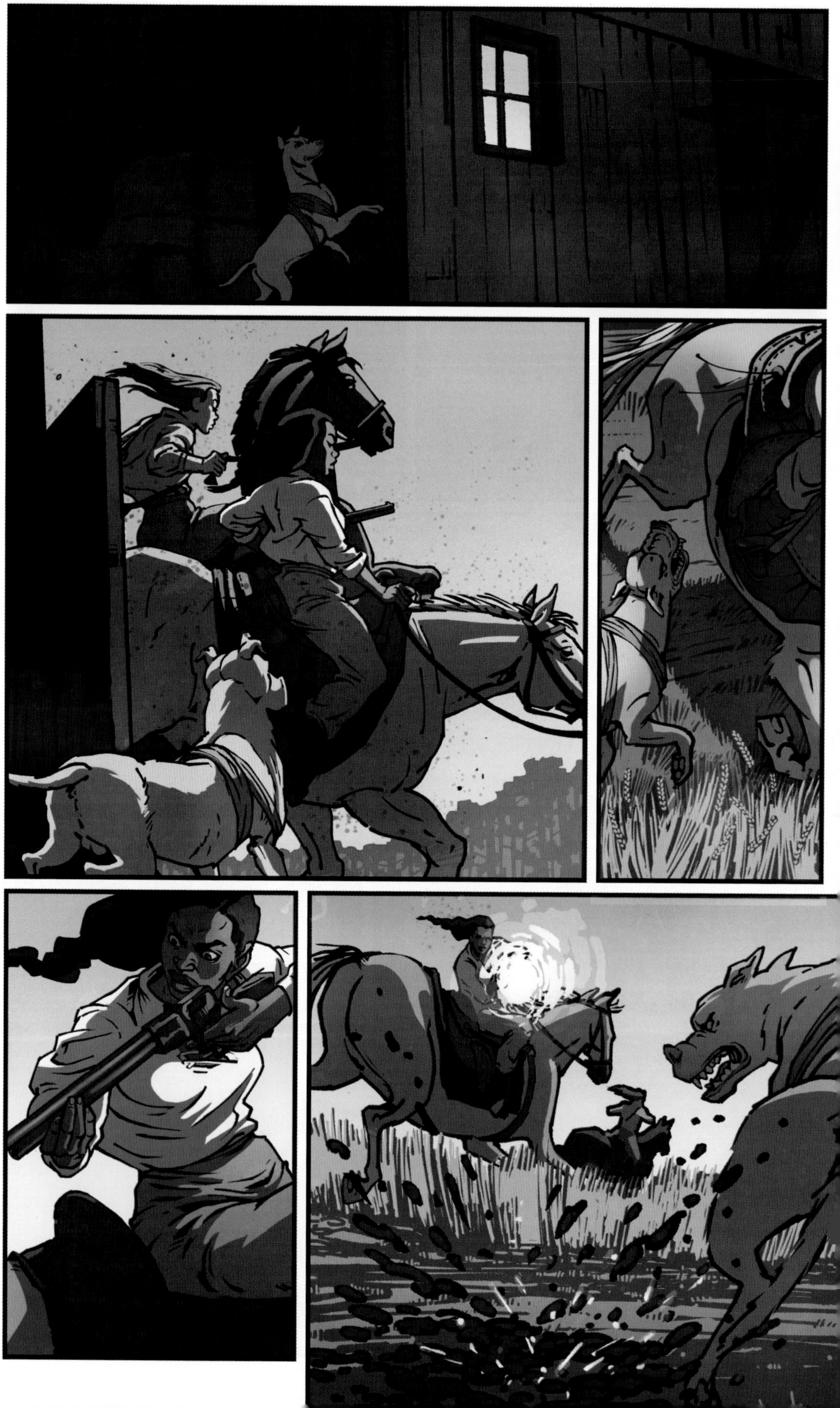

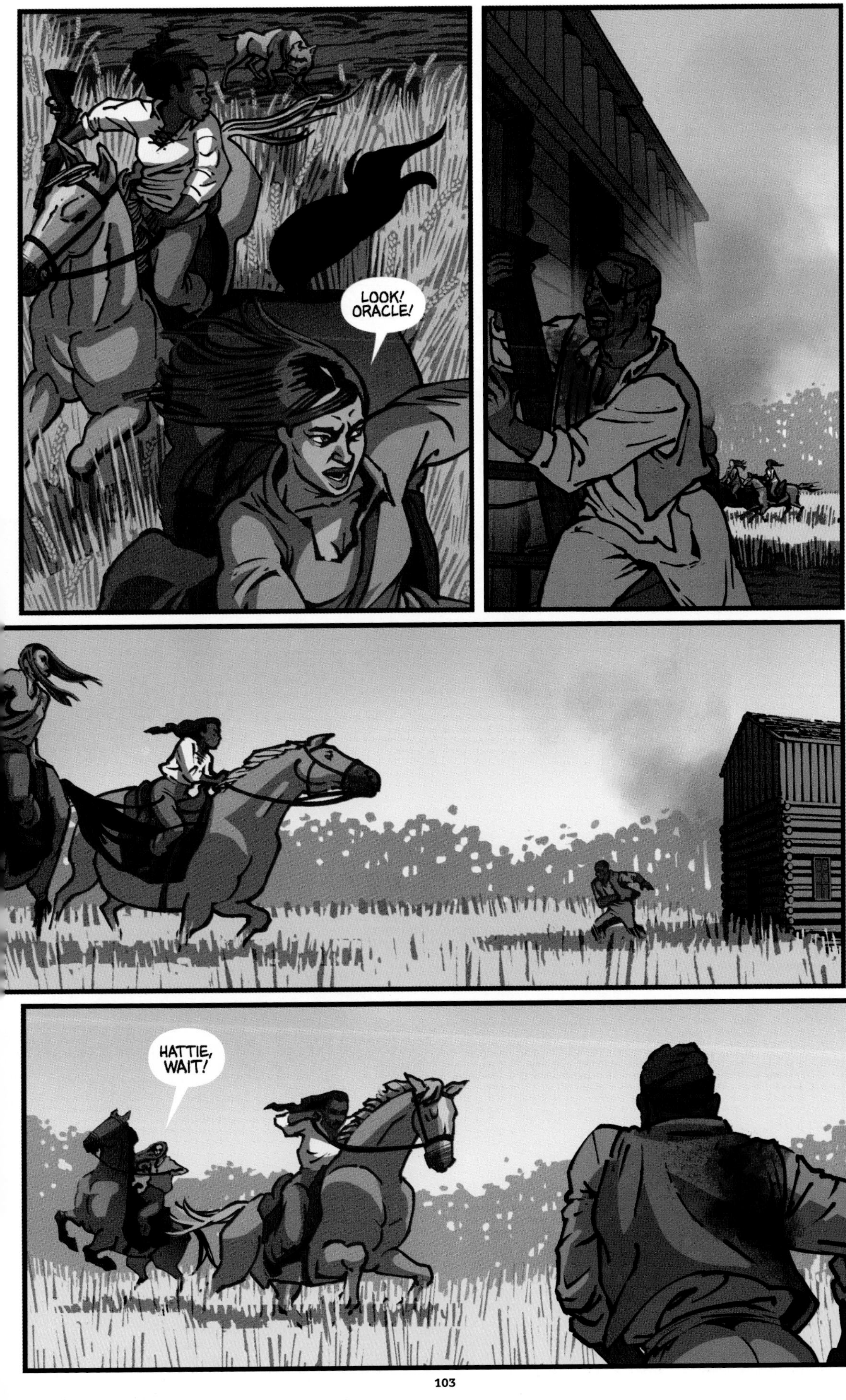
LOOK! ORACLE!
HATTIE, WAIT!

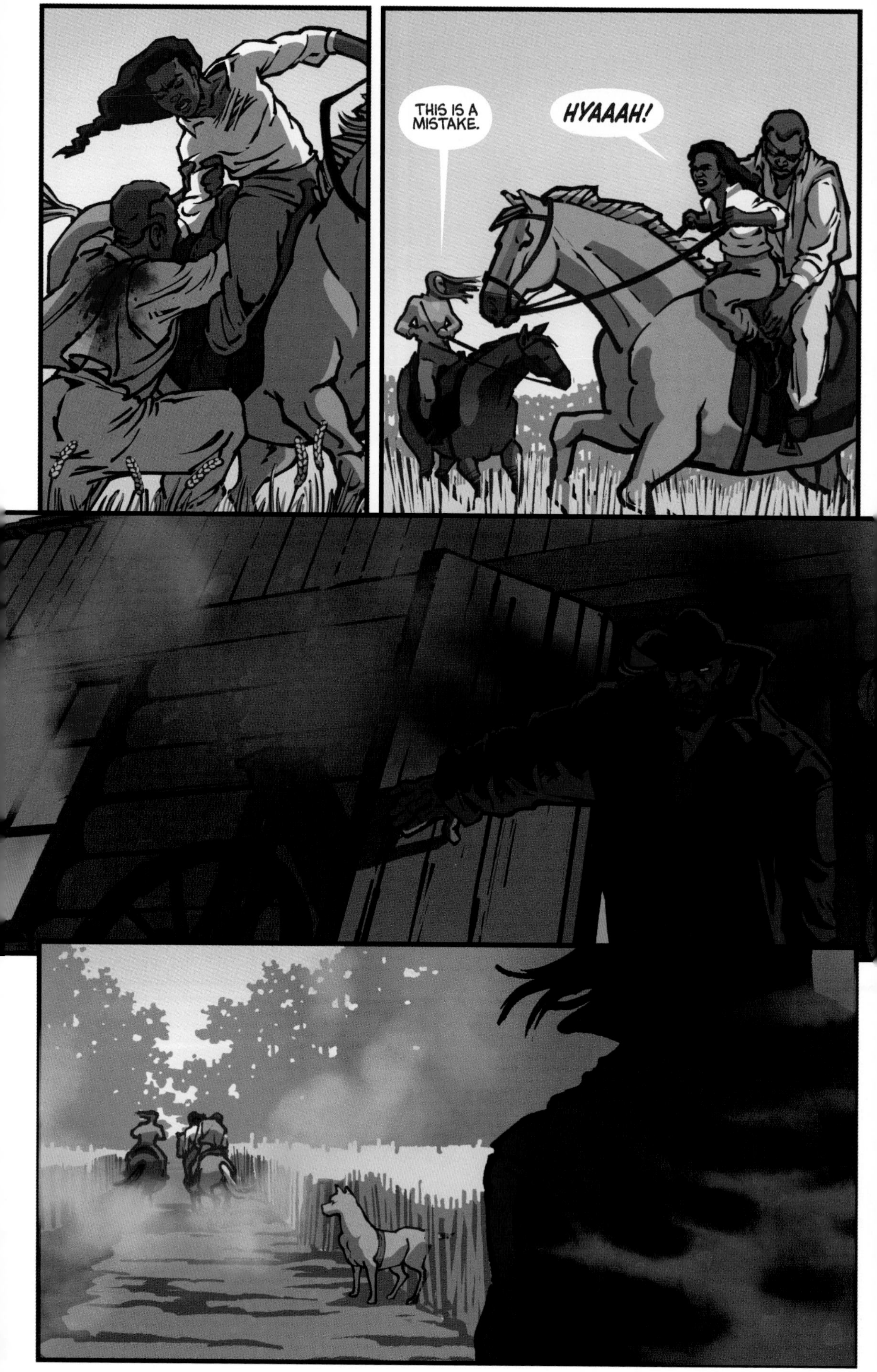
THIS IS A MISTAKE.
HYAAAH!

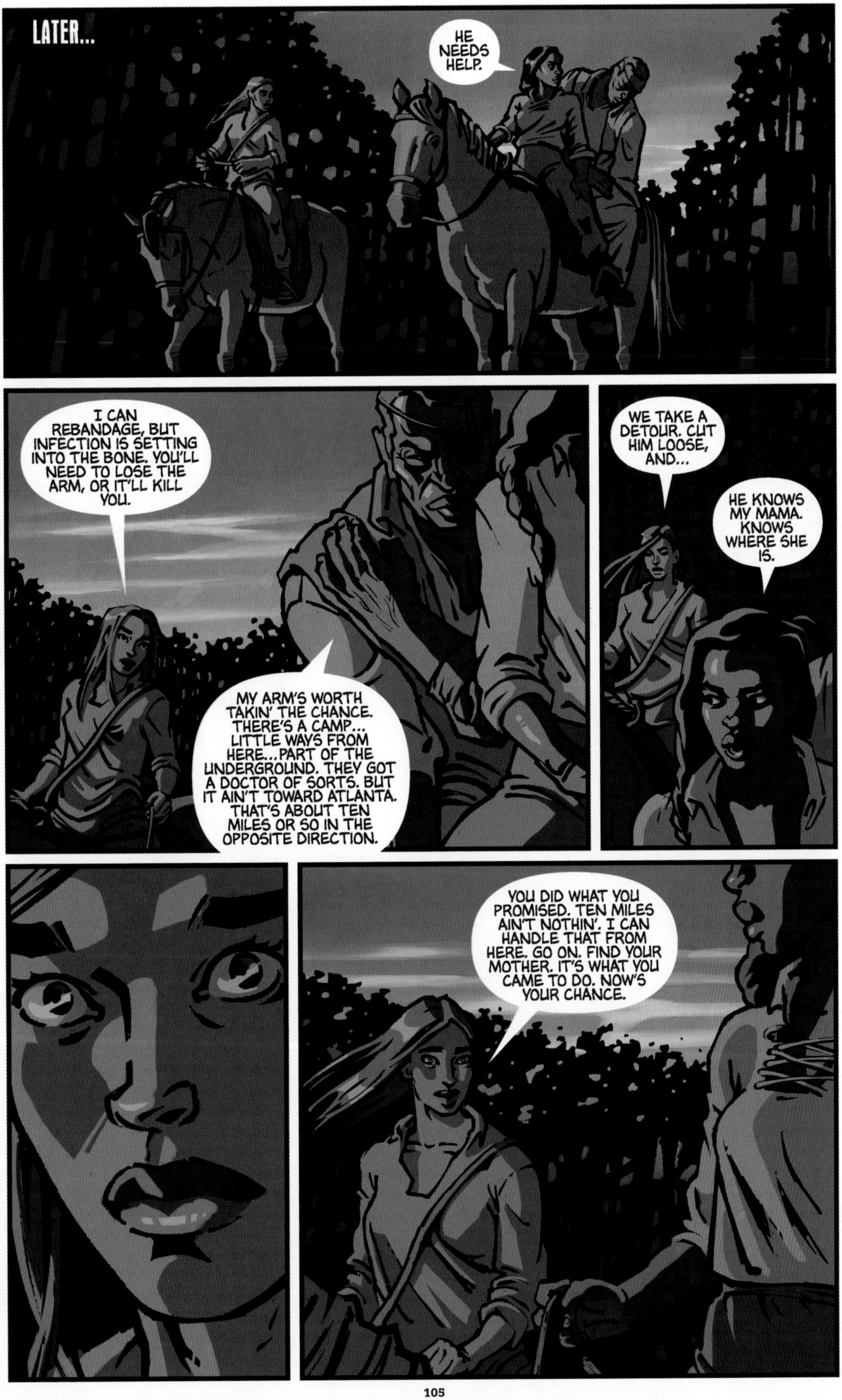
LATER...
HE NEEDS HELP.
I CAN REBANDAGE, BUT INFECTION IS SETTING INTO THE BONE. YOU'LL NEED TO LOSE THE ARM, OR IT'LL KILL YOU.
MY ARM'S WORTH TAKIN' THE CHANCE. THERE'S A CAMP... LITTLE WAYS FROM HERE...PART OF THE UNDERGROUND. THEY GOT A DOCTOR OF SORTS. BUT IT AIN'T TOWARD ATLANTA. THAT'S ABOUT TEN MILES OR SO IN THE OPPOSITE DIRECTION.
WE TAKE A DETOUR. CUT HIM LOOSE, AND...
HE KNOWS MY MAMA. KNOWS WHERE SHE IS.
YOU DID WHAT YOU PROMISED. TEN MILES AIN'T NOTHIN'. I CAN HANDLE THAT FROM HERE. GO ON. FIND YOUR MOTHER. IT'S WHAT YOU CAME TO DO. NOW'S YOUR CHANCE.

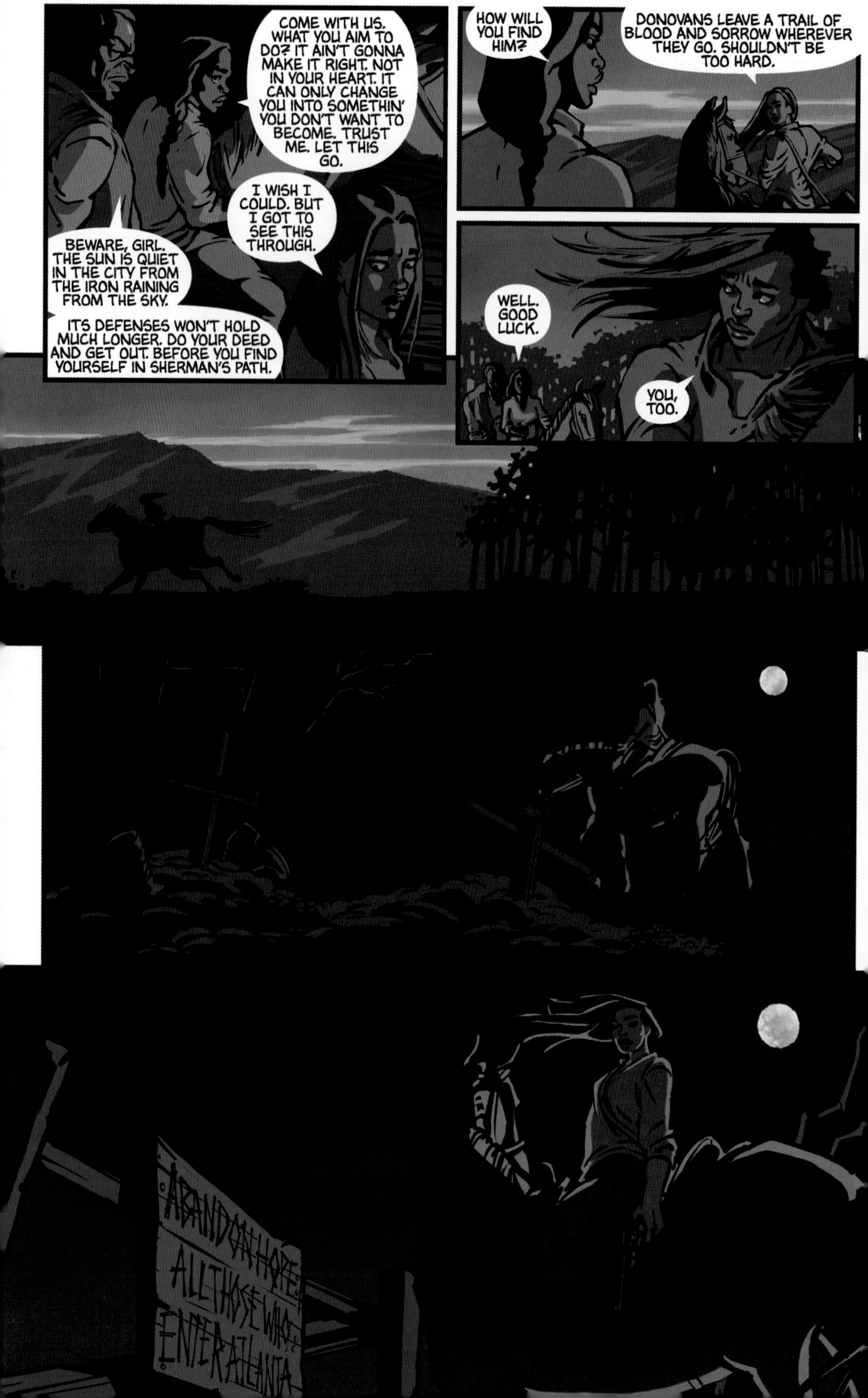
COME WITH US. WHAT YOU AIM TO DO? IT AIN'T GONNA MAKE IT RIGHT. NOT IN YOUR HEART. IT CAN ONLY CHANGE YOU INTO SOMETHIN' YOU DON'T WANT TO BECOME. TRUST ME. LET THIS GO.
I WISH I COULD. BUT I GOT TO SEE THIS THROUGH.
BEWARE, GIRL. THE SUN IS QUIET IN THE CITY FROM THE IRON RAINING FROM THE SKY.
ITS DEFENSES WON'T HOLD MUCH LONGER. DO YOUR DEED AND GET OUT. BEFORE YOU FIND YOURSELF IN SHERMAN'S PATH.
HOW WILL YOU FIND HIM?
DONOVANS LEAVE A TRAIL OF BLOOD AND SORROW WHEREVER THEY GO. SHOULDN'T BE TOO HARD.
WELL. GOOD LUCK.
YOU, TOO.
ABANDON HOPE ALL THOSE WHO ENTER ATLANTA

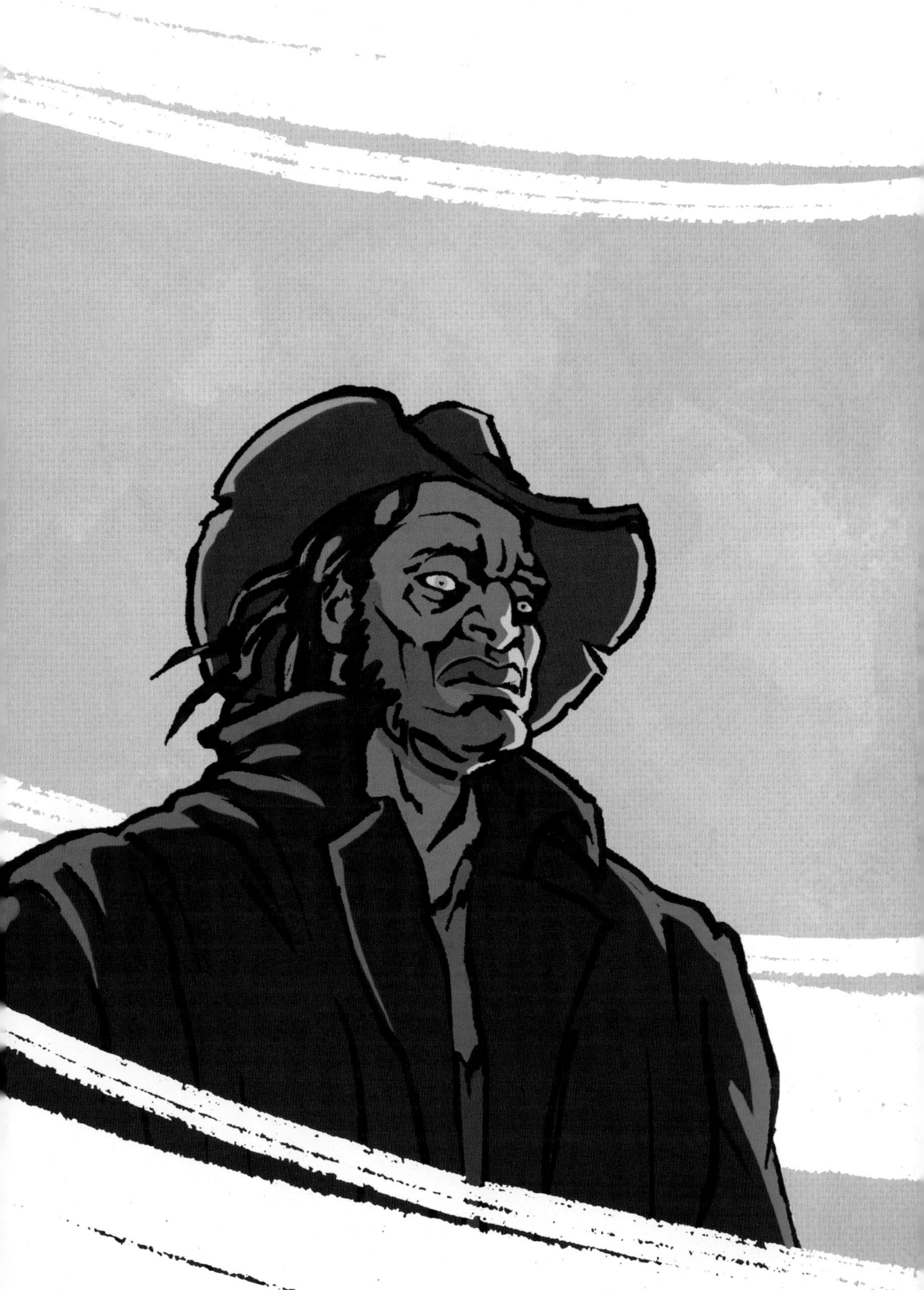

CHAPTER FIVE

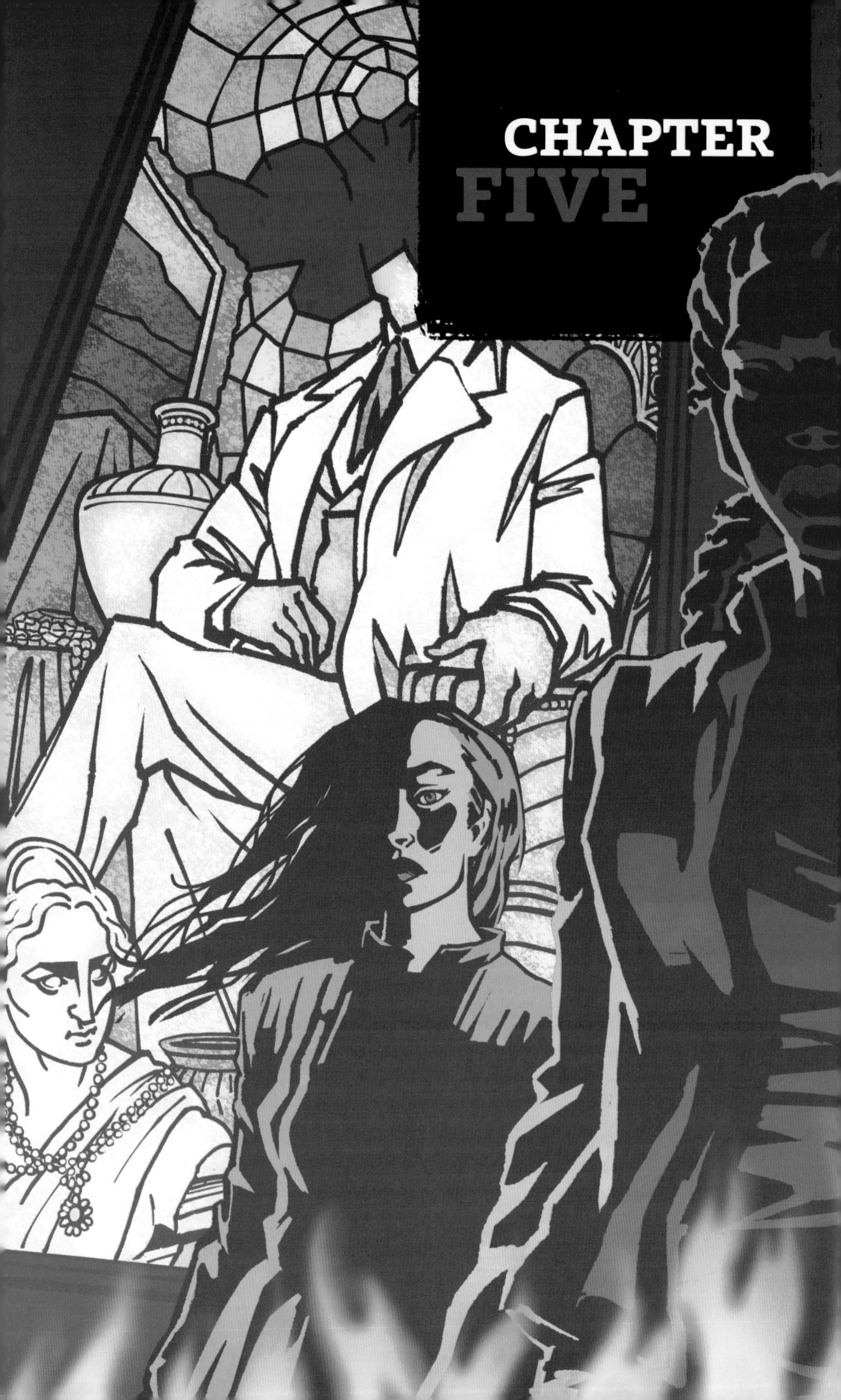

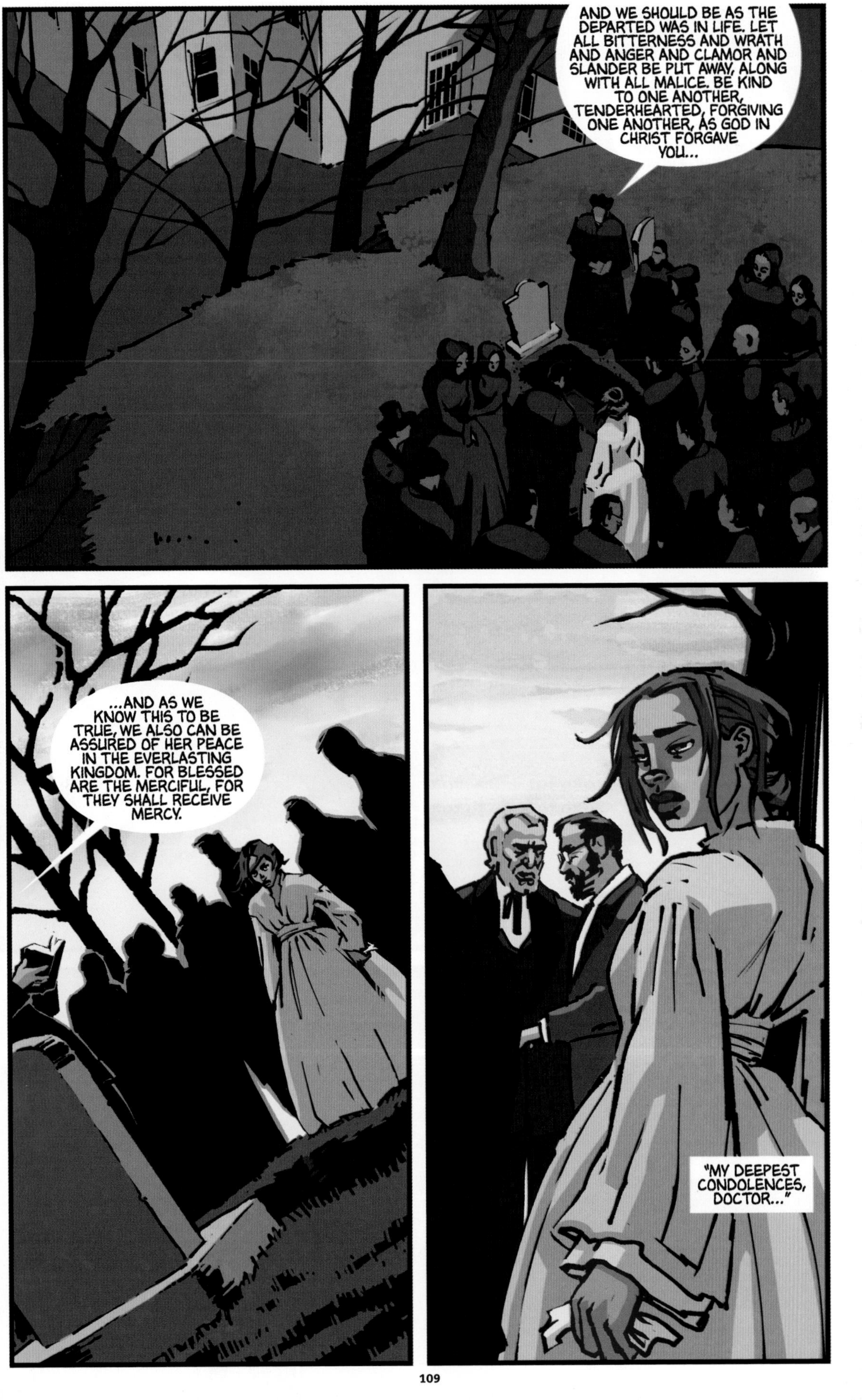
AND WE SHOULD BE AS THE DEPARTED WAS IN LIFE. LET ALL BITTERNESS AND WRATH AND ANGER AND CLAMOR AND SLANDER BE PUT AWAY, ALONG WITH ALL MALICE. BE KIND TO ONE ANOTHER, TENDERHEARTED, FORGIVING ONE ANOTHER, AS GOD IN CHRIST FORGAVE YOU...
...AND AS WE KNOW THIS TO BE TRUE, WE ALSO CAN BE ASSURED OF HER PEACE IN THE EVERLASTING KINGDOM. FOR BLESSED ARE THE MERCIFUL, FOR THEY SHALL RECEIVE MERCY.
"MY DEEPEST CONDOLENCES, DOCTOR..."

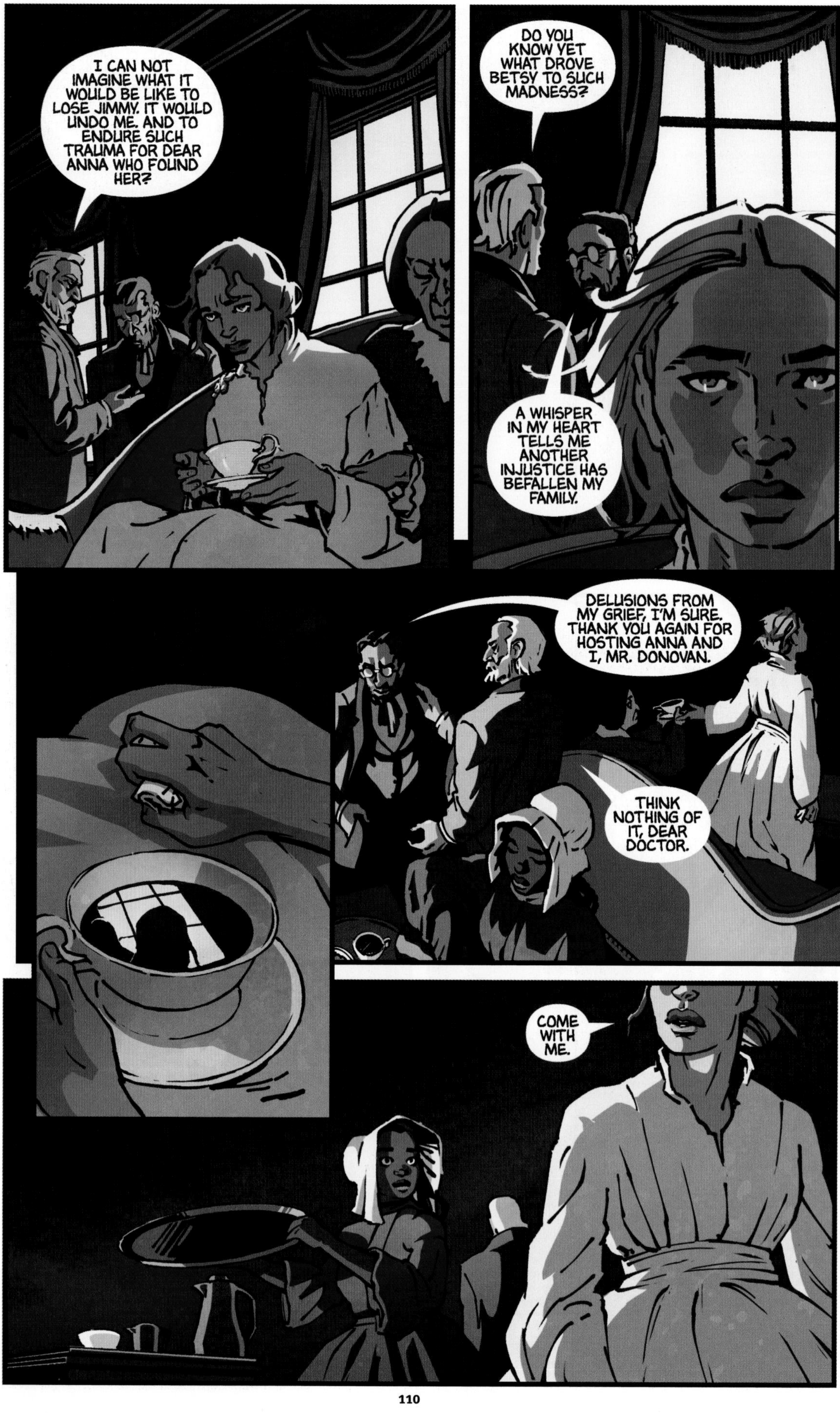
I CAN NOT IMAGINE WHAT IT WOULD BE LIKE TO LOSE JIMMY. IT WOULD UNDO ME. AND TO ENDURE SUCH TRAUMA FOR DEAR ANNA WHO FOUND HER?
DO YOU KNOW YET WHAT DROVE BETSY TO SUCH MADNESS?
A WHISPER IN MY HEART TELLS ME ANOTHER INJUSTICE HAS BEFALLEN MY FAMILY.
DELUSIONS FROM MY GRIEF, I'M SURE. THANK YOU AGAIN FOR HOSTING ANNA AND I, MR. DONOVAN.
THINK NOTHING OF IT, DEAR DOCTOR.
COME WITH ME.

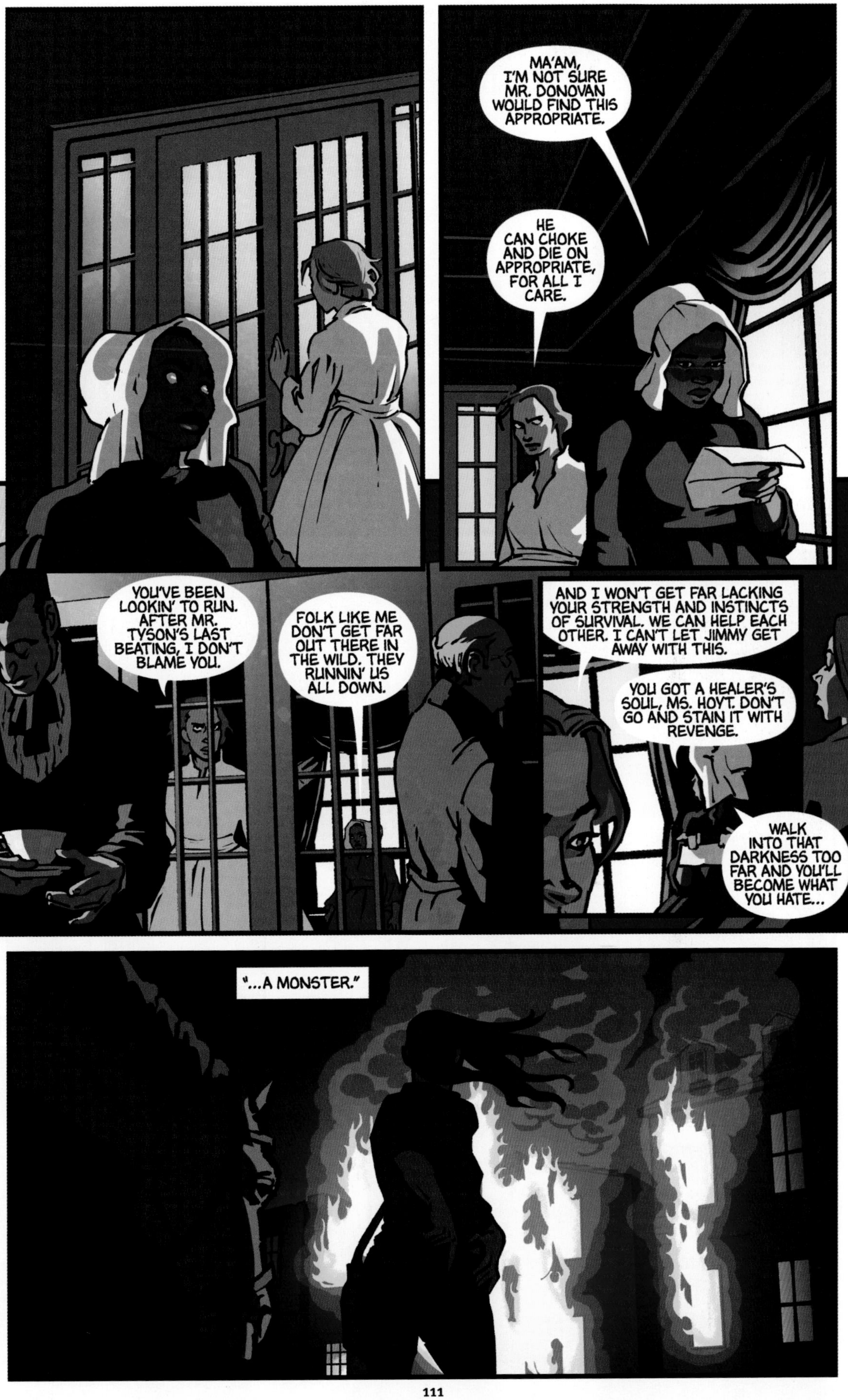
MA'AM, I'M NOT SURE MR. DONOVAN WOULD FIND THIS APPROPRIATE.
HE CAN CHOKE AND DIE ON APPROPRIATE, FOR ALL I CARE.
YOU'VE BEEN LOOKIN' TO RUN. AFTER MR. TYSON'S LAST BEATING, I DON'T BLAME YOU.
FOLK LIKE ME DON'T GET FAR OUT THERE IN THE WILD. THEY RUNNIN' US ALL DOWN.
AND I WON'T GET FAR LACKING YOUR STRENGTH AND INSTINCTS OF SURVIVAL. WE CAN HELP EACH OTHER. I CAN'T LET JIMMY GET AWAY WITH THIS.
YOU GOT A HEALER'S SOUL, MS. HOYT. DON'T GO AND STAIN IT WITH REVENGE.
WALK INTO THAT DARKNESS TOO FAR AND YOU'LL BECOME WHAT YOU HATE...
"...A MONSTER."

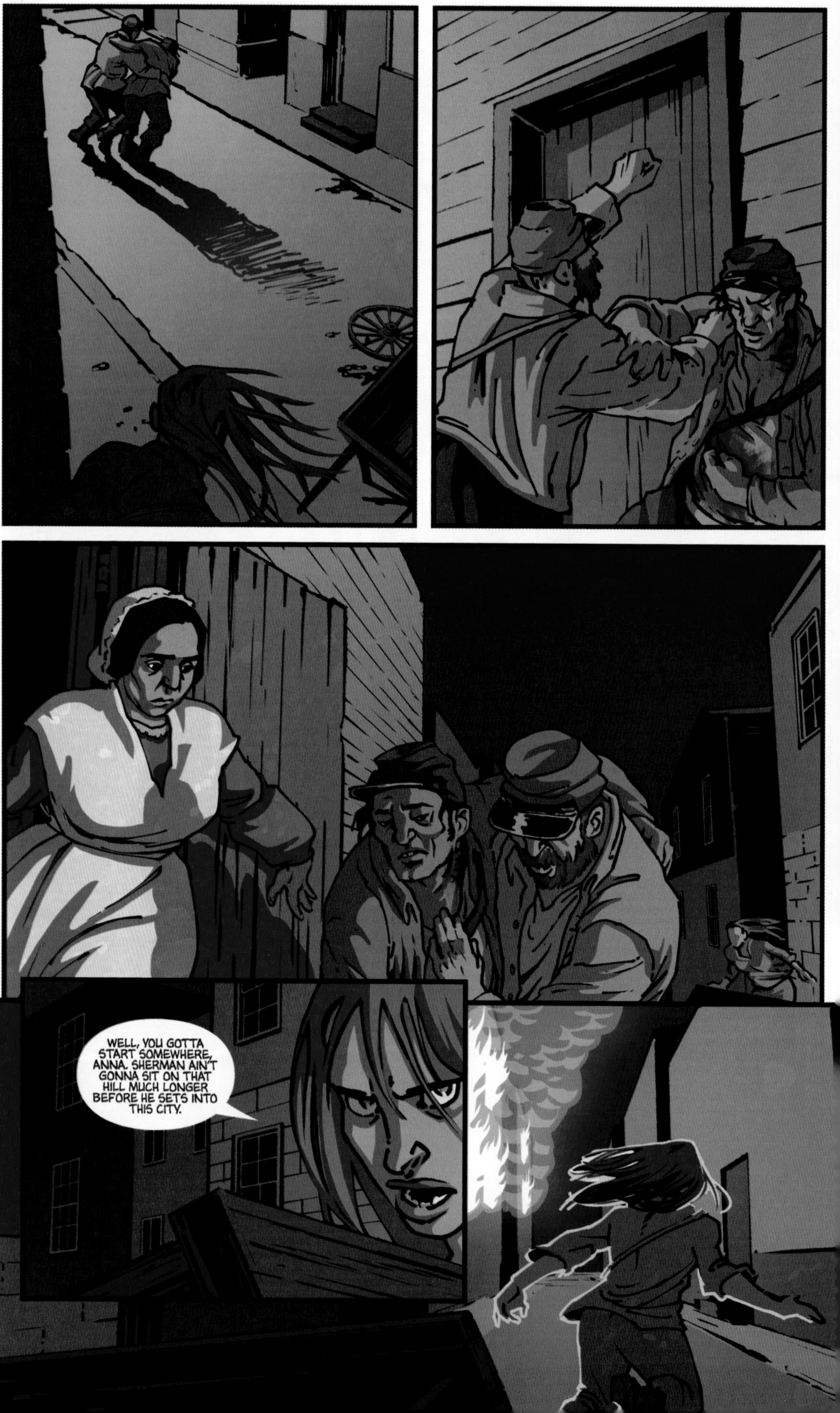
WELL, YOU GOTTA START SOMEWHERE, ANNA. SHERMAN AIN'T GONNA SIT ON THAT HILL MUCH LONGER BEFORE HE SETS INTO THIS CITY.

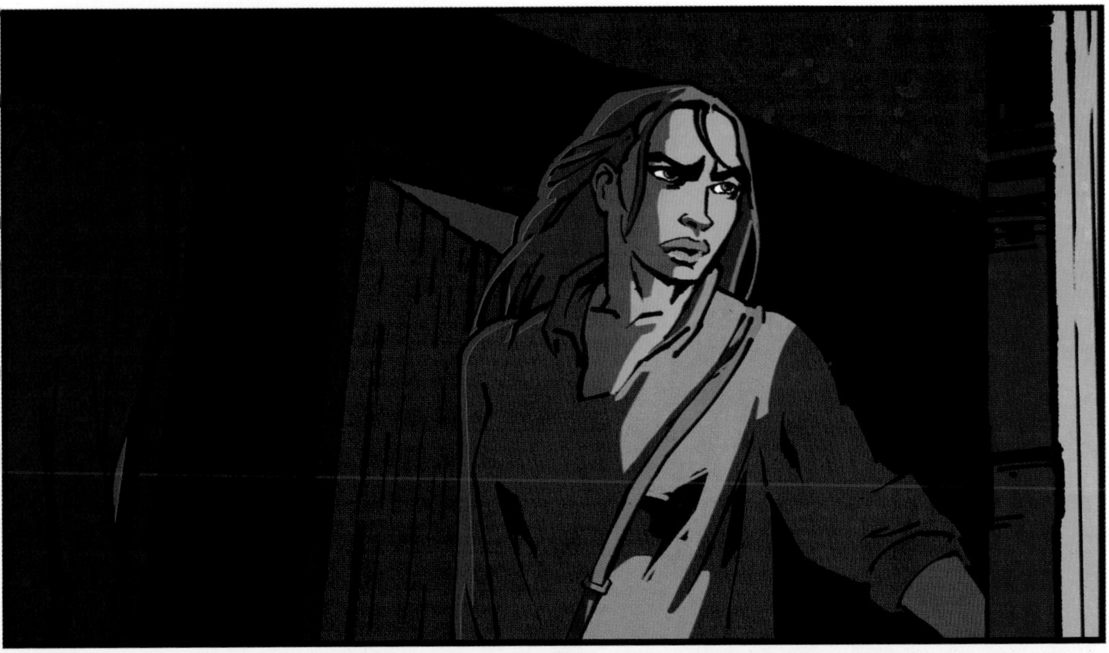

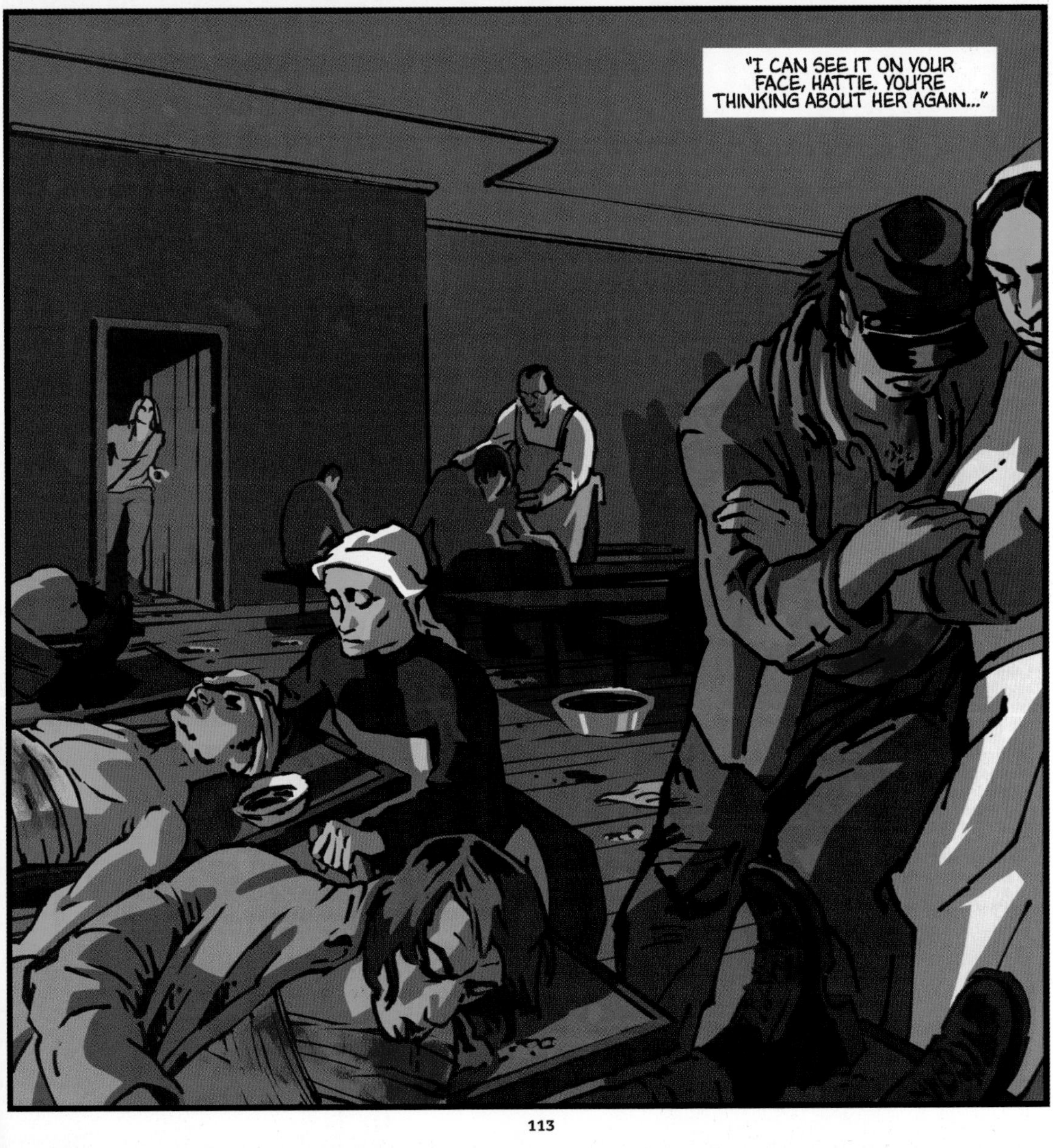
"I CAN SEE IT ON YOUR FACE, HATTIE. YOU'RE THINKING ABOUT HER AGAIN..."

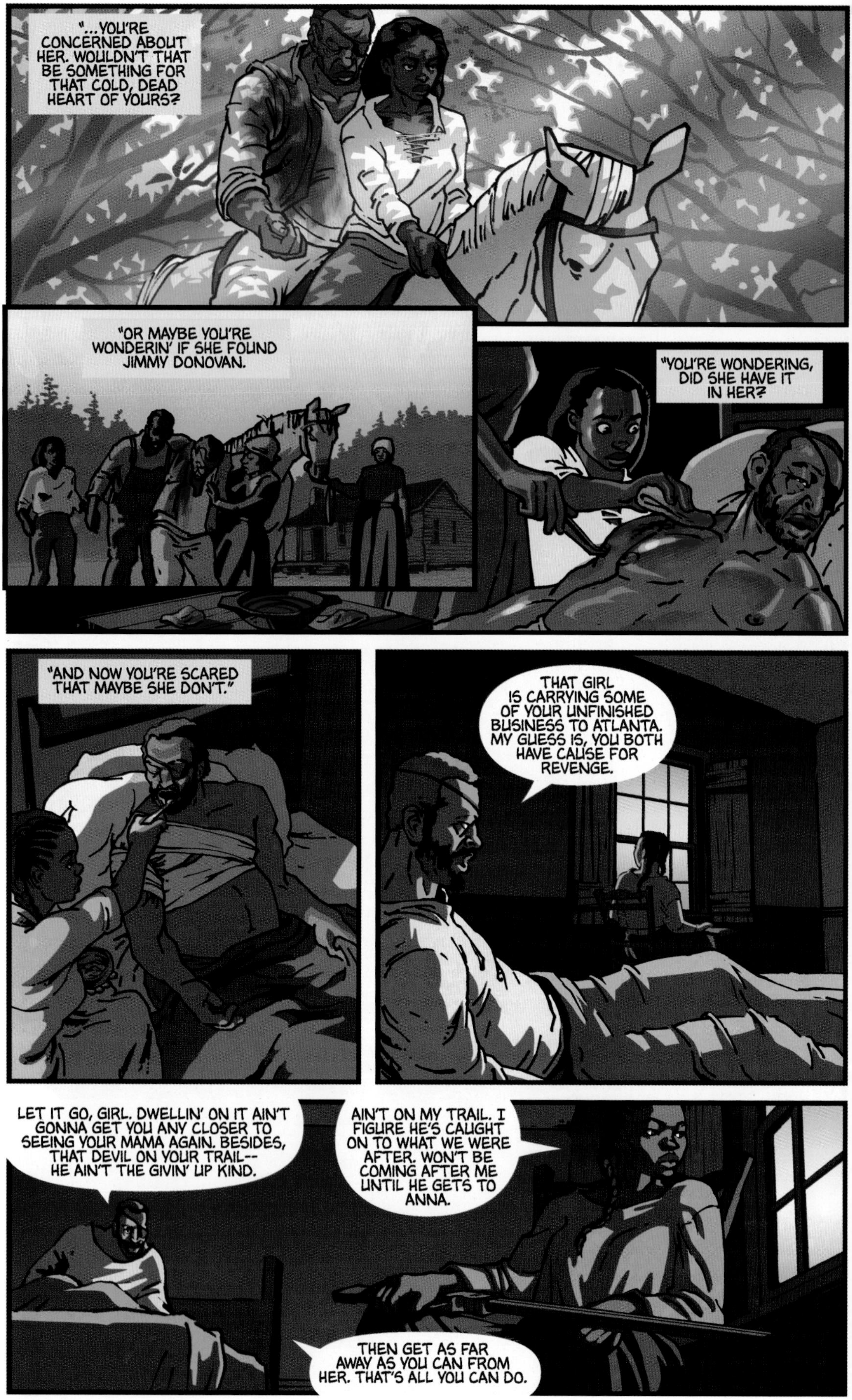
"...YOU'RE CONCERNED ABOUT HER. WOULDN'T THAT BE SOMETHING FOR THAT COLD, DEAD HEART OF YOURS?
"OR MAYBE YOU'RE WONDERIN' IF SHE FOUND JIMMY DONOVAN.
"YOU'RE WONDERING, DID SHE HAVE IT IN HER?
"AND NOW YOU'RE SCARED THAT MAYBE SHE DON'T."
THAT GIRL IS CARRYING SOME OF YOUR UNFINISHED BUSINESS TO ATLANTA. MY GUESS IS, YOU BOTH HAVE CAUSE FOR REVENGE.
LET IT GO, GIRL. DWELLIN' ON IT AIN'T GONNA GET YOU ANY CLOSER TO SEEING YOUR MAMA AGAIN. BESIDES, THAT DEVIL ON YOUR TRAIL-- HE AIN'T THE GIVIN' UP KIND.
AIN'T ON MY TRAIL. I FIGURE HE'S CAUGHT ON TO WHAT WE WERE AFTER. WON'T BE COMING AFTER ME UNTIL HE GETS TO ANNA.
THEN GET AS FAR AWAY AS YOU CAN FROM HER. THAT'S ALL YOU CAN DO.

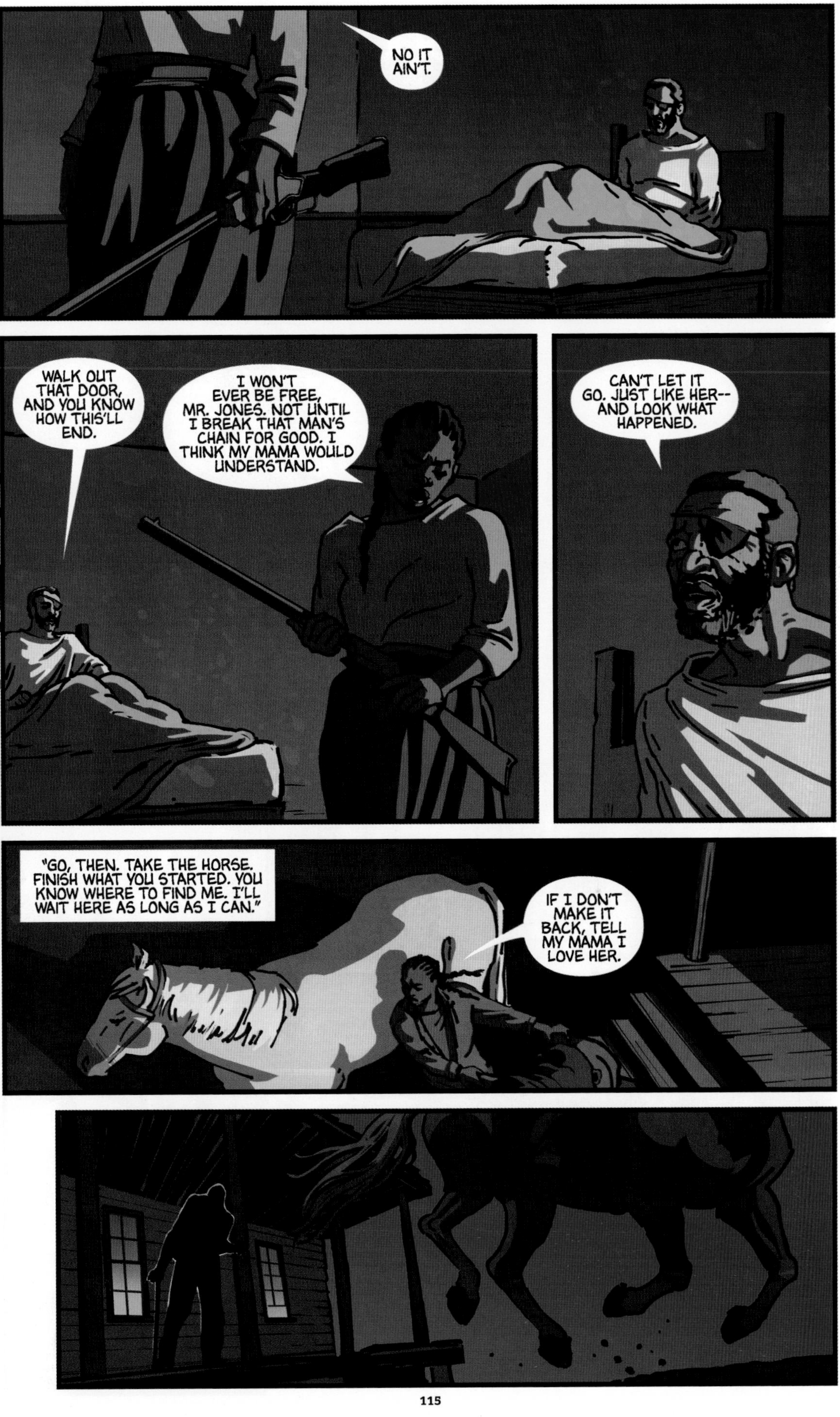

NO IT AIN'T.
WALK OUT THAT DOOR, AND YOU KNOW HOW THIS'LL END.
I WON'T EVER BE FREE, MR. JONES. NOT UNTIL I BREAK THAT MAN'S CHAIN FOR GOOD. I THINK MY MAMA WOULD UNDERSTAND.
CAN'T LET IT GO. JUST LIKE HER--AND LOOK WHAT HAPPENED.
"GO, THEN. TAKE THE HORSE. FINISH WHAT YOU STARTED. YOU KNOW WHERE TO FIND ME. I'LL WAIT HERE AS LONG AS I CAN."
IF I DON'T MAKE IT BACK, TELL MY MAMA I LOVE HER.

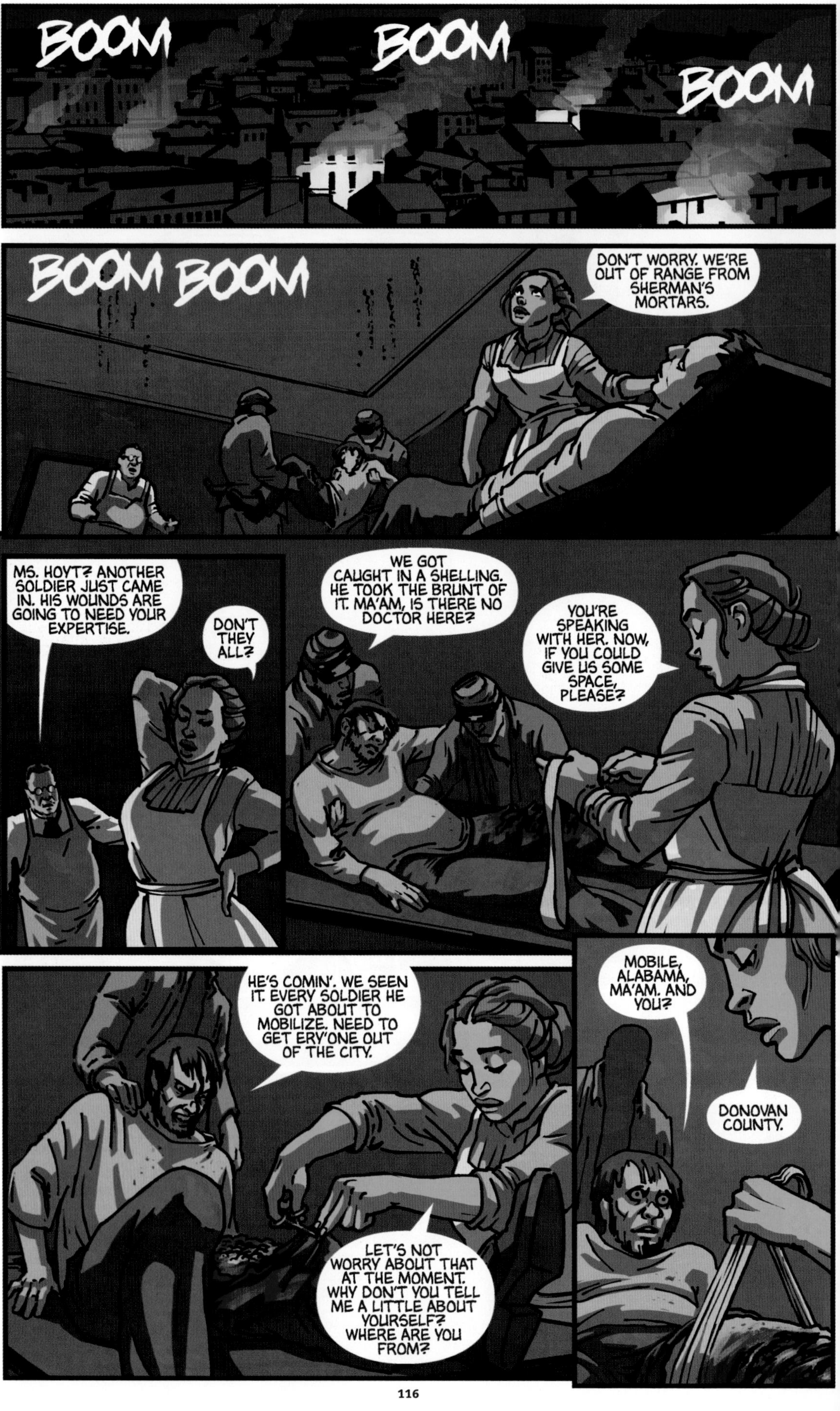

BOOM
BOOM
BOOM
BOOM BOOM
DON'T WORRY. WE'RE OUT OF RANGE FROM SHERMAN'S MORTARS.
MS. HOYT? ANOTHER SOLDIER JUST CAME IN. HIS WOUNDS ARE GOING TO NEED YOUR EXPERTISE.
DON'T THEY ALL?
WE GOT CAUGHT IN A SHELLING. HE TOOK THE BRUNT OF IT. MA'AM, IS THERE NO DOCTOR HERE?
YOU'RE SPEAKING WITH HER. NOW, IF YOU COULD GIVE US SOME SPACE, PLEASE?
HE'S COMIN'. WE SEEN IT. EVERY SOLDIER HE GOT ABOUT TO MOBILIZE. NEED TO GET ERY'ONE OUT OF THE CITY.
LET'S NOT WORRY ABOUT THAT AT THE MOMENT. WHY DON'T YOU TELL ME A LITTLE ABOUT YOURSELF? WHERE ARE YOU FROM?
MOBILE, ALABAMA, MA'AM. AND YOU?
DONOVAN COUNTY.

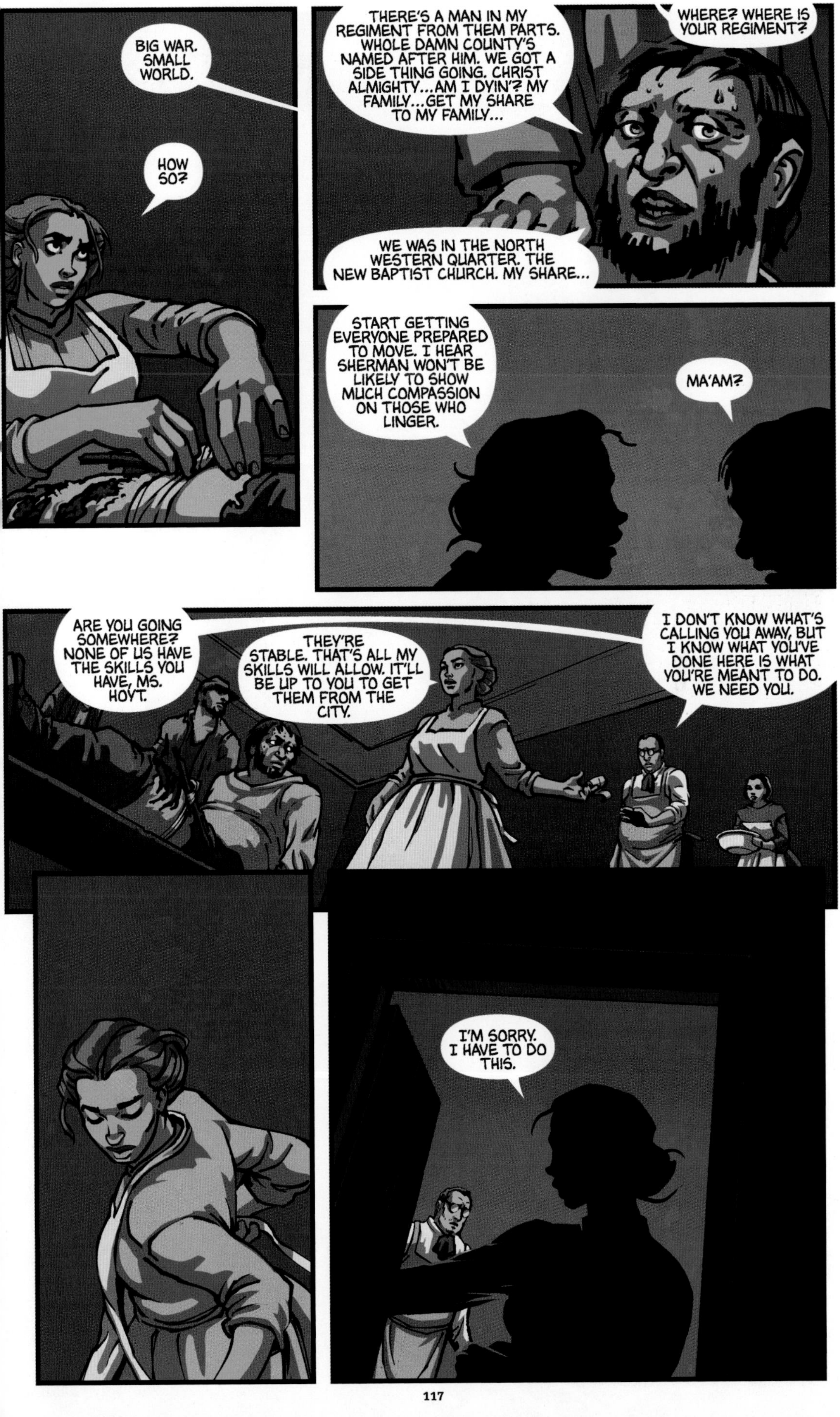
BIG WAR. SMALL WORLD.
HOW SO?
THERE'S A MAN IN MY REGIMENT FROM THEM PARTS. WHOLE DAMN COUNTY'S NAMED AFTER HIM. WE GOT A SIDE THING GOING. CHRIST ALMIGHTY...AM I DYIN'? MY FAMILY...GET MY SHARE TO MY FAMILY...
WHERE? WHERE IS YOUR REGIMENT?
WE WAS IN THE NORTH WESTERN QUARTER. THE NEW BAPTIST CHURCH. MY SHARE...
START GETTING EVERYONE PREPARED TO MOVE. I HEAR SHERMAN WON'T BE LIKELY TO SHOW MUCH COMPASSION ON THOSE WHO LINGER.
MA'AM?
ARE YOU GOING SOMEWHERE? NONE OF US HAVE THE SKILLS YOU HAVE, MS. HOYT.
THEY'RE STABLE. THAT'S ALL MY SKILLS WILL ALLOW. IT'LL BE UP TO YOU TO GET THEM FROM THE CITY.
I DON'T KNOW WHAT'S CALLING YOU AWAY, BUT I KNOW WHAT YOU'VE DONE HERE IS WHAT YOU'RE MEANT TO DO. WE NEED YOU.
I'M SORRY. I HAVE TO DO THIS.

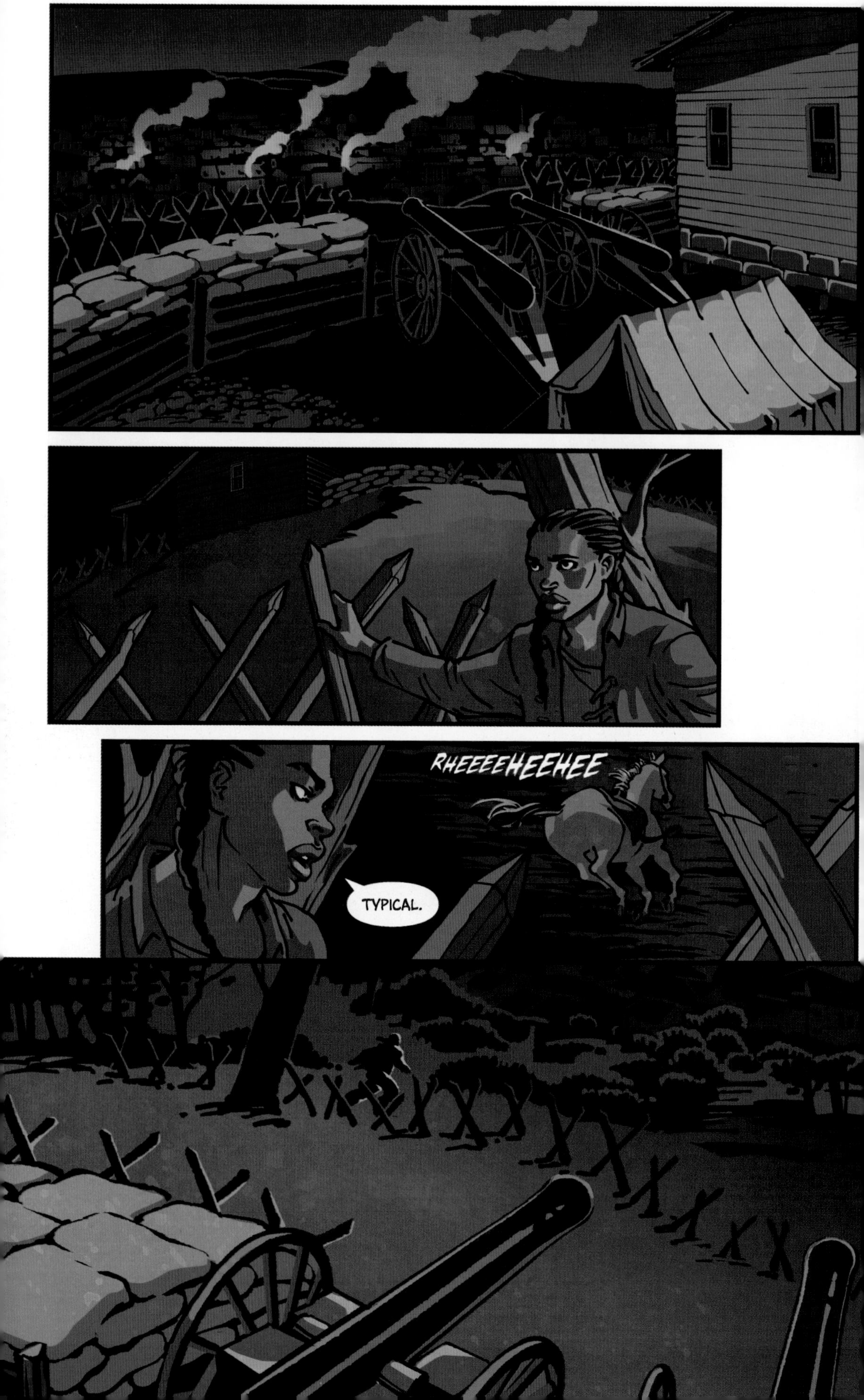
RHEEEEHEEHEE
TYPICAL.

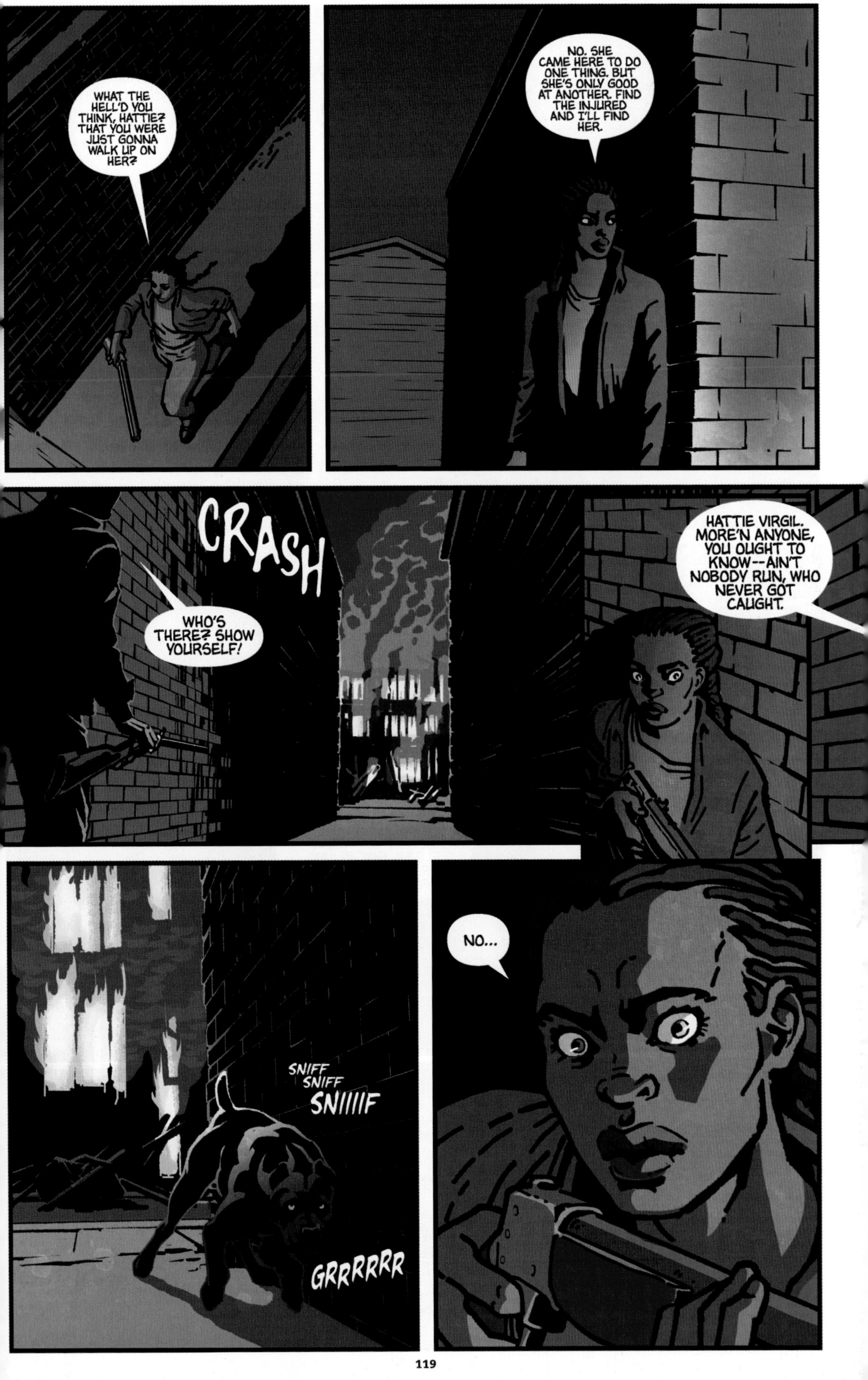
WHAT THE HELL'D YOU THINK, HATTIE? THAT YOU WERE JUST GONNA WALK UP ON HER?
NO. SHE CAME HERE TO DO ONE THING. BUT SHE'S ONLY GOOD AT ANOTHER. FIND THE INJURED AND I'LL FIND HER.
CRASH
WHO'S THERE? SHOW YOURSELF!
HATTIE VIRGIL. MORE'N ANYONE, YOU OUGHT TO KNOW--AIN'T NOBODY RUN, WHO NEVER GOT CAUGHT.
SNIFF
SNIFF
SNIIIIF
GRRRRRR
NO...

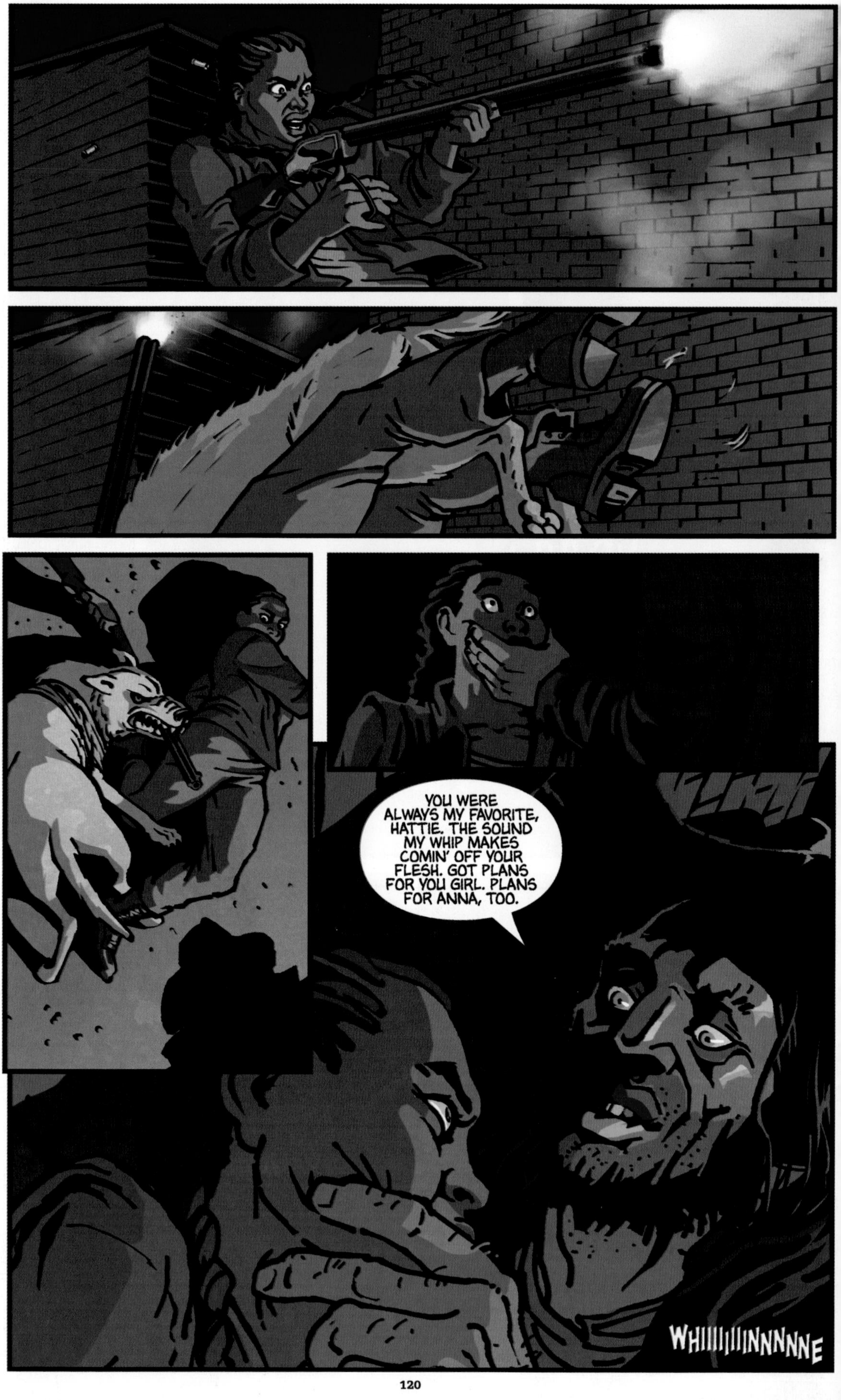
YOU WERE ALWAYS MY FAVORITE, HATTIE. THE SOUND MY WHIP MAKES COMIN' OFF YOUR FLESH. GOT PLANS FOR YOU GIRL. PLANS FOR ANNA, TOO.
WHIIIIIIINNNNNE

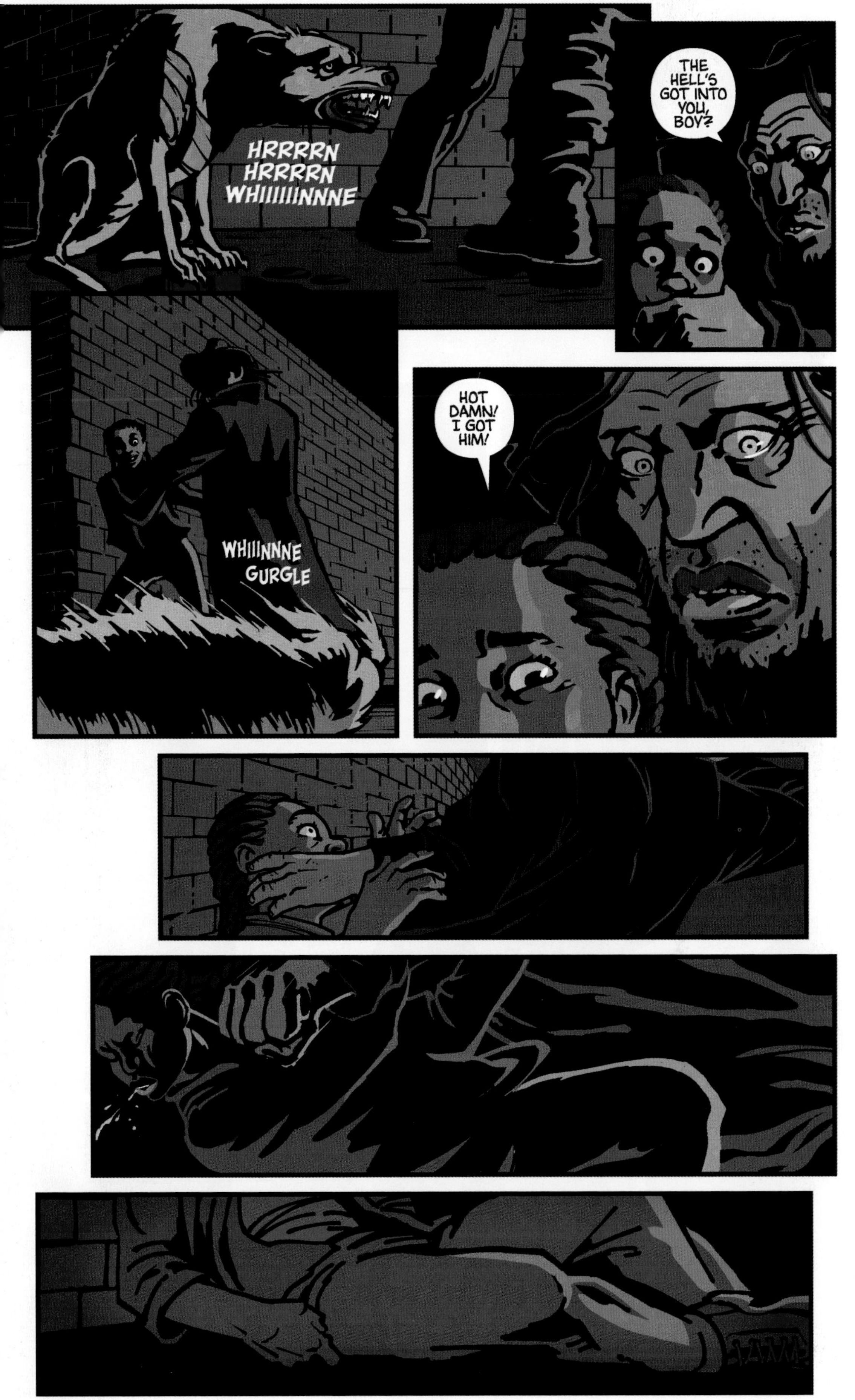
HRRRRN
HRRRRN
WHIIIIIINNNE
THE HELL'S GOT INTO YOU, BOY?
WHIIINNNE
GURGLE
HOT DAMN! I GOT HIM!

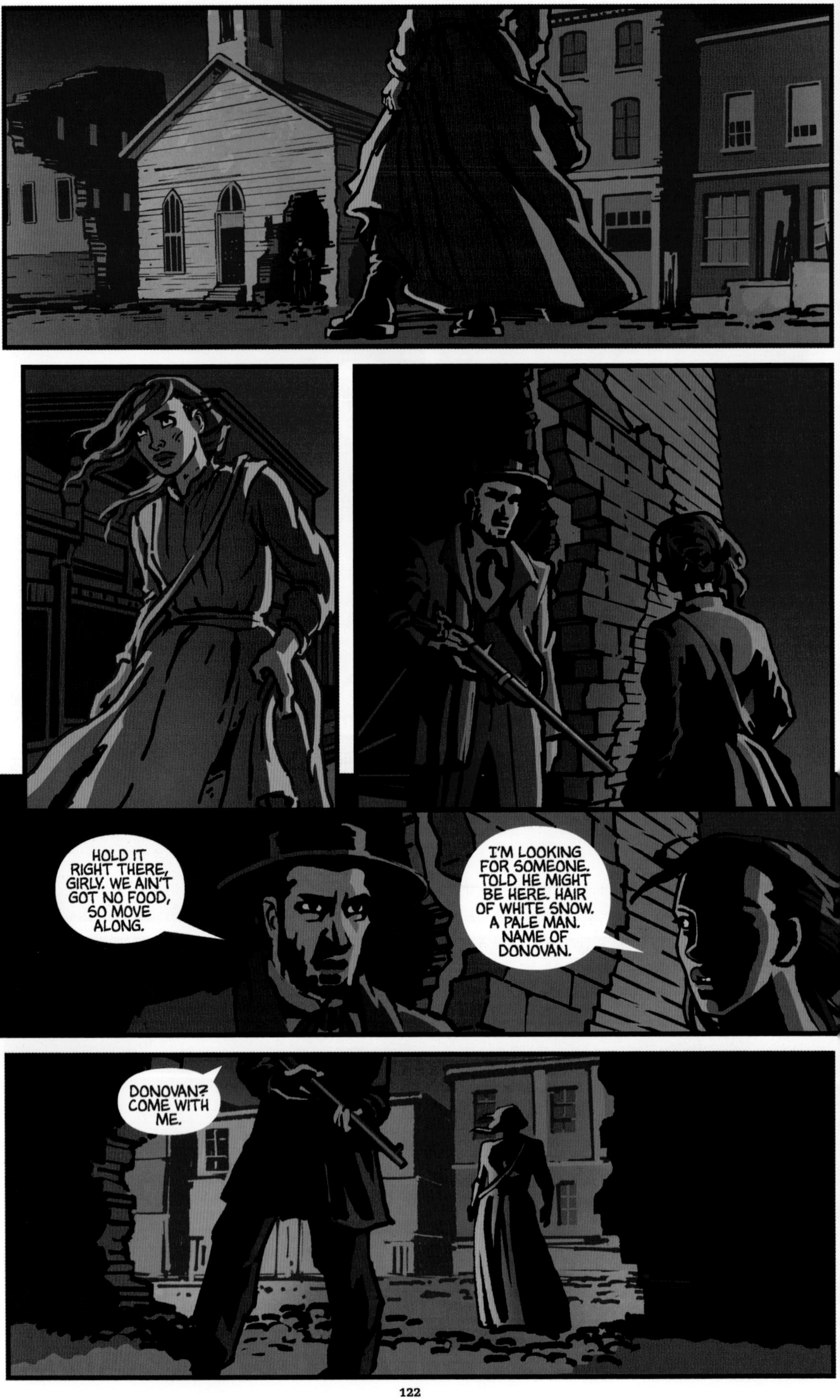
HOLD IT RIGHT THERE, GIRLY. WE AIN'T GOT NO FOOD, SO MOVE ALONG.
I'M LOOKING FOR SOMEONE. TOLD HE MIGHT BE HERE. HAIR OF WHITE SNOW. A PALE MAN. NAME OF DONOVAN.
DONOVAN? COME WITH ME.

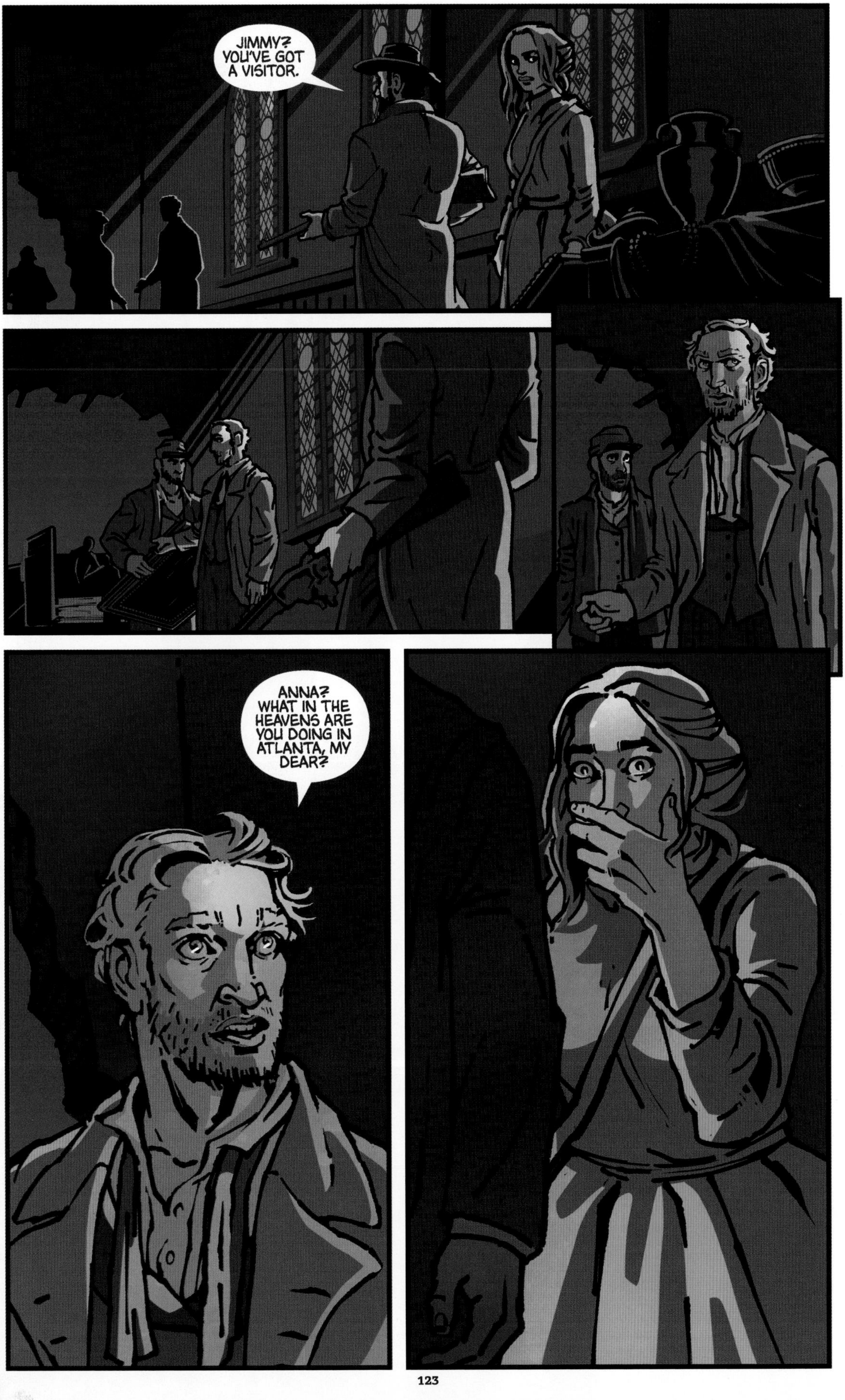
JIMMY? YOU'VE GOT A VISITOR.
ANNA? WHAT IN THE HEAVENS ARE YOU DOING IN ATLANTA, MY DEAR?

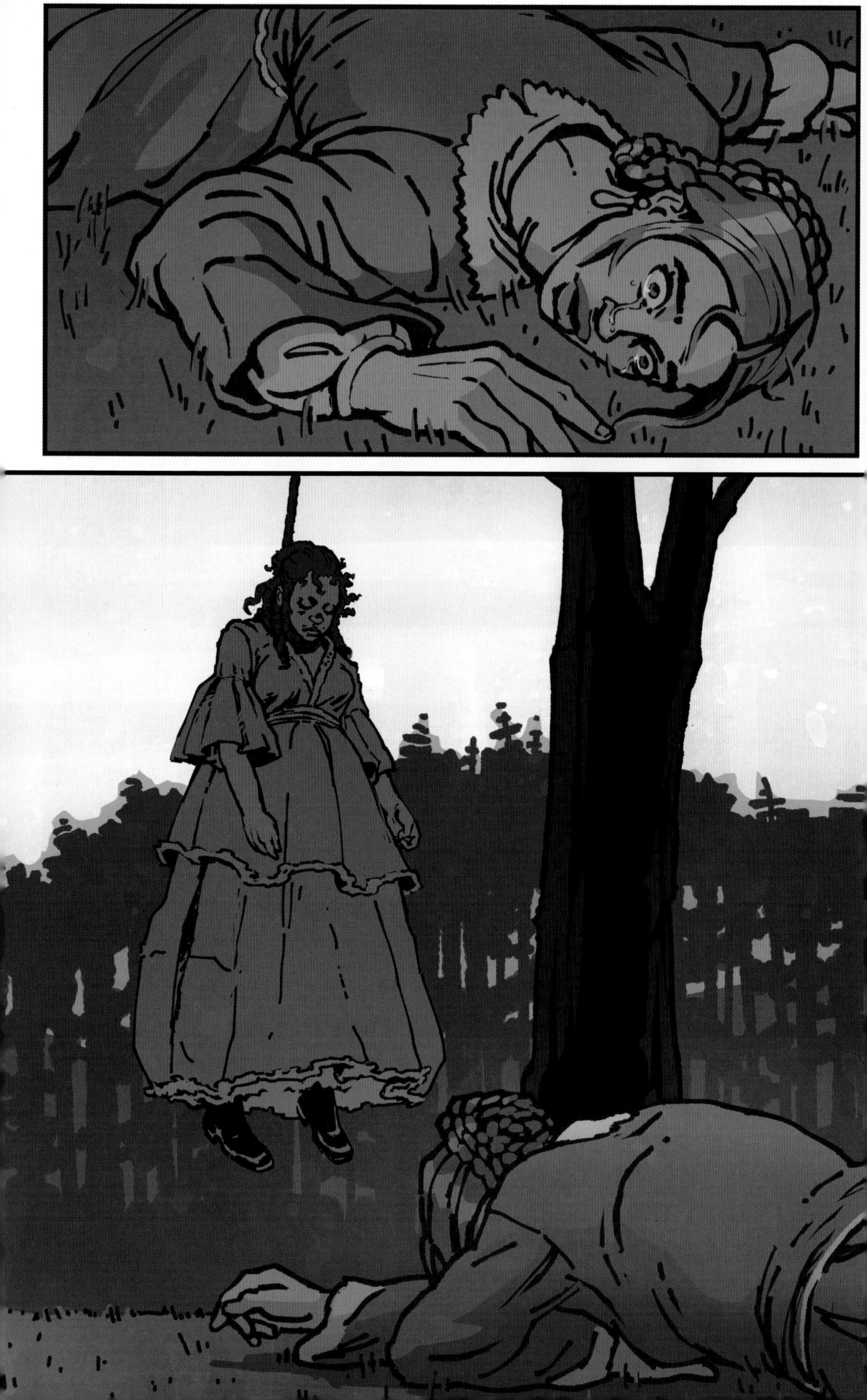

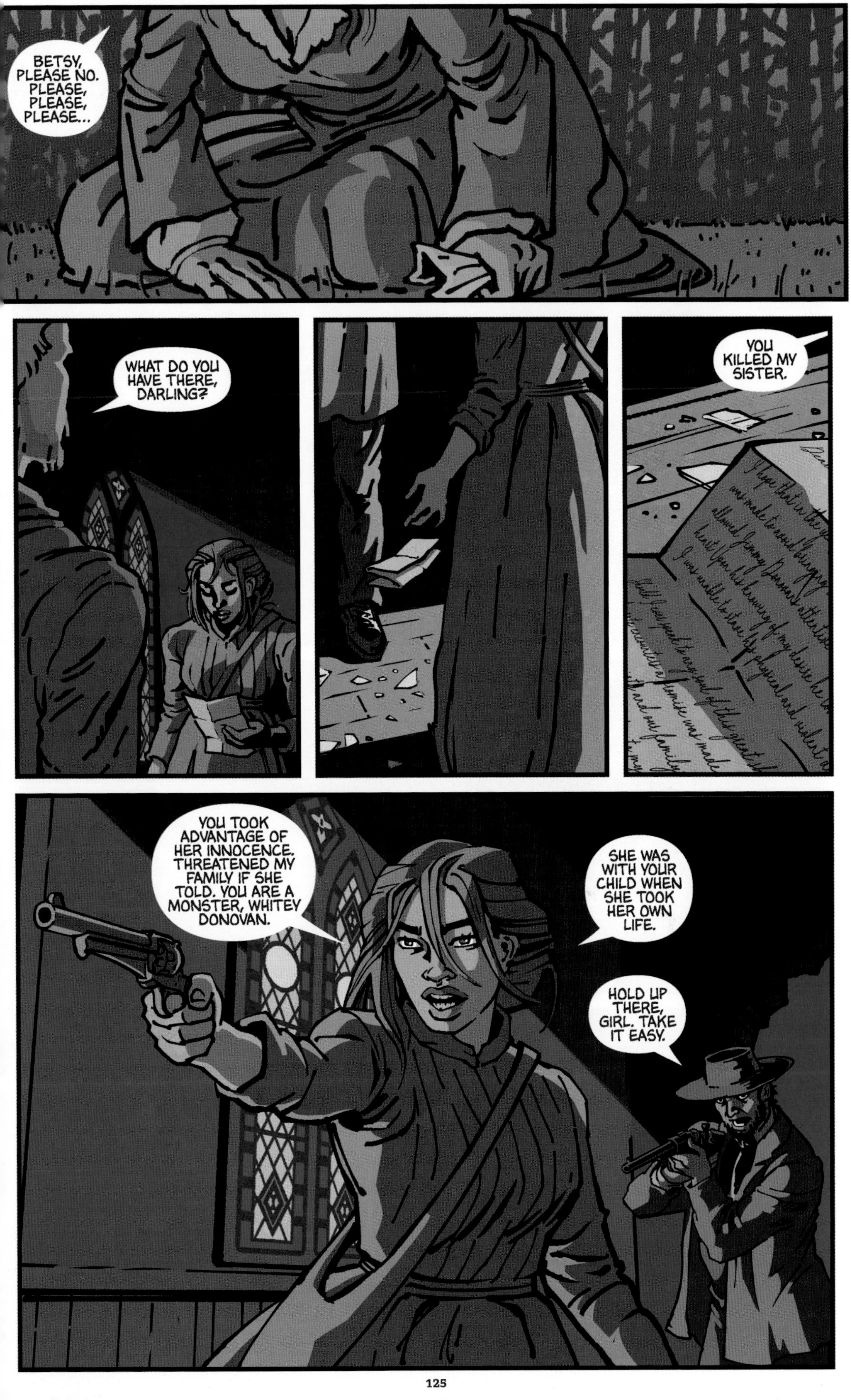
BETSY, PLEASE NO. PLEASE, PLEASE, PLEASE...
WHAT DO YOU HAVE THERE, DARLING?
YOU KILLED MY SISTER.
YOU TOOK ADVANTAGE OF HER INNOCENCE. THREATENED MY FAMILY IF SHE TOLD. YOU ARE A MONSTER, WHITEY DONOVAN.
SHE WAS WITH YOUR CHILD WHEN SHE TOOK HER OWN LIFE.
HOLD UP THERE, GIRL. TAKE IT EASY.

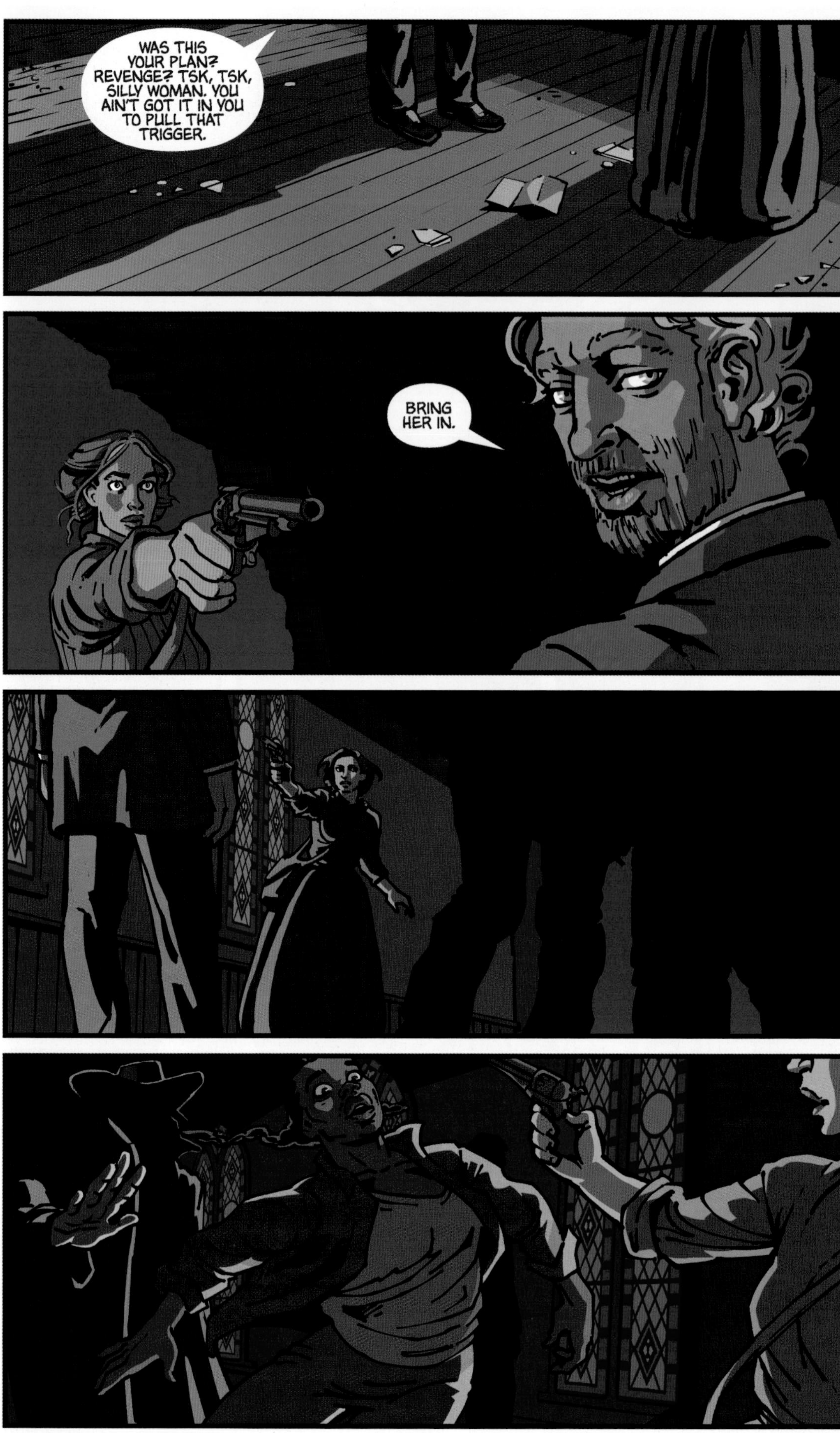
WAS THIS YOUR PLAN? REVENGE? TSK, TSK, SILLY WOMAN. YOU AIN'T GOT IT IN YOU TO PULL THAT TRIGGER.
BRING HER IN.

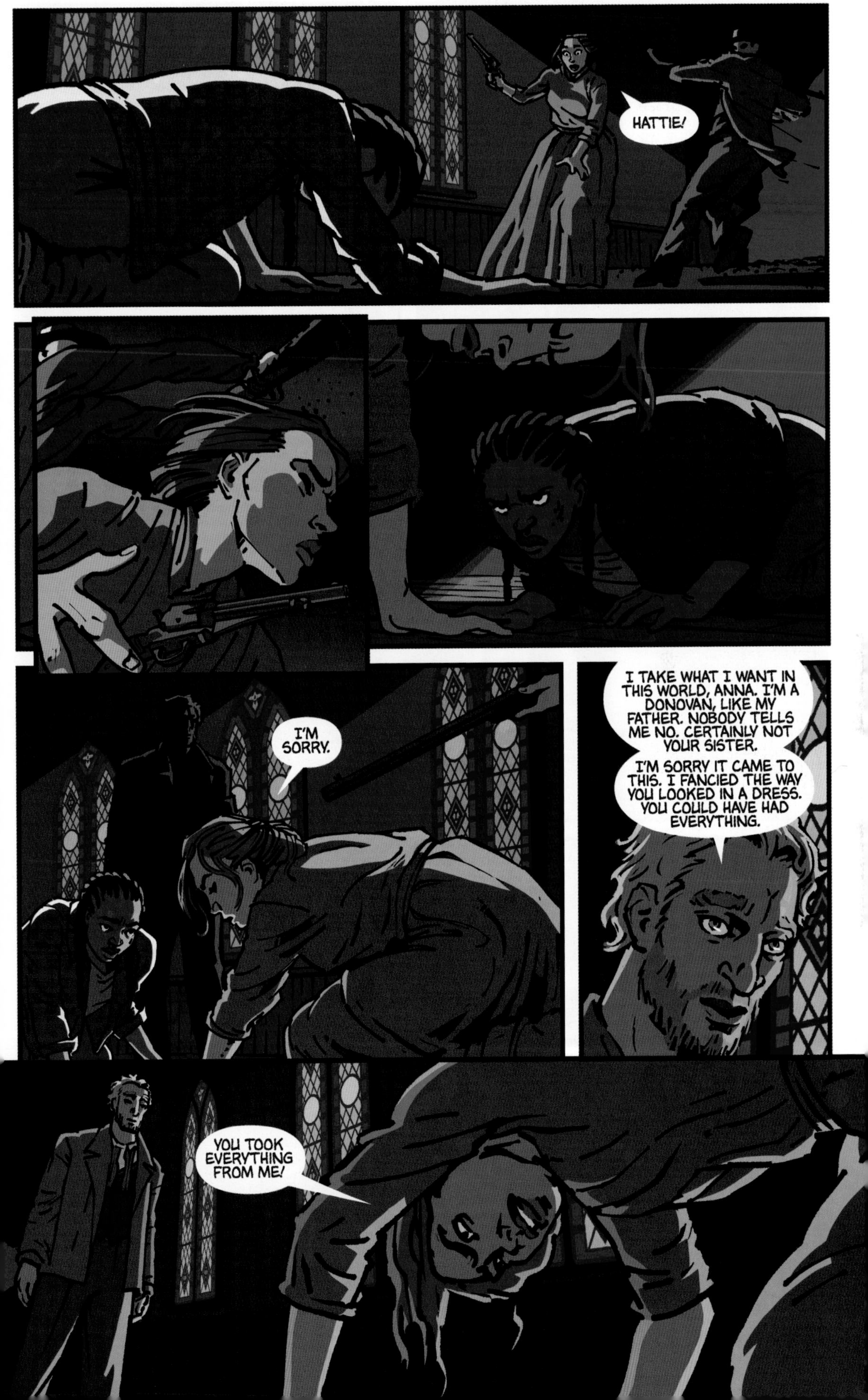
HATTIE!
I'M SORRY.
I TAKE WHAT I WANT IN THIS WORLD, ANNA. I'M A DONOVAN, LIKE MY FATHER. NOBODY TELLS ME NO. CERTAINLY NOT YOUR SISTER.
I'M SORRY IT CAME TO THIS. I FANCIED THE WAY YOU LOOKED IN A DRESS. YOU COULD HAVE HAD EVERYTHING.
YOU TOOK EVERYTHING FROM ME!

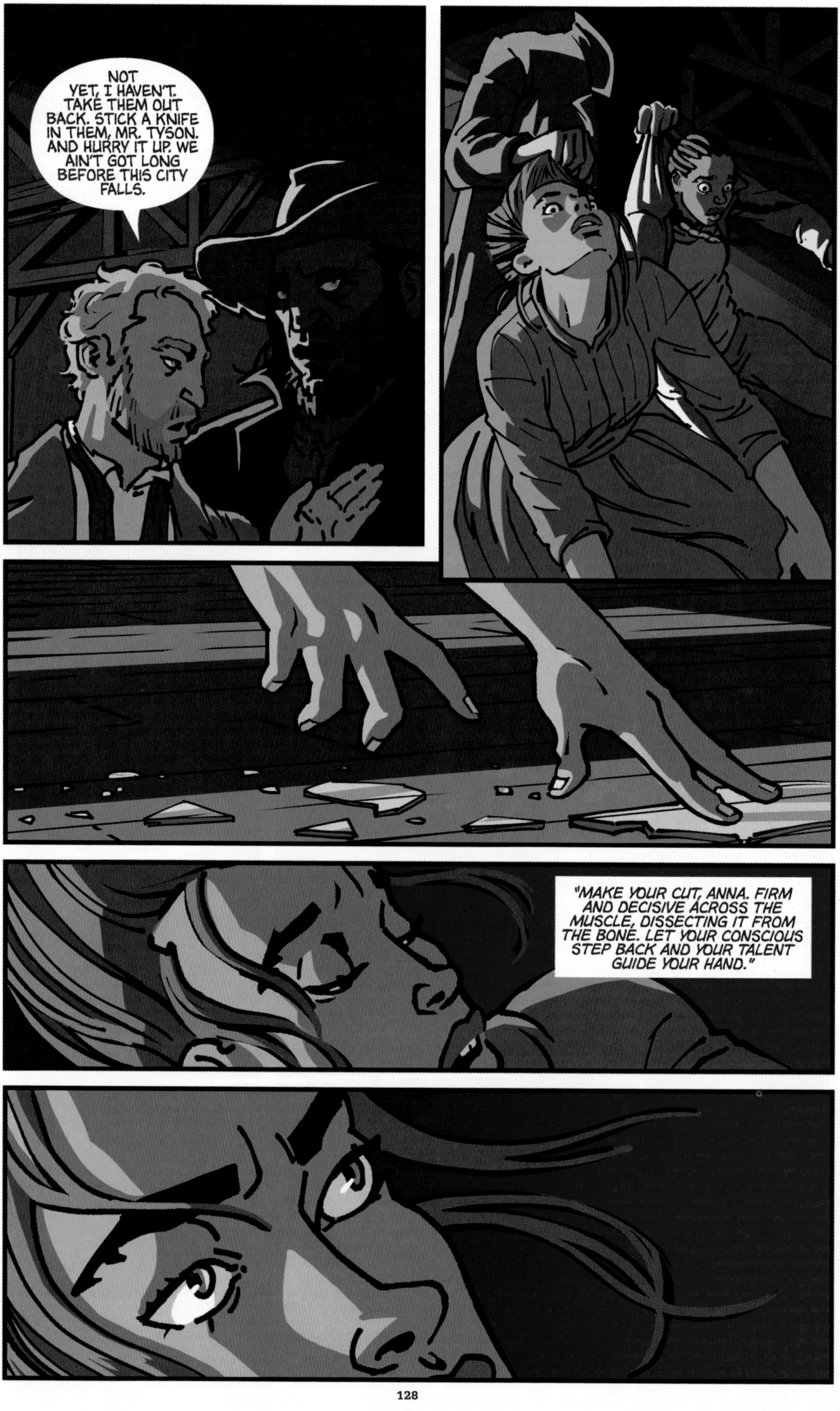
NOT YET, I HAVEN'T. TAKE THEM OUT BACK. STICK A KNIFE IN THEM, MR. TYSON. AND HURRY IT UP. WE AIN'T GOT LONG BEFORE THIS CITY FALLS.
"MAKE YOUR CUT, ANNA. FIRM AND DECISIVE ACROSS THE MUSCLE, DISSECTING IT FROM THE BONE. LET YOUR CONSCIOUS STEP BACK AND YOUR TALENT GUIDE YOUR HAND."

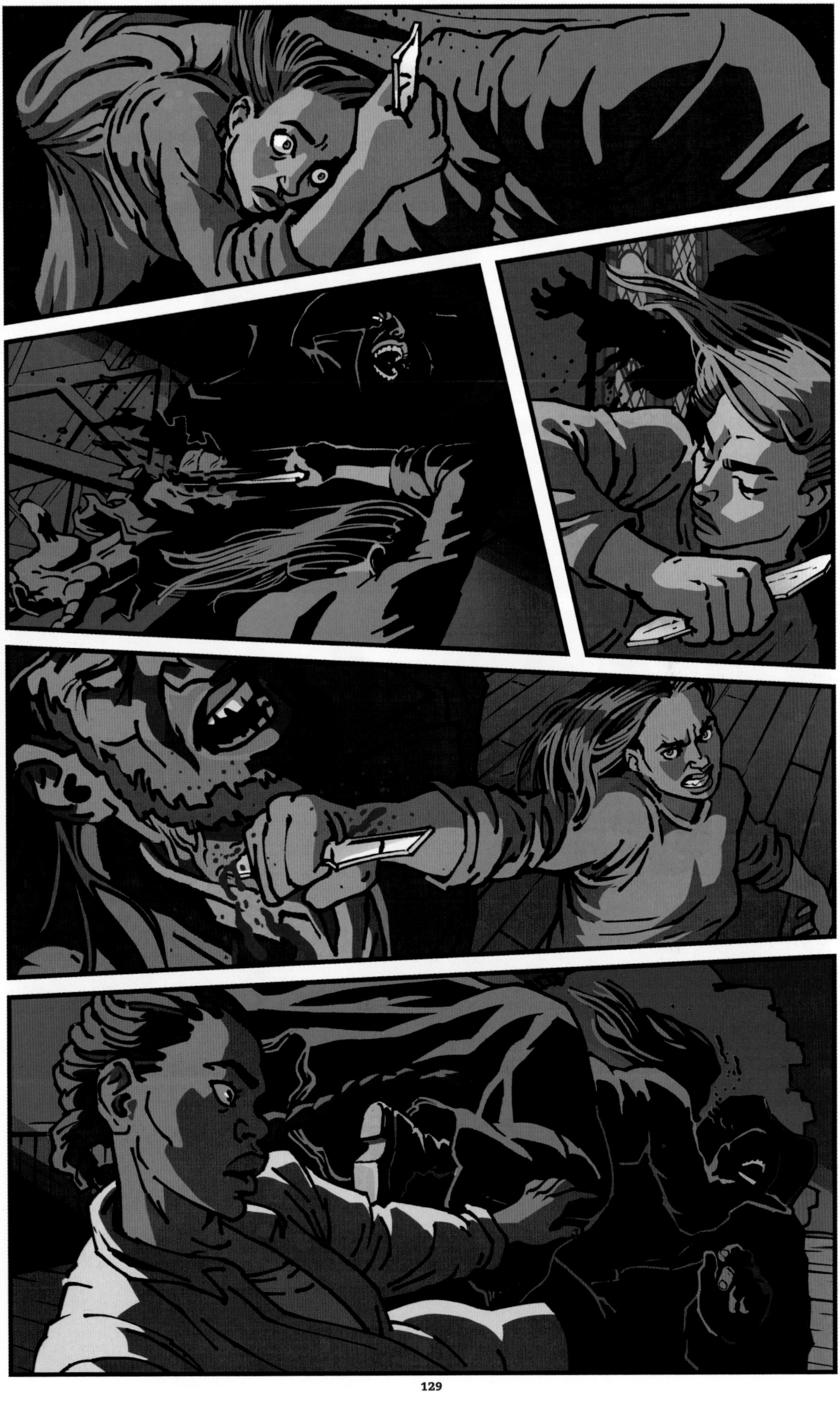

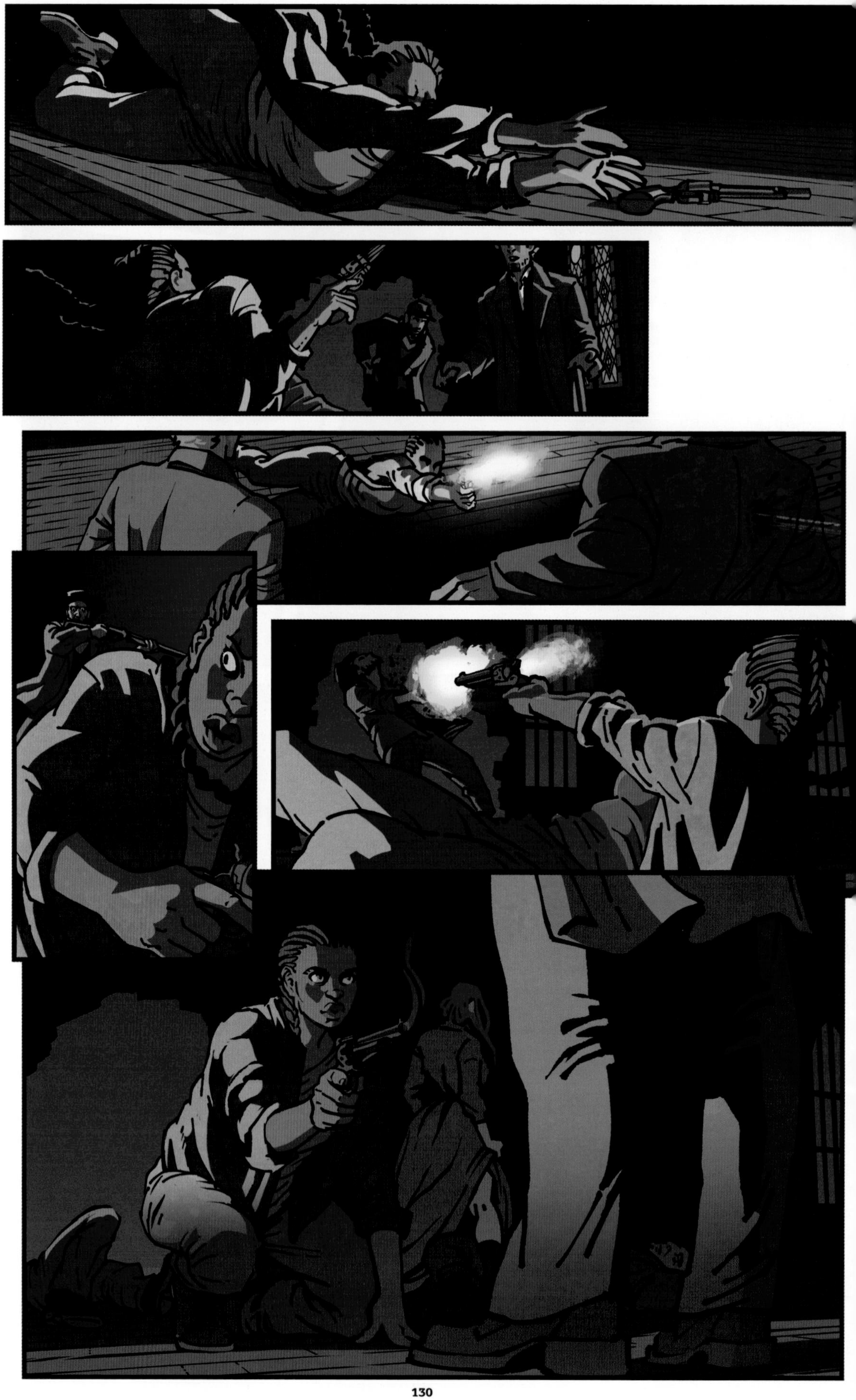

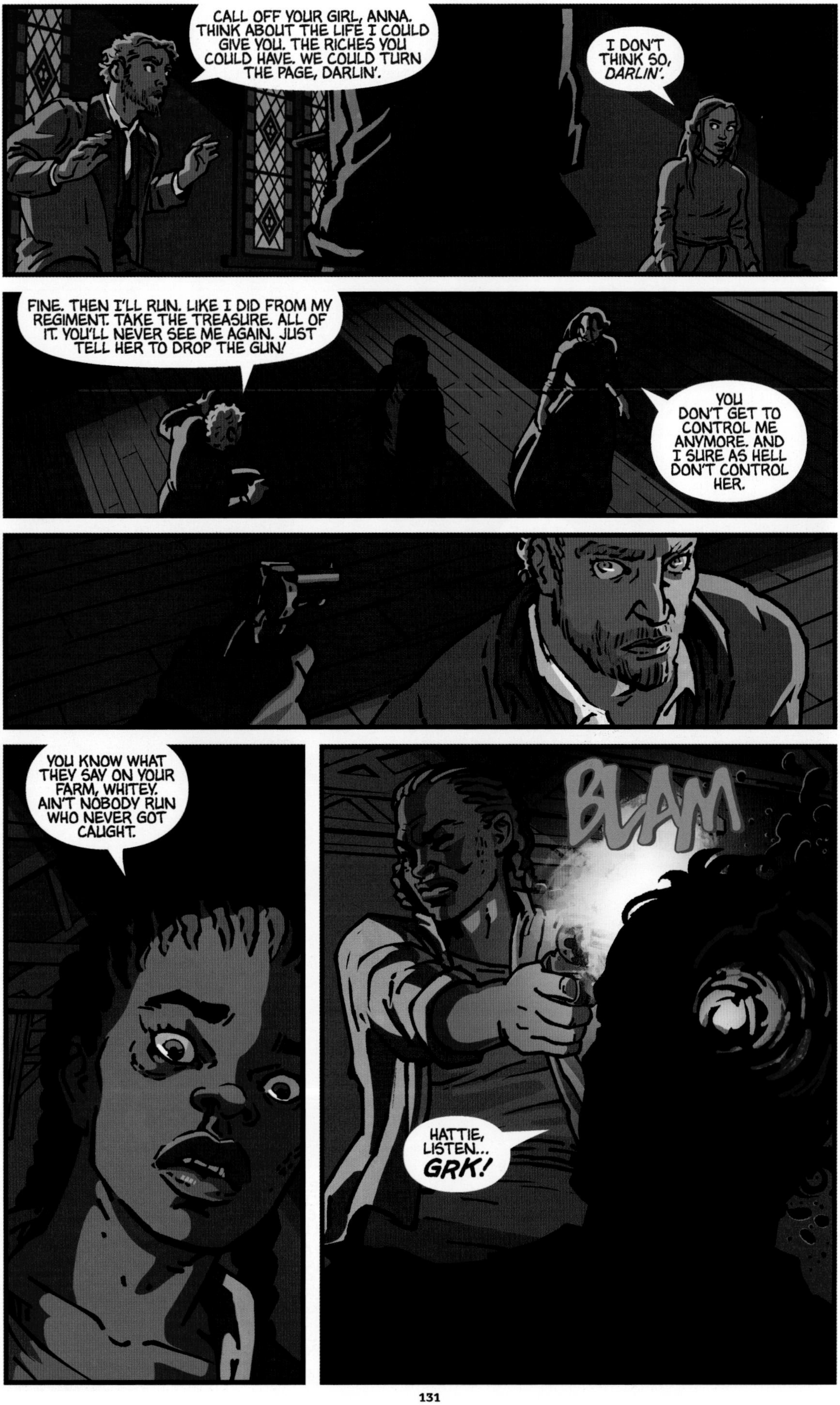
CALL OFF YOUR GIRL, ANNA. THINK ABOUT THE LIFE I COULD GIVE YOU. THE RICHES YOU COULD HAVE. WE COULD TURN THE PAGE, DARLIN'.
I DON'T THINK SO, *DARLIN'*.
FINE. THEN I'LL RUN. LIKE I DID FROM MY REGIMENT. TAKE THE TREASURE. ALL OF IT. YOU'LL NEVER SEE ME AGAIN. JUST TELL HER TO DROP THE GUN!
YOU DON'T GET TO CONTROL ME ANYMORE. AND I SURE AS HELL DON'T CONTROL HER.
YOU KNOW WHAT THEY SAY ON YOUR FARM, WHITEY. AIN'T NOBODY RUN WHO NEVER GOT CAUGHT.
BLAM
HATTIE, LISTEN... **GRK!**

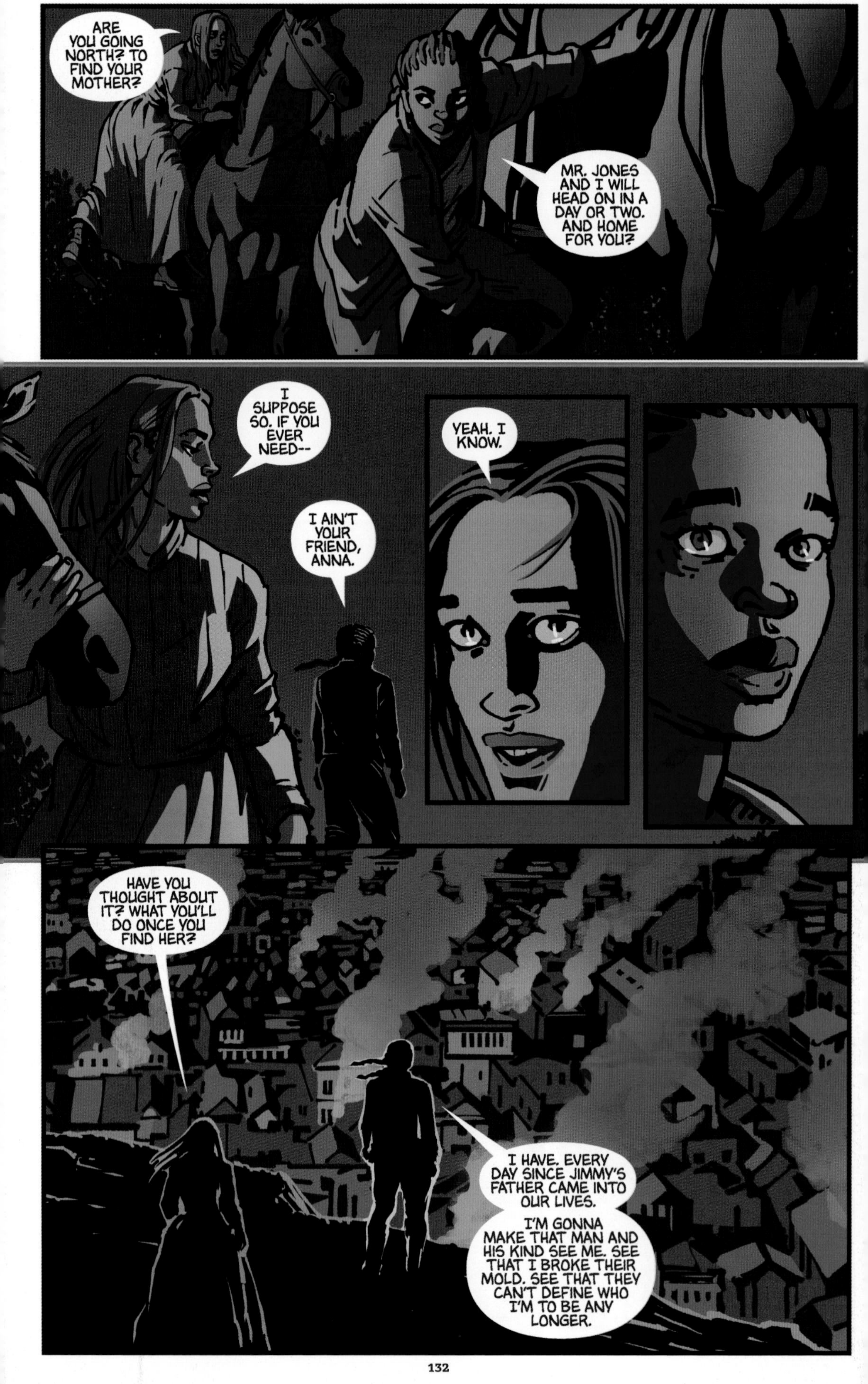
ARE YOU GOING NORTH? TO FIND YOUR MOTHER?
MR. JONES AND I WILL HEAD ON IN A DAY OR TWO. AND HOME FOR YOU?
I SUPPOSE SO. IF YOU EVER NEED--
I AIN'T YOUR FRIEND, ANNA.
YEAH. I KNOW.
HAVE YOU THOUGHT ABOUT IT? WHAT YOU'LL DO ONCE YOU FIND HER?
I HAVE. EVERY DAY SINCE JIMMY'S FATHER CAME INTO OUR LIVES.
I'M GONNA MAKE THAT MAN AND HIS KIND SEE ME. SEE THAT I BROKE THEIR MOLD. SEE THAT THEY CAN'T DEFINE WHO I'M TO BE ANY LONGER.

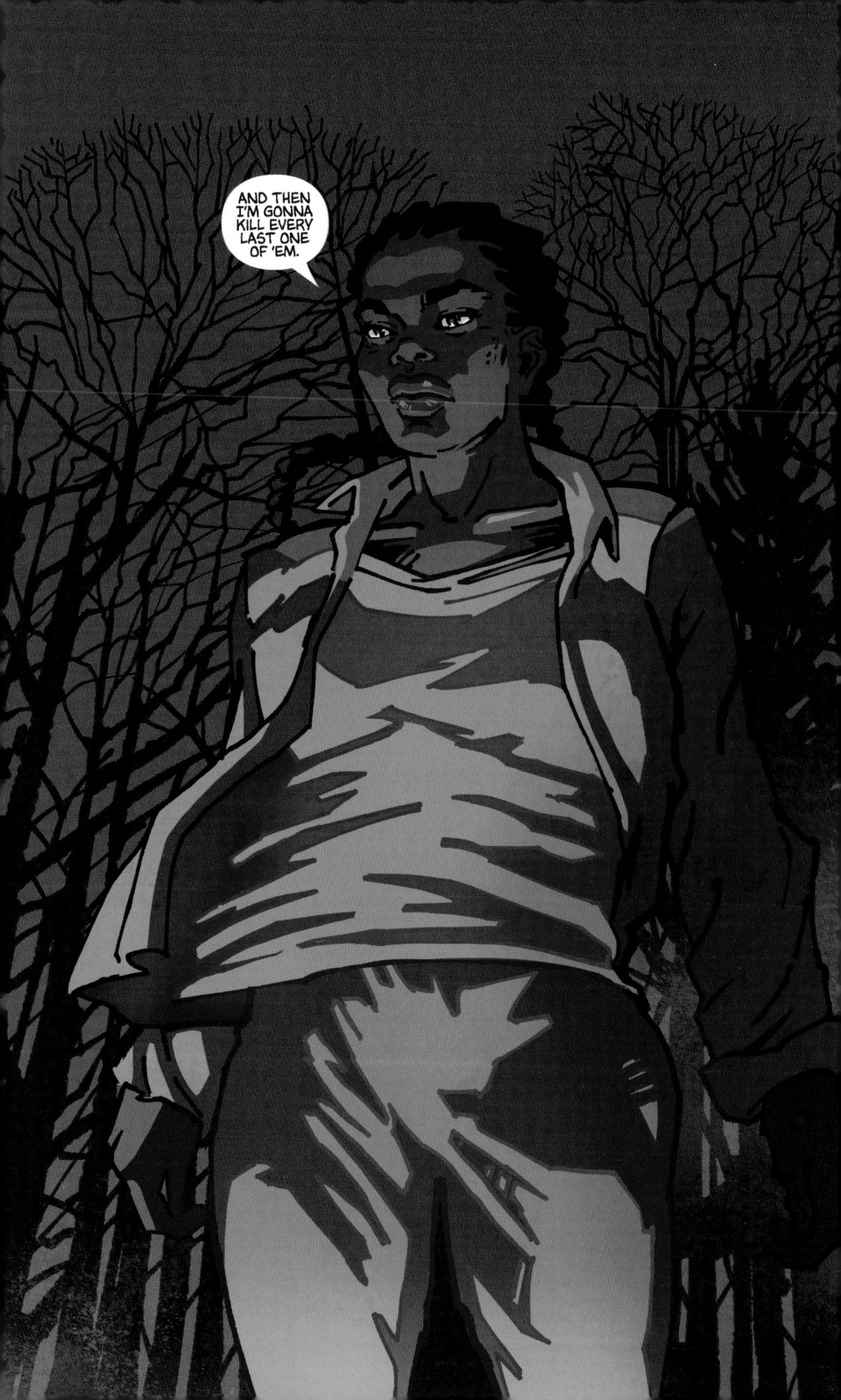
AND THEN I'M GONNA KILL EVERY LAST ONE OF 'EM.

HATTIE VIRGIL

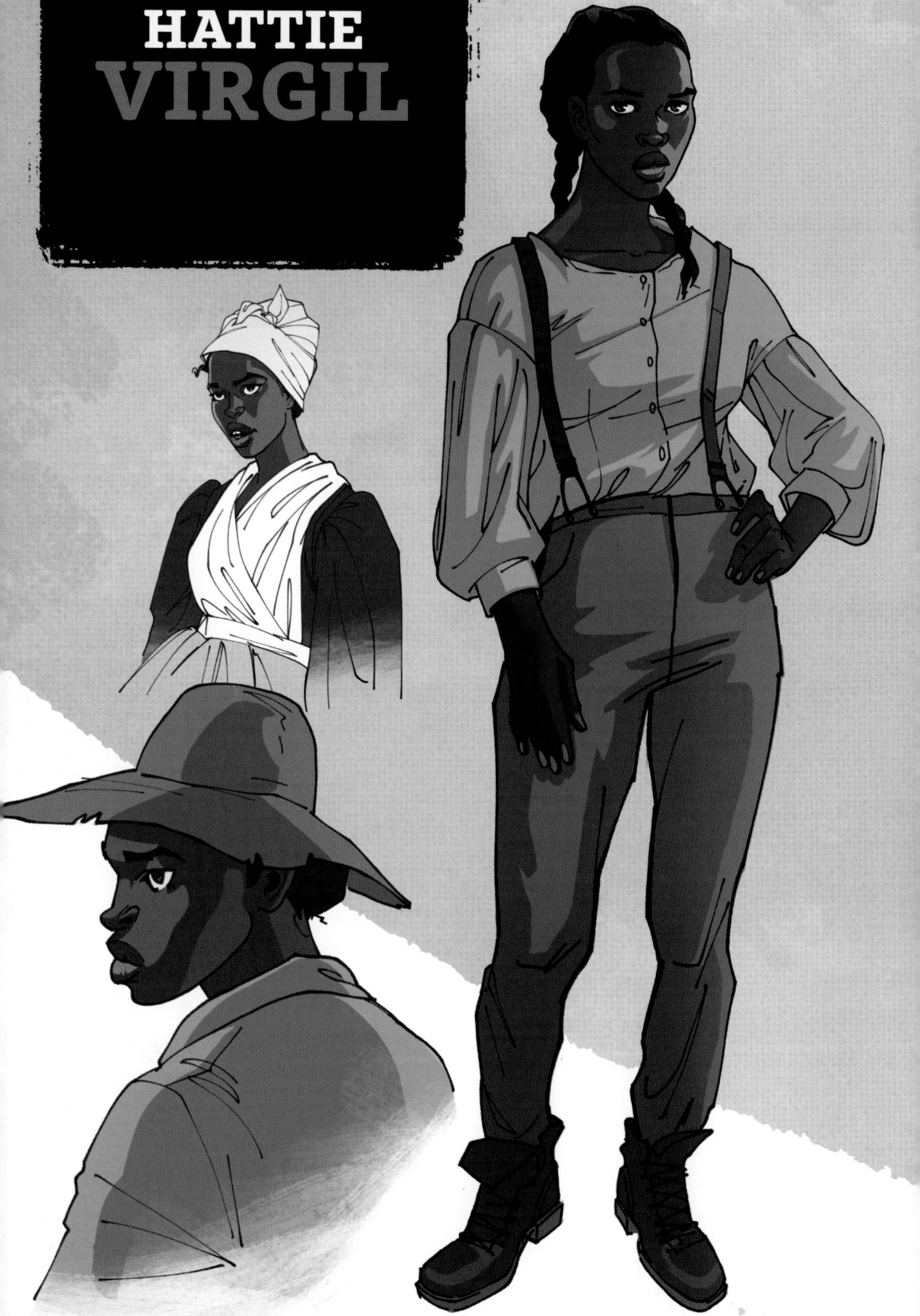

Character Designs by
NATALIE BARAHONA

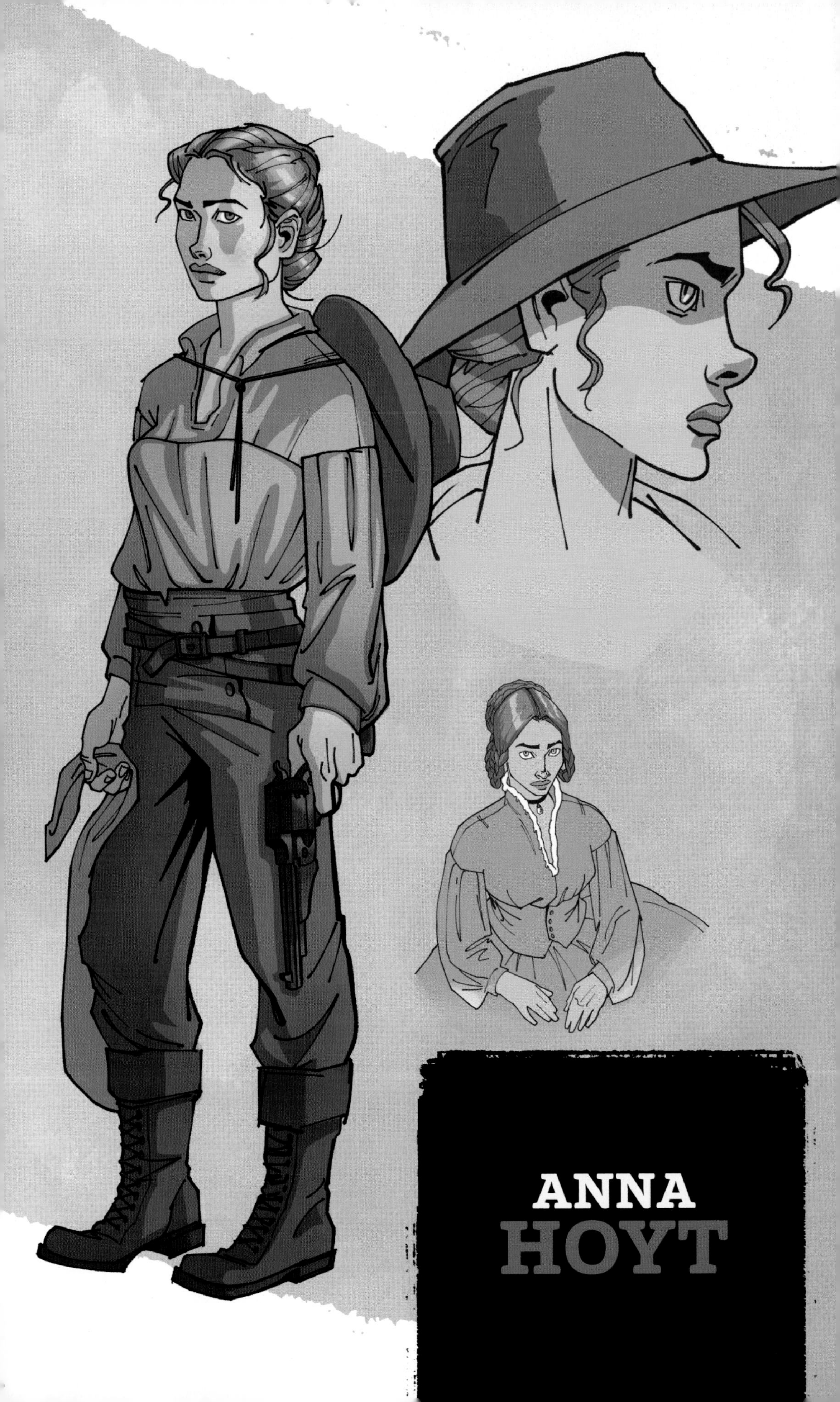
ANNA
HOYT

COVER GALLERY

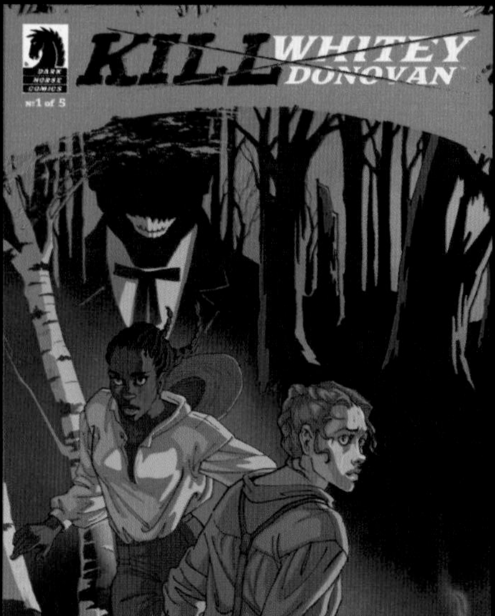
KILL WHITEY DONOVAN
№1 of 5
Sydney Duncan
Natalie Barahona

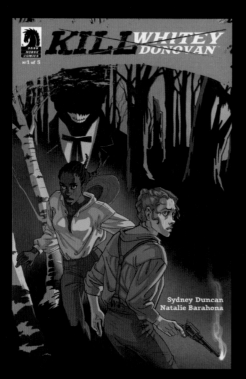

Issue #1 Variant
NATALIE BARAHONA

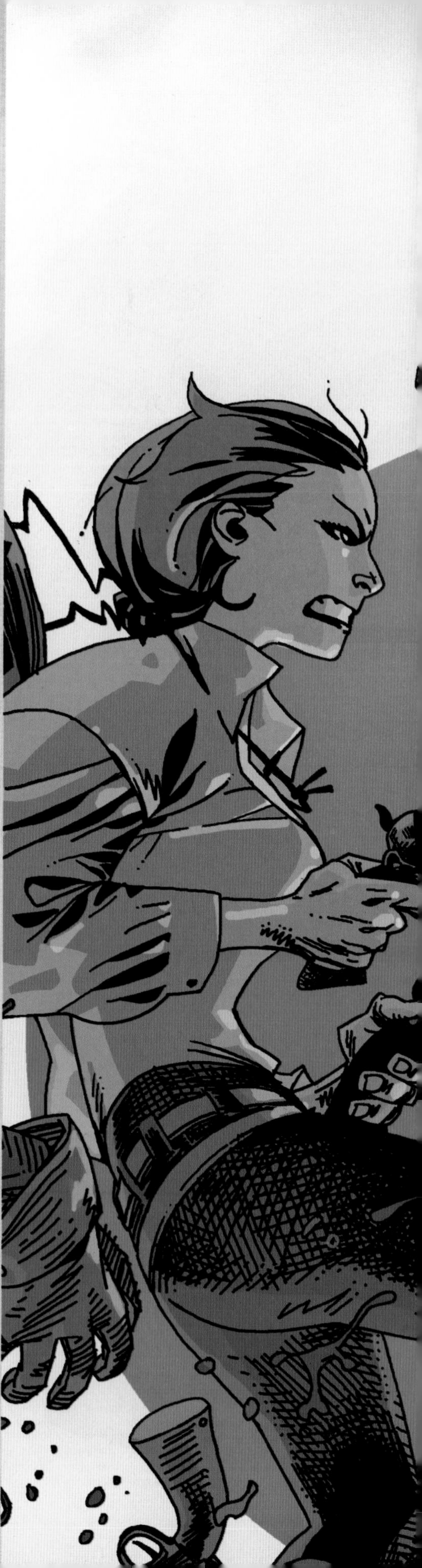

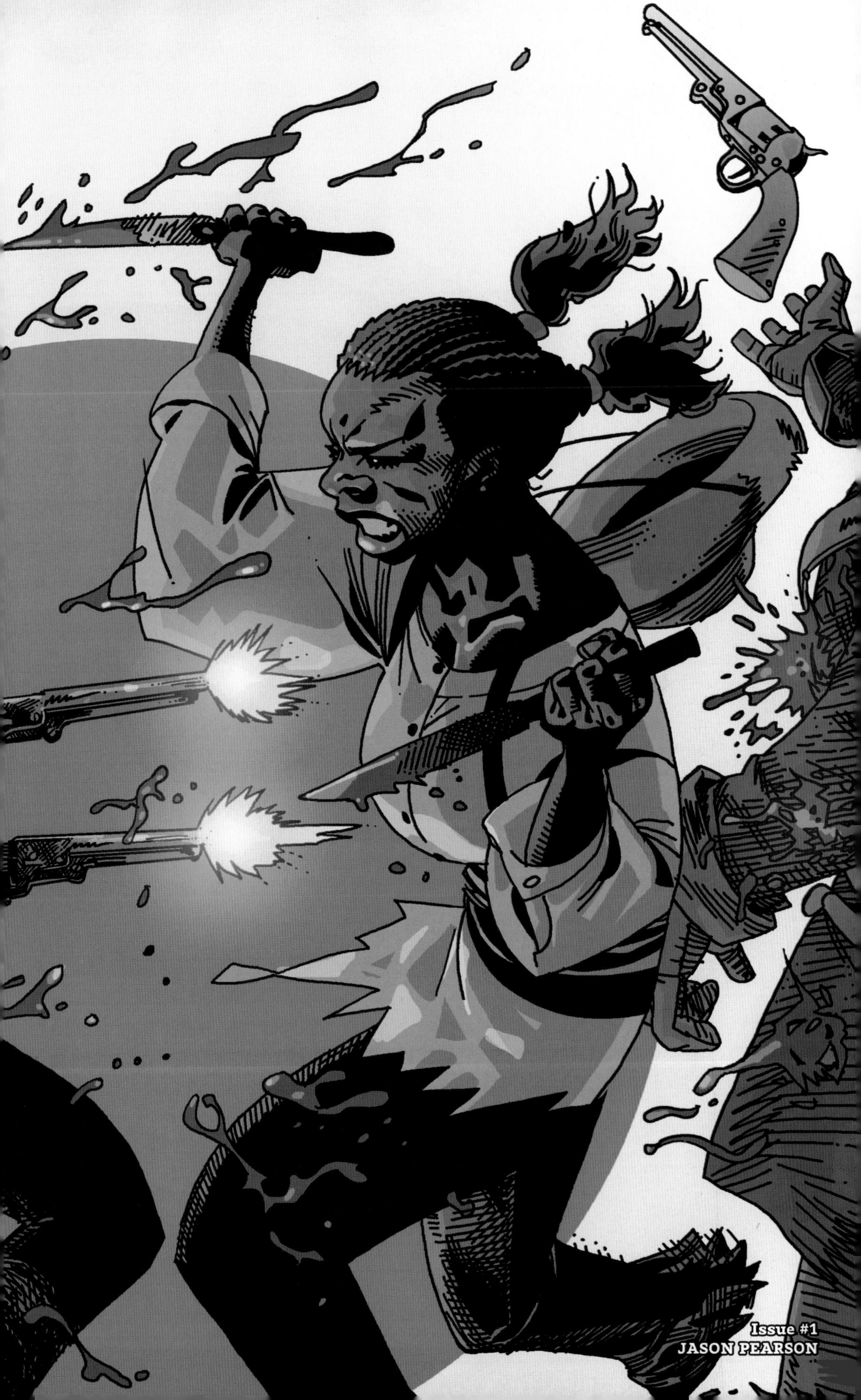

Issue #1
JASON PEARSON

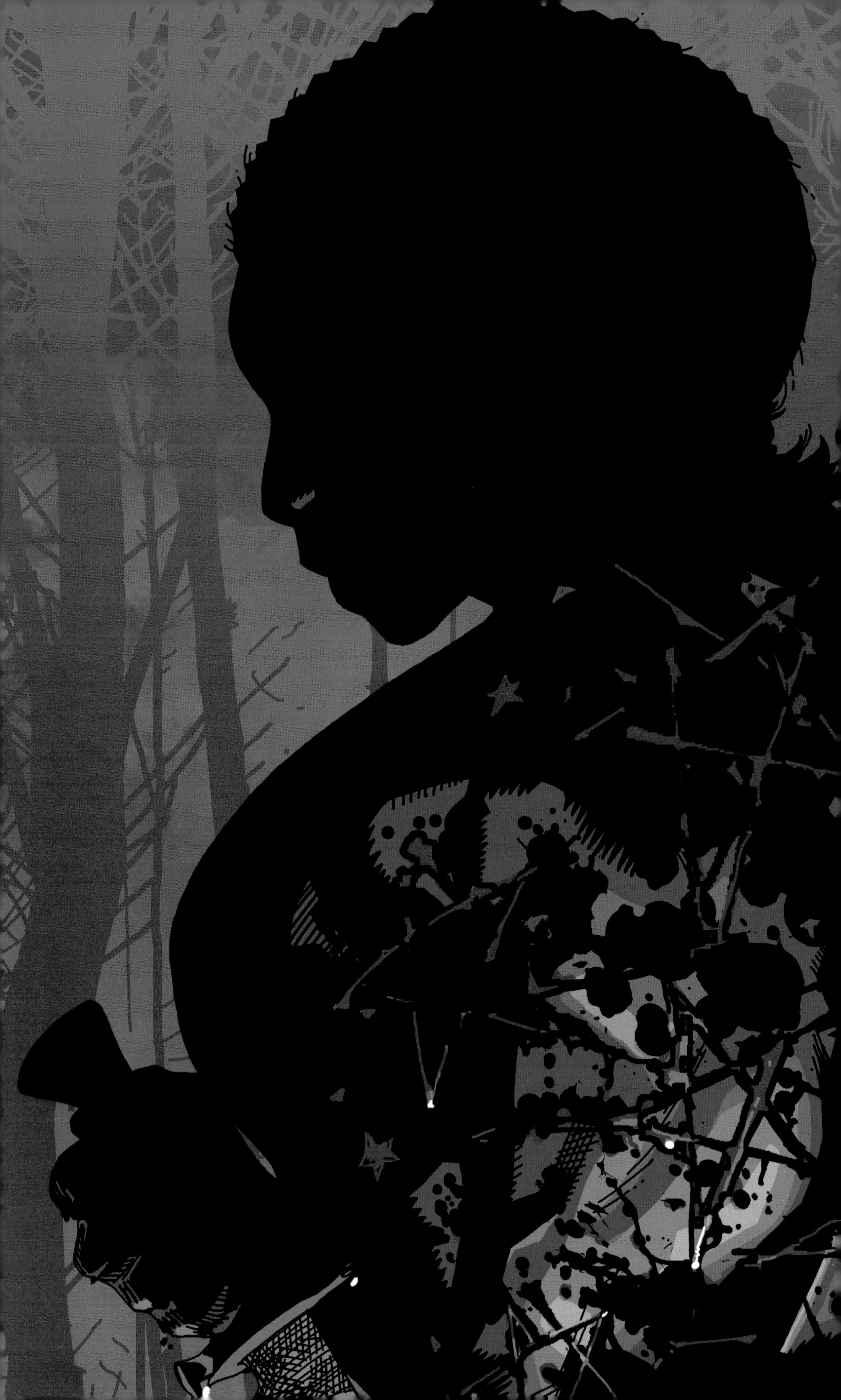

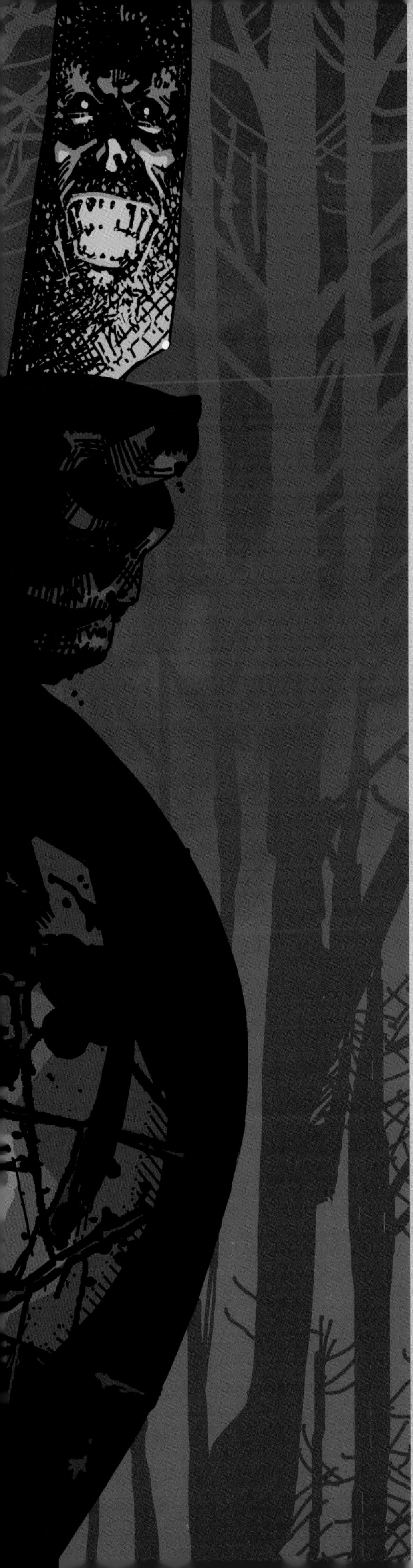

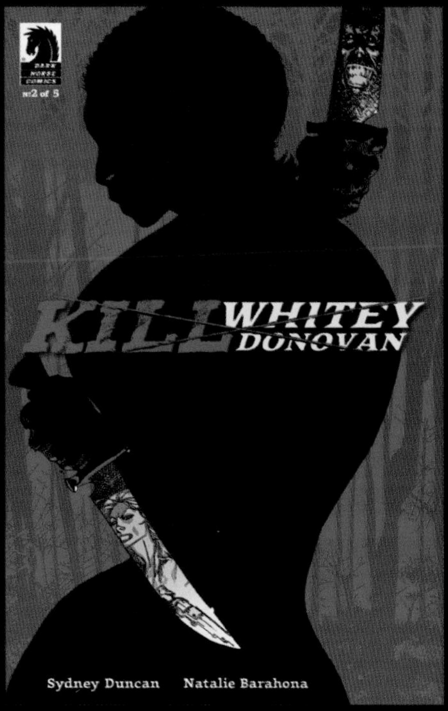
DARK HORSE COMICS
№2 of 5
KILL WHITEY DONOVAN
Sydney Duncan
Natalie Barahona

Issue #2
JASON PEARSON

JASON PEARSON'S UNEDITED ISSUE #2 COVER

"Jason's original cover was a commentary on the Civil War and the scars slavery left on our nation (the whip marks on Hattie's back represent the stars on the American flag, with the trees behind Hattie representing the stripes). However, as powerful as this cover was, I felt it was a little too provocative for this particular story. Jason was kind enough to alter the cover to show Hattie in full silhouette, which was a great cover in its own right, but we are all pleased to present his original vision here for the first time."

— Keven Gardner

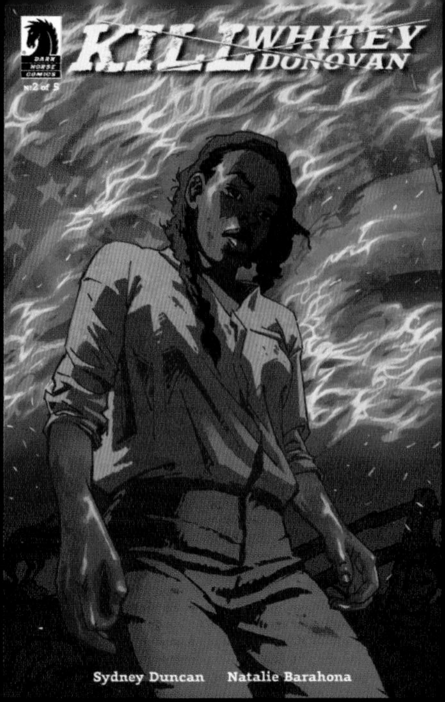
DARK HORSE COMICS
KILL WHITEY DONOVAN
№2 of 5
Sydney Duncan
Natalie Barahona

Issue #2 Variant
NATALIE BARAHONA

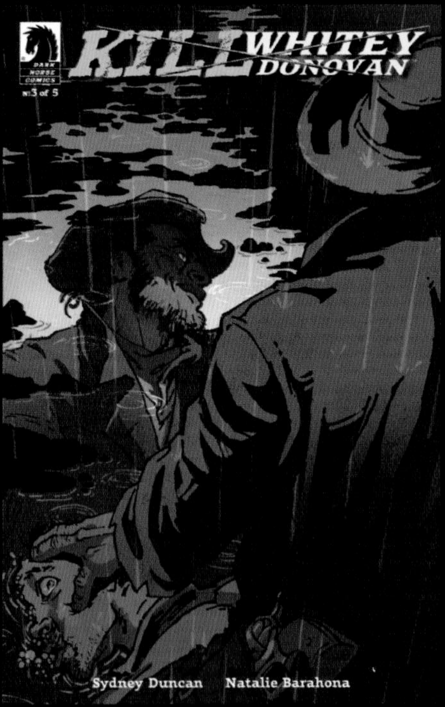
DARK HORSE COMICS
KILL WHITEY DONOVAN
№3 of 5
Sydney Duncan
Natalie Barahona

Issue #3 Variant
NATALIE BARAHONA

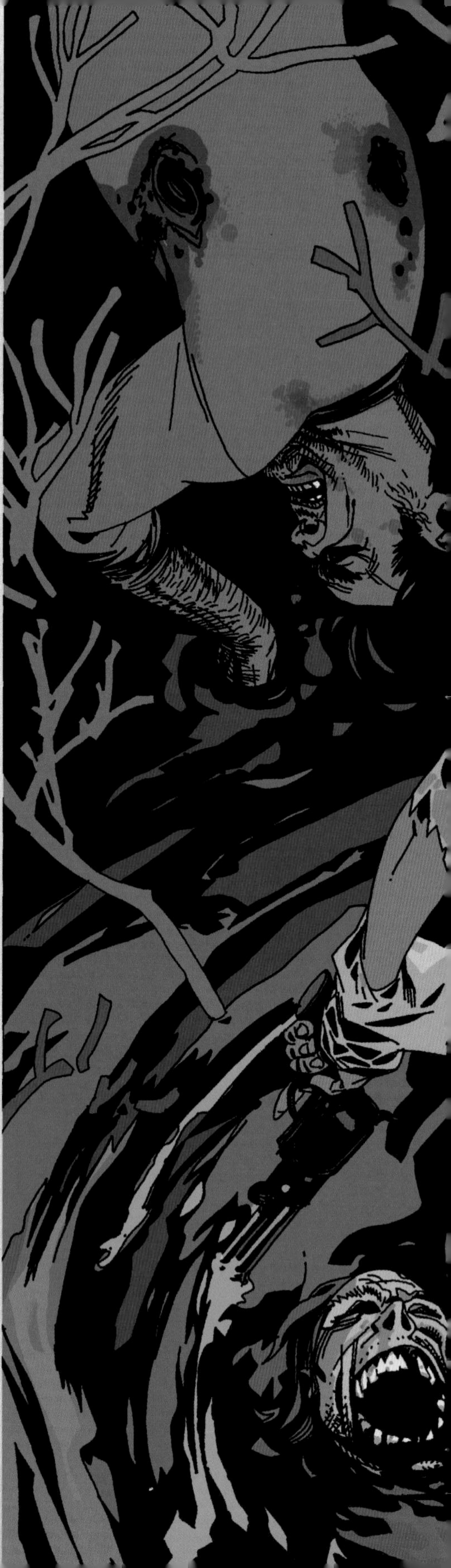

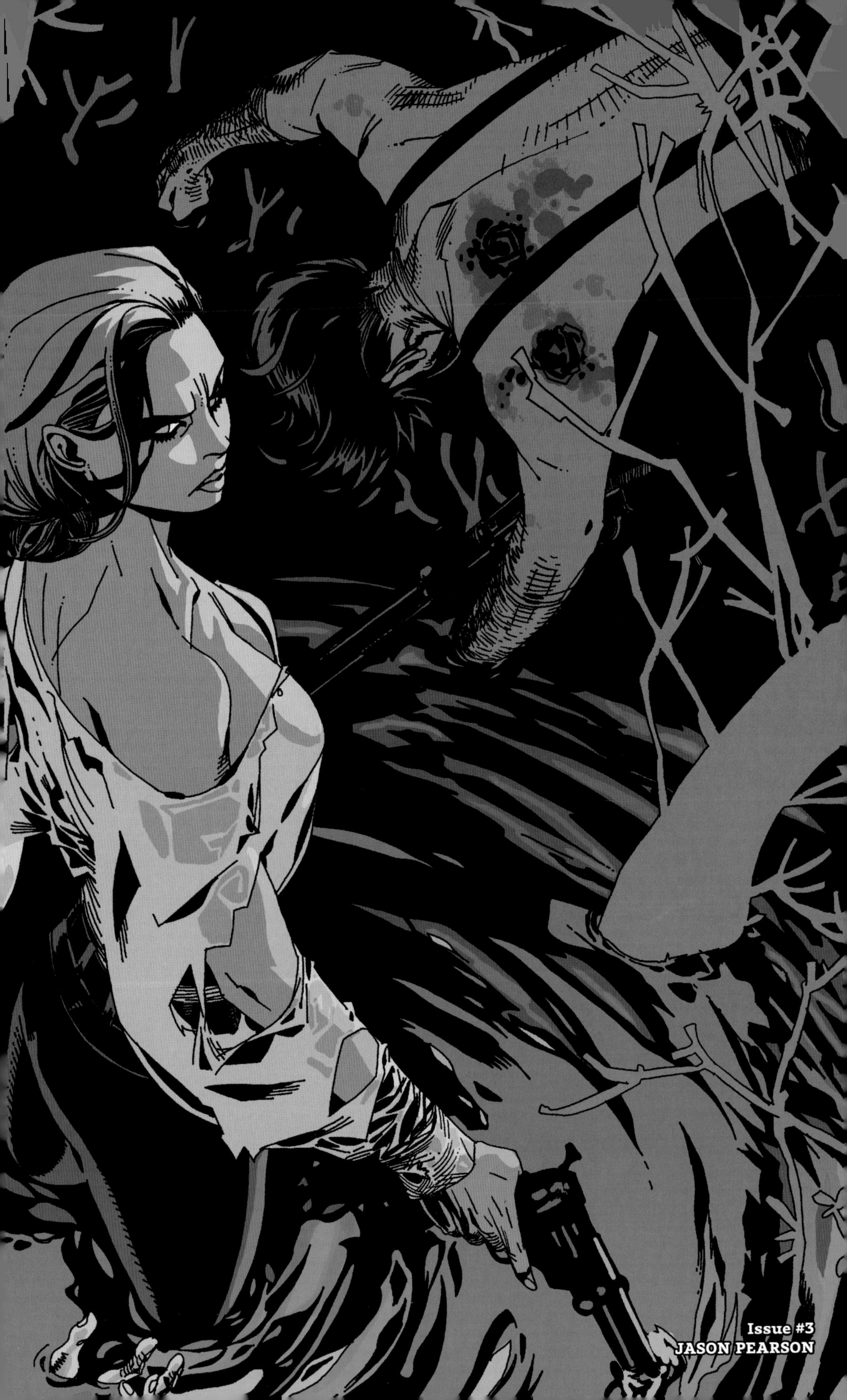

Issue #3
JASON PEARSON

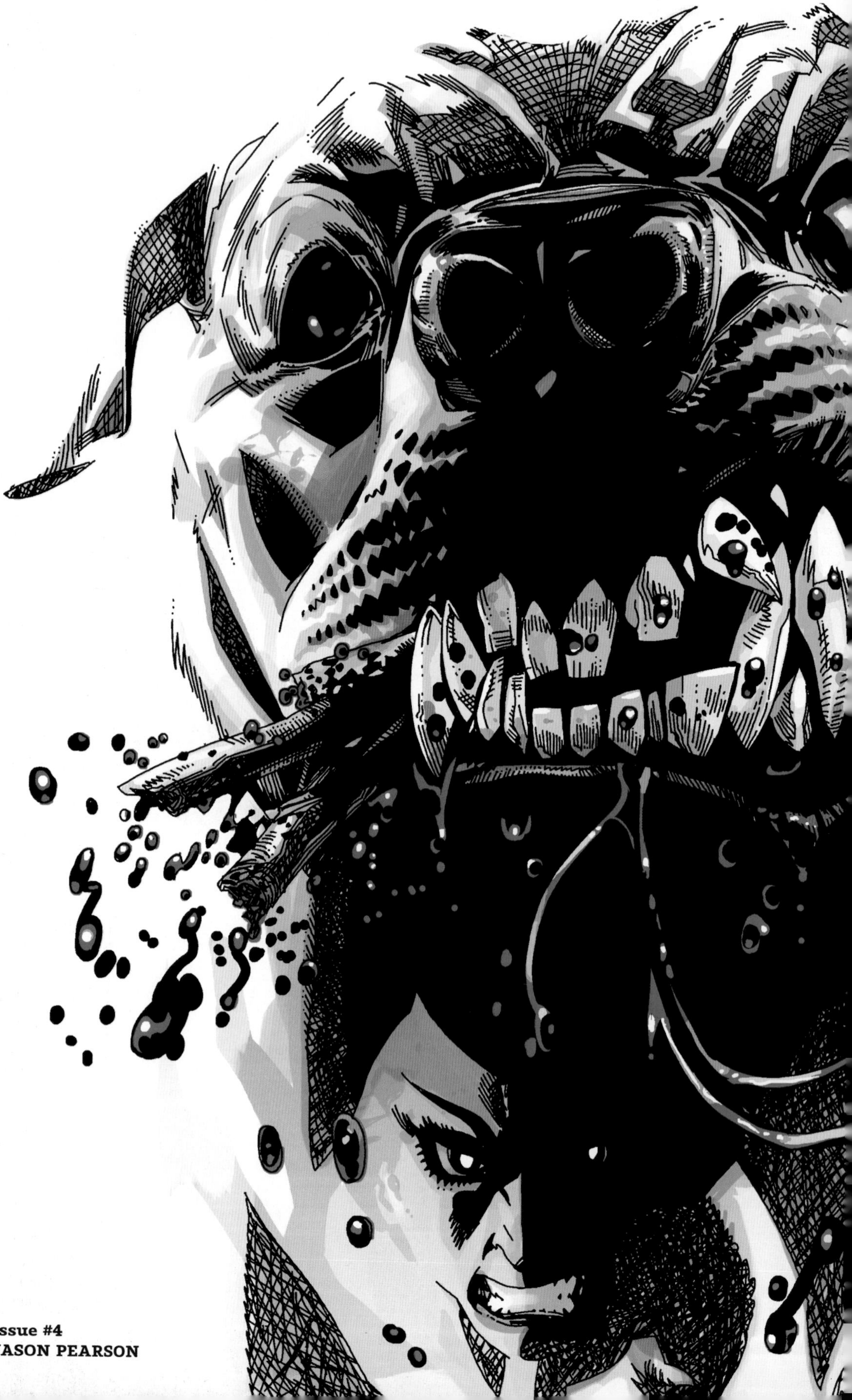

Issue #4
JASON PEARSON

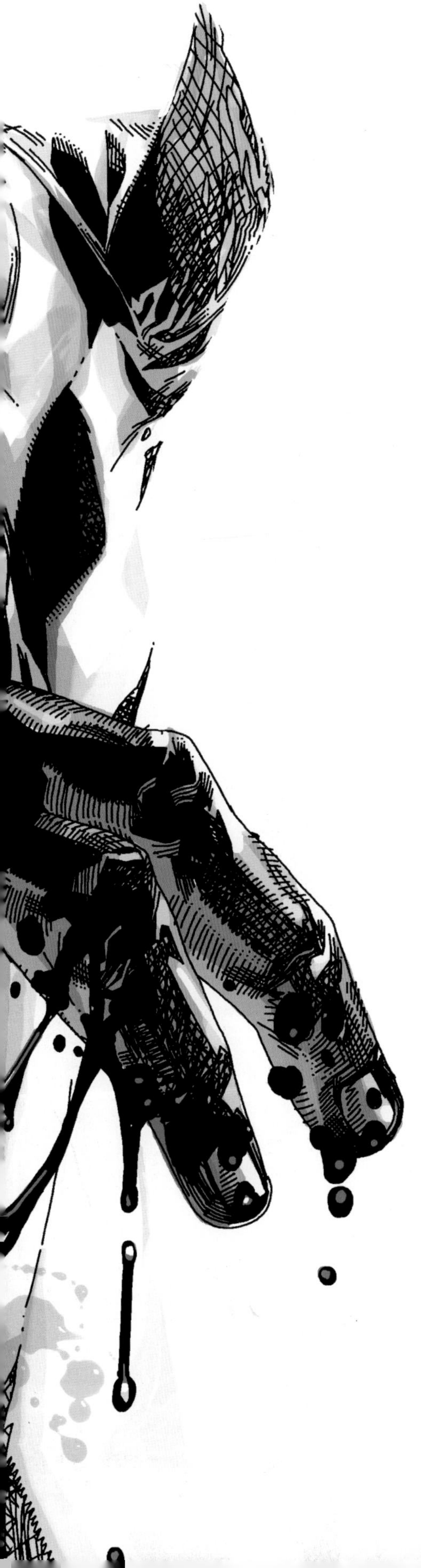

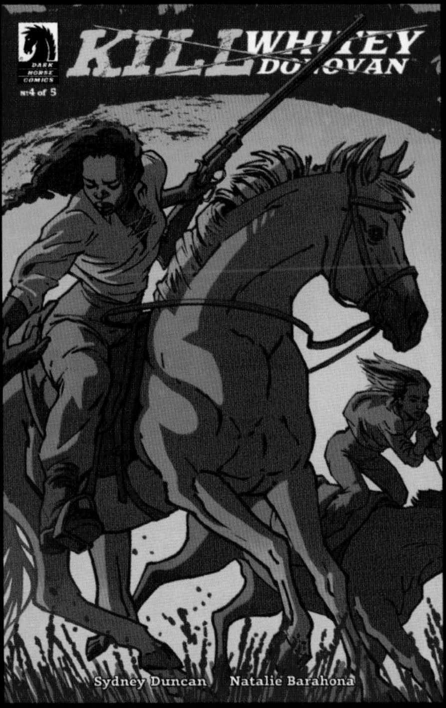
KILL WHITEY DONOVAN
DARK HORSE COMICS
№4 of 5
Sydney Duncan
Natalie Barahona

Issue #4 Variant
NATALIE BARAHONA

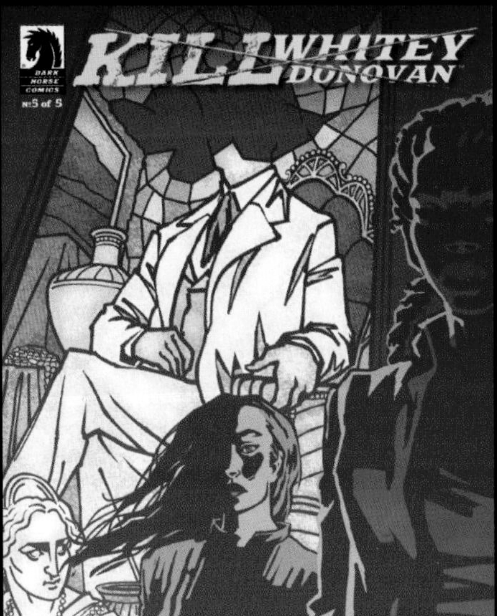
KILL WHITEY DONOVAN
DARK HORSE COMICS
№5 of 5
Sydney Duncan
Natalie Barahona

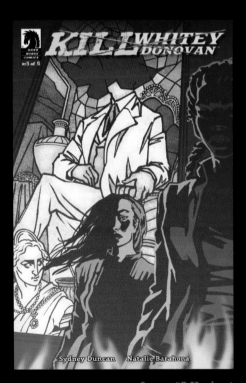

Issue #5 Variant
NATALIE BARAHONA

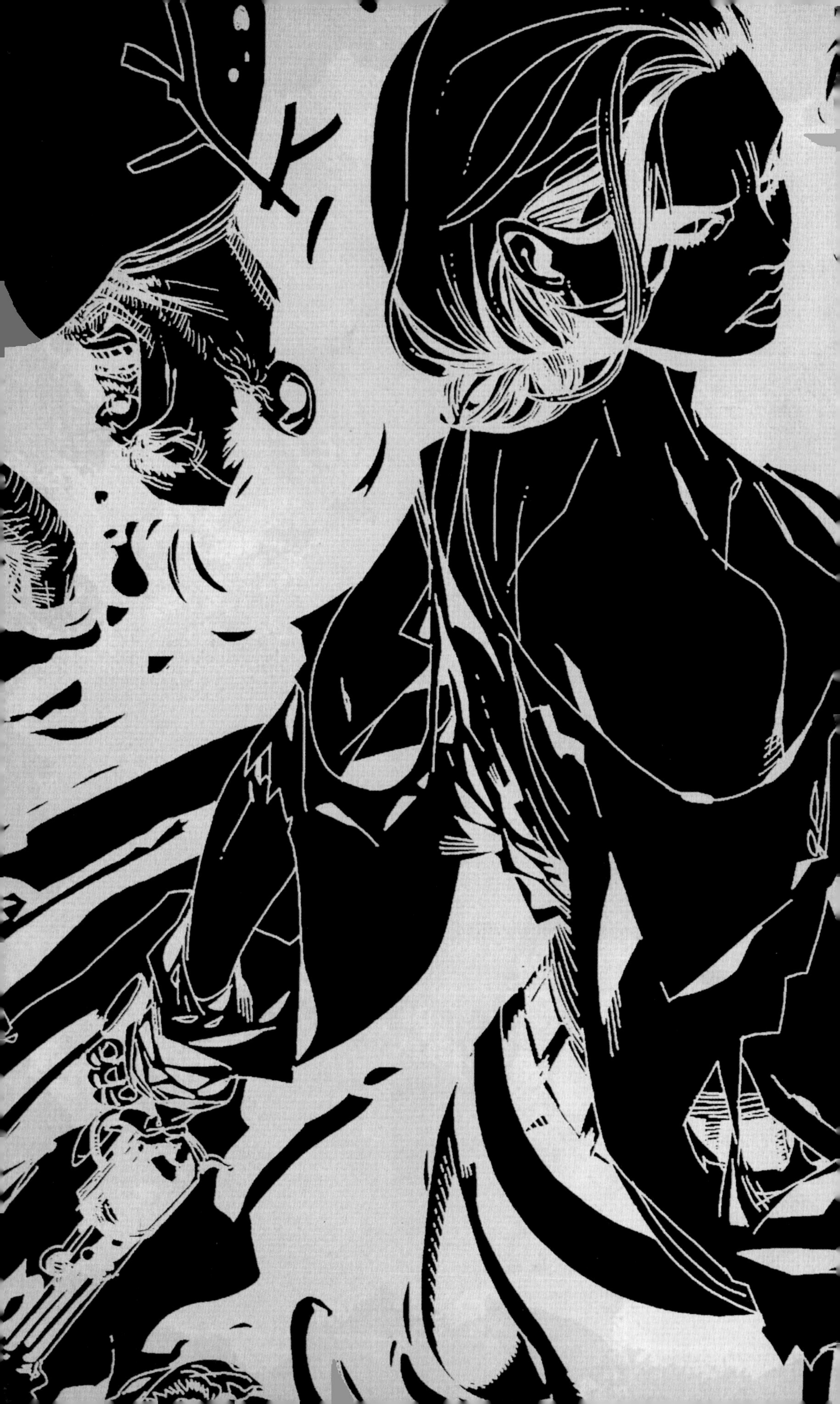